HERE'S WHAT THE EXPERTS ARE SAYING ABOUT STA...
AND HIS NEW BOOK, *BEYOND THE ABSOLUTE L.....*

"Stan's book is packed with winning methods for practice and game competition. Excellent reading for the coach and the athlete looking for the edge in building confidence."

Dean Smith, Head Basketball Coach, University of North Carolina

"Stan Kellner has helped me win more basketball games than any coach or clinic I know of. No one knows more about the inner game. That's why I've passed his book on to our coaching staff."

Frank Layden, President, Utah Jazz

"Stan Kellner's innovative training program integrates the physical and mental aspects of the game like no other book around. If playing with confidence, concentration, composure, and consistency is important to you, I recommend you read it cover to cover as I did."

Dr. Hal Wissel, Noted basketball author, scout and special assistant coach to the New Jersey Nets

"If you want to be the best you can be, you owe it to yourself to 'max out' physically and mentally. I know Cybernetics Training works. It's been more than half my game and will always be a part of my life."

Mitch Kupchak, General Manager, Los Angeles Lakers and former NBA star

"Anybody who is serious about peak performance would have to be crazy not to buy this book and wear it out."

Dr. Peter Greider, Sports psychologist and author of *80%, How You Can Shoot Foul Shots Better Than The Pros*

"Improving as a player is as much psychological as it is physical. No one understands this better than Stan Kellner. Stan gives you the path toward personal success. Follow it and you will be a winner."

Richard Conover, National Coaching Officer, Irish Basketball Association

"Stan is ahead of his time. He has been preaching Basketball Cybernetics for over two decades. Since using his visualization and relaxation techniques, we have made 10 "final four" appearances in the last 11 seasons, including 3 Ontario Provincial "AA" Championships. For coaches who are prepared to look beyond X's and O's, Stan's program might be the decisive edge they have been looking for."

Hugh Meyer, Timmins High School, Ontario, Canada

"Finally... the basketball success book that should have been written years ago."
Karen McConnell, Head Women's Basketball Coach, Heidelberg College

"Stan Kellner, whom I have known and respected for 20 years, has outdone himself with this great publication. 'Beyond The Absolute Limit' should be on every coach's desk or bookshelf."
Tom Penders, Head Basketball Coach, University of Texas

"Thank you, thank you, thank you. At last, a manual explaining and implementing mental techniques for sports performance that high school and college athletes can understand! I truly believe that anyone interested in doing the best they can at anything they desire should have this book at their fingertips. It has already changed my life."
Bruce Boguski, The Winner's Edge

"The crown prince of the kingdom of Cybernetics Training has done it again — produced a well-written, well-organized Ultimate Success Formula for playing basketball with more confidence, concentration, and more effectiveness."
Scholastic Coach Magazine

"We shot over 80% from the line as a team and led the league shooting 53% from the three-point arc. The Cybernetics shooting method created by Stan Kellner was the key to our success."
Denny Dearden, 1994 Coach of the Year, Grand Junction High School, Colorado

"Stan Kellner's Ultimate Shooting Method is an exciting technique that works! It is a great tool for all players at any level."
Marian E. Washington, Head Women's Basketball Coach, University of Kansas

"The method doesn't teach shooting —it teaches shooting success."
Dr. Ron Slaymaker, 1986 NAIA Coach-of-the-Year, Emporia State University, Kansas

"Stan Kellner's book is not only informational... it's motivational. He tells players how to reach their potential in a language they can understand. Then, he moves them to want to do it."
Mark Ehlen, Head Women's Basketball Coach, University of Toledo

The possible dream . . .

BEYOND THE ABSOLUTE LIMIT

STAN KELLNER'S
NATIONALLY ACCLAIMED
"YES, I CAN!"
BASKETBALL SUCCESS PROGRAM
featuring **BASKETBALL CYBERNETICS**

---

*A **Yes, I Can!** Publication*

Fourth Printing, October, 1998
Third printing, May, 1996
Second printing, March, 1995
First printing, June, 1994

Published by
"Yes, I Can!" Publications
Long Island, New York

Editorial and design services by
L.N. Raptis
Melville, New York

Typesetting and graphic services by
Peter G. Meade
Williston Park, New York

Printing by
Edwards Brothers, Inc.
Ann Arbor, Michigan

Photography by
Pat Colombraro
Nesconset, New York

Manufactured in the United States of America
ISBN # 0-9644175-0-2

This book is dedicated to the memory of
Cliff Lennon, Frank Mackwich and Don Ronan.

"To live in the hearts left behind is not to die."
Anonymous

ACKNOWLEDGEMENTS

Both the writing of this book and the evolutionary journey of the "Yes, I Can!" program would not have been possible without the contributions of many fine people. They serendipitously appeared in my life at the right time. I will always be deeply indebted to them.

To my wife Martha. She is not only my most loving and caring friend, but this book would never have been written without her daily editorial guidance.

To Bill and Marilyn Immler, for his guidance in the writing of this book and their joint effort making the Ohio camps as successful as they are.

To Ron Slaymaker, who placed his reputation on the line, took a risk and brought my New York accent to the great state of Kansas.

To Lou Raptis, for the final creative editing and production of this book.

To Frank Skubis, Tom Hughes, Wayne Smith, Karen McConnell, Ed Dolinar, Jim Kelly, Marty Riger, Allan Silva, Jeff Loughry, Sam Washington, Harold Manaskie, and Denny Dearden. Thank you for seeing the bigger picture and spreading the news.

To Herman Masin, editor of *Scholastic Coach*. Thank you for the literary start.

To an extraordinary staff of coaches, who did more than teach the "Yes, I Can!" Camp program. They lived it.

To Dave Cross and Joe Kolodka. Thank you for bringing "Yes, I Can!" into the fantastic sport of volleyball.

To Mitch Kupchak, an incredibly great basketball player and an even better person.

To Chet Jaworski, who taught me how to play and coach winning basketball.

To all the athletes I have known who were unafraid to look in an inner direction for help. Especially to my first varsity basketball team. Thank you for not quitting on me.

And to the creative minds of the real innovators of the "Yes, I Can!" program ... authors Maxwell Maltz, Anthony Robbins, Richard Bandler, Denis Waitley, Robert Schuller, John-Rogers, Peter McWilliams, Sephen Covey, Wayne Dyer, Tim Gallwey, and Martin Seligman. Read their inspirational wisdom and discover their formulas for the good and happy life.

An Important Note

As an aid to the reader,
Stan Kellner has included a
Glossary of important terms
beginning on page 195.
Please use it liberally as you read
this book to help you truly
understand each step
in his inner-game method.

TABLE OF CONTENTS

PART ONE. . . IN THE MIND

PART TWO. . . THE BATTLE WITHIN

PART THREE. . . ON THE COURT

PART FOUR. . . AND BEYOND

*"Did you ever hear about a frog
that dreamed of being a king
and then became one?"*

From the Neil Diamond song *"I Am...I Said"*

A WORD ABOUT THE AUTHOR

Stan Kellner is a celebrated author, educator, coach, television analyst and lecturer. His first book, *Taking It To The Limit,* has been read by more than 100,000 athletes and coaches. His most recent book, *Vollyball Cybernetics,* has already attracted rave reviews. Coauthored by one of vollyball's best teachers, Dave Cross, their book has become a must read success formula on what it takes to be a winner on the vollyball court. The *Living The Miracle* audio cassette and acclaimed video, *The Ultimate Shooting Method,* are being distributed internationally.

When Stan Kellner first introduced his inner-game techniques and drills of Basketball Cybernetics, it was to help his high school and later college teams find their winning ways. They did – in dramatic fashion – winning 9 consecutive championships.

Among his best known players is 6'10" Mitch Kupchak, a former North Carolina All-American and Los Angeles Lakers pro star. Mitch is currently the General Manager of the Lakers.

In 1978, Stan Kellner developed the **Yes, I Can! Basketball Camps**. Today, over four thousand athletes attend his camps each summer from Hawaii to Europe.

A frequent lecturer on Cybernetics Training, Stan Kellner earned his bachelor's degree from Adelphi University in 1957 and his master's from C.W. Post in 1965.

A WORD FROM THE AUTHOR

What's holding you back from living your basketball dream? Is it a lack of talent, good coaching or catching the right breaks? Only if you're ready to trade these excuses for excellence, and take personal responsibility for your destiny, is this book for you.

You're about to discover an **inside-out** training process that's been around for a long time helping athletes live their dreams. The name of this success program is **Basketball Cybernetics.** Because of it, you'll find a computer-like inner success system... one that you've always had buried inside your head. **Basketball Cybernetics** will also provide you with the **Ultimate Formula for Success**, complete with drills and methods that will help you master the winner's mind game. Soon, you'll know how to activate your **internal cybernetic system** to develop the skills and attitudes you'll need to live your basketball dream.

In my first book *Taking It To The Limit* (1978), I referred to my system of fast-acting techniques as **Basketball Cybernetics**. After the book's publication, surprisingly, I received a flood of letters and calls from athletes of other sports who had unlocked their hidden powers to succeed by employing the methods of **Basketball Cybernetics**. There was a wrestler, well beyond his prime, who achieved an Olympic Medal. A sky diving team shattered a long existing time record for international team sky diving. Marathon runners, weight-lifters, golfers, tennis, baseball, softball, volleyball, soccer, and football players all improved their performance level as a result of discovering the benefits of **Basketball Cybernetics**.

> Realizing there are no sports boundaries to my inner-game success plan, I've decided to refer to **Basketball Cybernetics** throughout this book as **Cybernetics Training**. Please be aware that these two terms are interchangeable and synonymous.

So, if you're ready to take it to the limit of your potential and beyond ... turn the page and discover the magic of **Cybernetics Training**. Commit to it and I promise your life on the court and off will never be the same.

THE BUTTON MARKED SUCCESS

Have you ever wondered what life on the basketball court would be like if you awakened one morning to find a **Success Button** on the night table next to your bed? Imagine what your game would be like if it really was a magical **Success Button**. Suppose by simply pressing it, you could realize any one of your favorite basketball dreams ... including the one you had just before you awakened. The one where you drill that 20-footer at the buzzer to win the big game!

Think of it! By simply pressing this button, you could become a step-up, prime time performer. Or perhaps you'd be thrilled just to make the team; push the button and presto ... you'd be on the roster. If reaching your basketball dream meant that you needed to be more aggressive or develop a power game ... all you'd have to do is press the **Success Button** and abracadabra, like magic, you'd be playing bigger and stronger.

Sound too good to be true? Maybe not! Thanks to **Cybernetics**, the science that produced the electronic computer, you're about to discover that an actual, honest-to-goodness mechanism for success does exist. No, it's not on the night table next to your bed. It's located inside the cyberspace of your head. Cyberneticians call it the power mechanism responsible for human behavior. Behavioral psychologists have another name for it ... they call it the subconscious. Regardless of what you want to call it ... getting it to operate with the power and reliability of an automatic success mechanism is what this book is all about.

Although it may not be as easy as pressing a button, getting your subconscious to produce the level of performance you'll need to live your basketball dream could be as simple as changing the way you think, talk to yourself and move your body. Interested? You ought to be. As soon as you learn the operating principles of your subconscious, you will change the course of your life on the court. Before we look in an outward direction to show you how to systematically improve all facets of your game in the gym, we will first look inwardly to learn more about your cybernetically designed subconscious and the rest of the inner machinery sitting there between your ears.

You're about to examine Cybernetics Training (CT), an **inside-out** success program that has been around since 1968 helping athletes of all sports live their dreams. If you're ready to commit to employing its principles and methods on a daily basis, you will liberate the limitless power of your incredible internal success system. Give CT the honest shot it deserves and you'll notice the following changes in your game:

- **Shooting:** You'll consistently drill the jumper!
- **Free Throw Shooting:** You'll find a remarkable shooting groove!
- **Quickness and Aggressiveness:** You'll wonder where the new found power came from!
- **Power Game:** You'll be tougher inside and play bigger!
- **Defense:** You'll be able to stop the dribbler!
- **Transition Game:** You'll see the entire court and finish the break!
- **Ball Handling:** You'll value the ball!
- **Playing Weaknesses And Attitudes:** You'll turn glitches into glory!
- **Clutch Performance:** You'll be unafraid to step-up in prime time.
- **Playing Basketball Will Be More Fun:** You'll be free to experience the real joy of playing basketball!

And you'll learn about the **Ultimate Success Formula of Cybernetics Training ... FAST,** and how to access the **Power State of Mind** ... instantly.

In addition to learning how to play with more overall confidence, concentration and composure, you'll have a proven dream fulfillment plan you can apply to other areas of your life. So if you're ready to travel from where you are now to where you'd like to be as a basketball player, let's take a closer look at your inner success system and the Science of Cybernetics. You'll be amazed at what you find. Enjoy your inner journey.

PART ONE

...IN THE MIND...

"Your dreams are the touchstones for success."
Henry David Thoreau

YOUR CYBERNETIC INNER SUCCESS SYSTEM

"All glory comes from daring to begin."
Eugene Ware

Can you recall watching Michael Jordan cleverly penetrate a defense with a reverse pivot, change speed to avoid an opponent, go up for a shot only to drop the ball off to an open teammate at the last possible second? You may think you saw the world's greatest basketball player performing with uncanny accuracy. You were actually observing a precisely programmed human computer execute its wizardry. The memory of this great player is stocked with thousands of past experiences of similar situations which help him evaluate the present game situation. In a millisecond Jordan's subconscious mind scans both his past successes and failures and matches them to the current circumstances. Simultaneously, he is perceiving the movements of others, searching for cues to an open lane, the location of the basket and finally seeing the open teammate. Never once does he focus his attention on his dribble, become distracted by the screaming fans or concern himself about the importance of the basket. Six hundred muscles, over two hundred bones, and miles of nerve fibers are activated in perfect harmony to produce the appropriate winning response ... miraculous proof of one man's internal successs system operating cybernetically!

THE WORLD'S GREATEST COMPUTER

The road CT takes leads you straight to the control center for your performance ... your mind. Take it easy, this book won't present a Freudian approach to playing basketball. No inkblot test, no delving into your childhood, or looking for unresolved conflicts. Your mind is explored in a cybernetic light—as the world's greatest computer system. Just think of this book as an owner's manual.

The learning process will include…
• understanding the capabilities of your biological computer.
• discovering the key operational rules of your subconscious.
• introducing you to your Reticular Activating System. ("My what?" you ask. Read on and find out.)
The key to living your basketball dream will be to take control of all three.

Since the analogy of the human brain and the electronic computer is well established (again, no debate necessary) your brain receives, processes, records and acts upon input just like any man made computer … with one exception. The instructions it receives are not always valid. Your inner computer receives its vital input from the internal representations (or inner responses) of your past experiences. Everything you do on the court, every thought you think, every action you take, everything you feel, hear and see is first subjectively defined and then stored inside your mental computer.

As a player … you are what you are, not always because of reality but because of the personal interpretations of past experiences you have processed and stored. These mental recordings are not necessarily accurate experiences, but your impression of those experiences.

Insert the wrong software into any mechanical computer and you can expect a wrong response. The cybernetic law, "input determines output" applies for both man and machine.This explains why "success breeds success" and "failure breeds frustration." Computer programmers have a great expression for it. They say, "garbage in … garbage out!"

The best chance for tapping your full potential is to stack as many positive internal representations as you can into your mental computer. Unless you think, feel, talk and especially interpret positively, you can bet the ranch that your game will be inconsistent. Before you run out of games to play you ought to take a hard look at what you're putting into cold storage inside your inner computer. Whatever it is … it's shaping your destiny.

With the shortcut methods of visualization, power talk, positive affirmation, modeling and acting as if, you'll be able to store thousands of success signals for easy access.

THERE'S NOTHING WRONG WITH YOUR COMPUTER

I don't care if you think you're the #1 underachiever on your team, there's absolutely nothing wrong with the operational ability of your inner computer. If you can see, imagine, feel and remember, your Inner Success System is prepared and ready to operate at full power. Check out its unparalleled potential:

• The human brain contains more storage cells than the largest man made computer. Latest estimation … over 100 billion storage cells.
• The brain needs only two basic inexpensive and highly available ingredients to operate— sugar and oxygen. And it rarely needs repairs.
• Its mechanical counterpart requires at least a thousand watts of expensive electrical energy to operate and its repairs are costly.
• If science could build a facsimile of the human computer (which it is fruitlessly trying to do), the cost would be in the billions!

- To house this mechanical computer, the storage space would be enormous. The largest building in the world, the World Trade Center, wouldn't be big enough!
- The human brain has over 7,000 miles of wiring, weighs 3 1/2 pounds and can be stored in 6 inches of cranial space.
- It has been estimated that the brain is capable of accepting 16 new facts for every second of your life. The speed of sending instructions to over 200 muscles of your body is a thousand times quicker than any mechanical computer's processing ability.

Are you impressed? The fact is, you have the greatest, most miraculous and incomparable prize sitting between your ears. And the great news is that it's user friendly!

DON'T KNOCK YOURSELF: REPROGRAM

A million dollar IBM computer won't give you the right time of day without correct programming. Do you think the computer programmers would junk the computer or insult it if it failed? I don't think so. The scientist would simply examine the feedback coming from its data base and, if it wasn't any good, better information would be programmed into it.

MEET YOUR SUCCESS MECHANISM

There's a powerful genie that's always been there, hidden away inside your mental computer. Operating as your habit maker, the subconscious is the performance muscle for your inner computer. It has enough power to perform all kinds of performance miracles, including getting you to jump several inches higher or making your basketball dream become a reality. The subconscious is the **Cybernetic Mechanism** that automatically supplies the know-how fire power for your basketall performance.

Identical to any cybernetic service device, the subconscious works directly upon:

1. **Clear-cut goals.**
2. **Informational signals which it receives from...your belief system, body language and self talk.**

Unfortunately, your subconscious has been unable to perform feats of success because of the negative feedback instructions it receives from your:

- limited belief system.
- the way you move your body before, during and after action.
- inner conversations.

Your powerful genie-like mechanism is equipped with fantastic powers, capable of granting you your most fervent desires and what have you done to it? You incarcerated its incredible capacity inside a narrow comfort zone and exposed it to the most stupid, most limited feedback signals you could produce. The penalty for subconscious abuse is **a basketball career of underachieving performance or at best fulfilling the unappreciated position of a role player.**

Unless you decide to expand your comfort zone and improve your self image, the only magic your genie will produce will be to make your basketball dream disappear.

THE MAGIC POWERS OF YOUR SUBCONSCIOUS

When you drive to the basket and finish it off with a power lay-in, do you have to think about releasing the ball on the first dribble before you picked up your pivot foot? Do you have to think about every low and hard step you make, or what your free arm is doing? Do you have to ponder the jump stop and soft kiss of the ball off the glass? When you shoot a free throw in competition, do you have to remember to breathe or clear your eyes by blinking, or keep your blood pressure under control so you don't explode?

You don't have to think about any of these essential life saving activities. If you do, you're in trouble! Whether it's a creative basketball skill or an autonomic nervous system habit, each action was automatically produced by the incomparable magnitude of your subconscious. Maybe it's time you appreciated its multi-dimensional talent.

In a nutshell, there are three basic functions of your magnificent and tireless subconscious mechanism:

1. Your subconscious is the mental engineer that handles all of your vital processes, including autonomic activities such as: blood pressure, pulse rate, breathing rhythm, swallowing, sneezing, digestion or muscular reflex action. Services that are rendered on a 24-hour basis. Never asleep, the subconscious is always on call.

2. Your subconscious is responsible for remembering all overlearned skills (habits), such as walking, running, talking, chewing, eating, and is in charge of all of your basketball fundamentals as well. These are automatic type skills that require no conscious thinking. Normally, it takes about three weeks of repetition to program an overlearned skill (one that you have to think about) into a skill that is automatic and requires no thinking. That's about the same amount of time the CT process needs to affect change. Psychology explains that the self image can be changed but it may take up to three weeks of positive and repetitive reinforcement.

Don't tell me you don't have enough time to spend on cybernetic training. You don't have enough time not to!

3. Your subconscious has a tremendous creative capacity, too, producing and controlling your feelings and expectations. Since it controls all of your actions and reactions, its inventive powers can construct or destruct a basketball dream in a heartbeat.

AN EXAMPLE OF THE CREATIVE POWERS OF YOUR SUBCONSCIOUS

Let's say you're on the foul line with two ticks left on the game clock and your team is down by two points. The official hands you the ball and signals **one and one**. Because you missed your last free throw earlier in the game, you're not in the most confident state of mind. A tightening feeling of anxiety is building within your body. You try to push the past out of your mind by taking a deep breath and slowly exhaling. You also focus harder on the front of the rim for a few seconds longer than usual, but the harder you try to concentrate, the more time you have to remember that nailing both ends of a **one and one** in pressure situations is not one of your strengths! Not only do your parents know this fact (they're praying), your coach knows it (he's sweating), the opposition knows it (they're smiling), but worst of all, your reliable and impersonal habit maker, the subconscious, knows it. Already it's gone to work producing a feeling of anxiety.

After converting the first freethrow, you miss the second shot (the ball falls short). The reason the second shot never felt right (even after the success of the first shot) was because the subconscious produced a negative expectation and an overtrying effort. Knowing that you usually make half of your shots from the line in clutch situations, you overtried. The faithful subconscious read your concern and overcompensated by sending too many signals. The wrong muscles of your shooting arm, responded by tightening up. The result was a short arm follow through and a flat, untrue trajectory. Thanks to the creative powers of your subconscious, **you successfully missed the freethrow!**

THE SUBCONSCIOUS HAS MANY NAMES

Would you like to know the other names of your powerful internal Genie? The list is impressive:

- The Cybernetics Mechanism
- The Unconscious Mind
- The Enforcer
- The Success Mechanism
- The Performance Mechanism
- The Creative Device
- Inner Intelligence
- The Inner Robot
- The Dream-Fulfillment Device
- Self-fulfilling Prophecy Device
- The Habit Maker
- The Subconscious Mind
- Automatic Pilot
- The Power Mechanism
- The Failure Mechanism
- The Destiny Device
- The Purpose Mechanism
- R2 D2
- Instinct
- The Genie
- Life Force
- Servo-Mechanism

With all these names and the power it yields, you would think a picture or at least a rendering of the subconscious could be found in some medical book. None exists. No one has ever seen a subconscious, located its exact location, touched or weighed it. No scientist, not even a surgeon has visually experienced its physical presence. So why should you believe that you have one? Read any book on the psychology of human behavior or in the area of self help and you'll find volumes written on the powers of the subconscious. I don't think it is a coincidence that as soon as I started to believe in the presence of a mechanism for success in my players (and in myself) that surprisingly good things started to happen in our lives.

At the beginning of my coaching career my philosophy was a pragmatic, "I'll believe it when I see it." Unfortunately a funny thing was happening to my team on the way to the championship each season—I wasn't seeing it!

Cybernetics brought the science of hope into my gym. I adopted a new concept about human capacity. I decided to believe in the ability of every one of my players in advance! When I accepted the cybernetic premise that each of my players had his own inner success system, I realized what the ultimate challenge was for me ... discover the best ways possible to activate my players' success systems.

BELIEVE IT FIRST AND YOU'LL SEE IT

Read Wayne Dyer's book *You'll See It When You Believe It,* and you'll understand that if you want to live a miracle of success on the court, you'll have to **believe** it first before you can **see** it. No matter how inconsistent my players' performance was, I focused on what was good. I also started to use the power of my imagination to anticipate success and not failure, as was my habit. Soon, happy coincidences (serendipitous events) were happening in our gym and my life. Not only were we winning games ... we were winning championships.

THE MAKING OF A SERENDIPITOUS EVENT
OR HOW TO SET THE INNER SUCCESS SYSTEM FOR SUCCESS

Can you recall reading what Duke coach Mike Krzyzewski said to his Blue Devils during that last timeout with his team down by a point to Kentucky in the 1992 NCAA semifinals? It's a classic illustration of how to make a serendipitous event happen.

Here's the game situation: with 2.1 seconds left on the clock, Duke had to advance 94 feet through Kentucky's tough full court press in order to score. An almost impossible task. All the Blue Devils had left was themselves, and the trust of their coach. In that last time-out, Krzyzewski said, "We're going to win. Whether you completely believe it or not, you have to have the conviction in your mind, the expression on your face and the words in your mouth that we're going to get a good shot to win." After receiving an 80-foot overhand pass from teammate Grant Hill, Christian Laettner (who did not miss a shot in the game) caught the pass, took one dribble, spun around and drilled the 17-foot game winner at the buzzer.

Why not believe in the presence of an internal system of success, one with an unlimited capacity for achievement and then commit to this concept? If I may redirect Coach Krzyzewski's classic expression of faith, "Whether you completely believe it or not, you have to have the conviction in your mind, the expression on your face and the words in your mouth" ... that you can become the player you want to be!

What if I told you that you have the exact same inner success system as Christian Laettner, Michael Jordan or Larry Bird? What would you say? Would it be ... show me and I'll believe it! What I'm trying to explain to you is ... **believe it first and you'll see it!**

HOW THE SUBCONSCIOUS TURNS OUT HABITS

Imagine your conscious mind as a deep well and your subconscious mind as a ditch around the well. Now imagine that every time you experience making a shot, a bucket of success is poured into the well of your conscious mind. The more baskets you make, the more buckets of success are poured into the well. Make enough shots and in time the well of your conscious mind eventually fills up and overflows filling the ditch, too. It's only at this point of time, when the flow of success reaches the subconscious mind, that an effective shooting habit is formed.

The Ultimate Shooting Method will show you how is to fill your conscious mind with enough buckets of success (both real and imagined) so that an overflow can reach your subconscious mind and become a habit.

YOUR FOCUSING DEVICE: THE RETICULAR ACTIVATING SYSTEM

I would be cybernetically irresponsible if I didn't tell you about another essential fixture of your inner success system ... your **Reticular Activating System** (RAS).

Picture a plank of wood 18 inches wide and 50 feet in length. Place this plank on the floor and imagine walking the length of it. Would you have any trouble accomplishing this challenge? No you wouldn't. But what if the plank was placed on the roofs between two tall buildings 400 feet high and then, I asked you to walk its length? Could you do it with the same ease? Would you do it for $1000? I doubt it. Why? Because you'd be imagining the worst outcome. Instead of centering your attention on the accommodating width of the plank, you'd be thinking death! Extraneous factors such as the slightest movement of the wind, the noise of the traffic below, the queasy sensation in the pit of your stomach and the unsureness of your legs become unecessary feedback for your subconscious. Still that wouldn't stop you from thinking about them ... unless you had mastered your RAS with the same proficiency of a high-wire performer.

Are you a high-wire performer when faced with an opportunity to step up and perform decisively with the game on the line? Are you focused or unfocused? Do you hear the noise of the crowd? Are you distracted by the movements of the opposing players? Are you thinking about your last missed shot, the score, your fatigue or the consequences of the play if you botch it up?

The internal mechanism responsible for screening all pertinent information around you is the **Reticular Activating System.** It's your focusing or concentration facilitator. Without the services of your RAS, you'd be bombarding your biocomputer with a litany of useless and distracting information.

If prime time performance is your goal, it is vital that you develop the centering ability of the **Reticular Activating System** to delete what is irrelevant and focus in on what is.

The game of basketball is like a kaleidoscope continuously changing. There are countless sights, sounds, actions and feelings that simultaneously occur during every second of play. The infinite powers of your subconscious are wasted unless your eyes, mind and Reticular Activating mechanism are all focused. You won't accomplish a single important goal on the road to your basketball dream unless you learn how to sharpen the concentration skills of your RAS.

Your conscious mind can only focus on a limited number of elements at any one time, so what you focus on must be relative to the success of your action.

At a **Yes, I Can! Camp**, a 16 year of girl learned to use her RAS more effectively to achieve a high priority goal. Because she focused on what was wrong with her game (and life) rather than what was right, she literally had been suffering from tension headaches that had endured for nine

9

months! When she realized the importance of asking herself smarter questions, she was able to redirect her RAS to pay attention to what was really important and distinguish what wasn't. The result was her headache disappeared as mysteriously as it had appeared.

A player, who could not drive and finish, discovered that as soon as he redefined his focus from **pass first** to **shoot first**, he was suddenly completing his drive to the basket. Another athlete with a habit of having his passes intercepted, found success by reading the defense first, and throwing the ball away from the defense. When a poor freethrow shooter learned to focus on **letting it happen** rather than **making it happen**, the flight of her freethrow traveled in a softer and more accurate trajectory. There are countless athletes who have shifted their game into high gear as soon as they were able to focus on what they wanted rather than what they wanted to avoid. There isn't a successful athlete who hasn't first developed the master skill of concentration. They learned how to pay attention to only those stimuli that are important by developing the power of their RAS.

With the concentration and relaxation exercises of CT, along with an ability to ask yourself more resourceful questions, you'll be able to set and activate your RAS at will. Then everything you need to know about your inner success system will be in place. That is, except for discovering the greatest secret of all about Cybernetics Training.

THE MASTER SECRET OF CYBERNETICS TRAINING

The greatest secret about your subconscious is not that it's a reliable and powerful servant, or that it does not know how to say no! The fact that it is impersonal and not at all interested in your success or failure, or whether you're right or wrong, isn't the big secret either. It's not the fact that you program your subconscious with your thinking, body language and self talk either ... although that's a close second. The most incredible secret about your habit maker is that it cannot tell the difference between a real or a vividly imagined experience! Now that's extraordinarily good news.

Just as cyberneticians (computer experts) discovered that computers accept wrong information, scientists learned that **the nervous system cannot always tell the difference between an imagined experience and a real one.** Again, man and machine react automatically to data. This law of the mind is graphically demonstrated in hypnotism. There is nothing supernatural about seeing a hypnotized 200-pound weightlifter suddenly become incapable of lifting a pencil off a table. What you're witnessing is the normal operating process of the human brain and nervous system. **The nervous system with its subconscious reacts naturally to what the individual thinks, imagines and believes to be true.**

A PROFESSOR'S GREAT DISCOVERY

Long ago, educators learned the importance of changing students' attitudes about themselves before their academic performance could be improved. A professor at Columbia University proved a theory that poor students could be turned into good students if their self image was first altered. Poor readers, spellers and math students suddenly became proficient at the same skills that once embarrassed them. The professor's technique was pure cybernetics. The educator, Prescott Lecky, theorized that if students had trouble learning, it could be because learning that particular subject would be inconsistent with their self concept.

In order for students to tap their real learning potential, he concluded they would first have to change, for the better, their system of beliefs about themselves as students. If a student could be induced to change his self-definition, his learning disability should also change. So this is what Prescott Lecky did. He took a bunch of poor students and placed them in a class by themselves testing them in several academic areas. As expected, they all failed the tests. What he did next was pure deception! He lied to half of them. He told them they had passed the test with flying colors. The other half of the class was given the painful truth. Then, he retested all of them without additional tutoring.

What happened was a real shocker! The group that was lied to, improved their scores—with many of them passing! The group that was living the truth, all flunked again. The experiment was repeated with similarly impressive results. Poor readers read better; poor spellers spelled better; poor math students added and subtracted better. The educator's theory became the foundation for a revolutionary way of learning. What the educator concluded:

1. What you think about yourself affects the way you behave and perform.
2. What you think about yourself does not have to be valid, only "believed!"

Think of the fantastic opportunities that lie ahead to achieve new skills and attitudes using the power of imagination to program new conditioned responses into your inner computer. The greatest genius of them all, Albert Einstein, understood the influence of imagination on his own life when he said, **"Imagination is more important than knowledge."** By the way, Einstein developed his Theory of Relativity by imagining himself riding on a moonbeam traveling through space.

The power of imagination is the key to the rest of this book and everything in it. Soon you'll be able to examine the past, learn from it and rehearse a new ending using the wings of your imagination to fly to a new playing destiny. It's time to recapture the same art of imagination you had as a child that allowed you to freely explore and experience a world filled with adventure not embarrassment, wonder not fear, happiness not frustration. A life that is full of fun and fascination, not fear and failure.

THE PROOF

Look no further than the phenomenon of hypnotism to demonstrate this fundamental principle of the mind. It's been documented that when a hypnotized subject was told that one of his hands was immersed in ice water, that hand actually showed a temperature drop. Another hypnotized subject, when told that he was holding a hot coal, immediately developed blisters on his hand.

A classic study of the effects of imagined experiences was reported in *Research Quarterly* years ago. The subject was mental practice in freethrow shooting. One group practiced foul shooting every day for 20 days and was scored on the first and last day. A second group did not practice at all and was scored on the first and last day. A third group was scored on the first and last day after spending 20 minutes a day imagining shooting one successful shot after another (all in their minds).

The results were startling. The first group, that practiced 20 minutes a day, improved 24%. The second group, that didn't practice at all, showed no improvement. The third group, that practiced mentally, improved 23% ... almost as much as the group that practiced physically. Are you starting to become convinced of the possibilities of CT? Just imagine the results when you combine mental practice and physical practice as you will do after you read the chapters on shooting and freethrow shooting.

The power of imagery has received even further dramatic affirmation. Clinical psychologists have recorded the electromyographic responses of athletes who were mentally summoning up the moment by moment imagery of their favorite sport's activity. The researchers attached an electromyograph to the muscles of these athletes who were visualizing themselves performing. Electrical signals were actually being received by the muscles. **The athletes were physiologically experiencing muscle reaction.** Since it's no secret that experience is the best method for learning, psychologists concluded that athletes could equally learn from the experiences of mental rehearsal.

The one advantage, of course, is that the imagined experience can always be completed successfully!

LOOKING FOR A PERSONAL EXPERIENCE

Here's a first person experience of how imagination affects your performance. Try this: Stand up and extend your right arm forward, pointing your index finger straight ahead. Make sure your right arm and wrist are perfectly straight, and your feet solidly planted on the floor (approximately shoulder width apart). In a clockwise direction, see how far you can twist and turn the upper part of your body around. Keep your feet firmly planted. As you swing your extended arm around, twisting your upper body with the pointer finger leading the way, how far are you capable of turning? Remember the exact location on the wall behind you where you were able to point your finger.

Now use the power of imagination to see how much further you can twist. Rest both arms at your side and close your eyes. Imagine your right arm is still extended in front of you with index finger pointing forward. Imagine feeling its weight. Now in your mind only, visualize that you are twisting your upper body and bringing your right arm around (again clockwise) but this time you are comfortably turning your body well beyond the point you attained earlier. Feel yourself pointing well past the first try. Mentally rehearse the successful twist again, feeling your arm pointing far beyond your first real try.

Now physically do it again. Extend your right arm, point your index finger forward and see how far you can swing the arm around. Compare the outcome with your first try. Surprised at how much further you turned after the visualization? What was it that Shakespeare said? **"Imagination rules your world."**

The implication is clear. My words affected an imagined picture in your mind. This action picture, synthetic as it was, was accepted by your subconscious as real, triggering a physical response of improved flexibility. In order to rule your world, the major CT technique you will utilize will be the power of visualization.

Now you know all about the physical components of your cybernetic success system ... your biological computer, the subconscious and the reticular activating system. They comprise the most powerful, complicated and unfathomable success producing system ever created by nature. Before you learn the four step **FAST Success Formula** that will activate it for optimal performance, you'll need to know more about the psychological components of your inner success system ... **the self image** and the **comfort zone**. Both have the power to either destroy or support your basketball dream.

THE PSYCHOLOGICAL COMPONENTS OF YOUR INNER SUCCESS SYSTEM

"I'll not be free until I believe in me."
Robert Schuller

THE SELF IMAGE

The mental picture you have of yourself ... the type of performer you consider yourself to be ... is your self image. The greatest psychological breakthrough of this century is the discovery of the self image as a predictor of human behavior. There is no factor more decisive in your life than the way in which you think about yourself.

Let me prove it to you. Close your eyes and think about a weak offensive skill that you have, one that frustrates you almost every time you're forced to use it in competition. Imagine that you're playing in a game with the score tied and your team down to its last possession. The ball finds you and you're forced to execute your weak offensive skill (let's say, a weak hand penetration dribble). What did you picture in your mind? Did you finish the play successfully and win the game or did you screw it up? If you're honest, you saw yourself blowing the opportunity ... just as you expected. Sitting in the director's chair was your self image.

As long as you define yourself with negative images, your performance will be limited to inconsistent play. The first step in your reprogramming process is to have an understanding and awareness about the influence that your self image has on your performance.

THE SELF IMAGE: A SYSTEM OF BELIEFS

The self image is not a true statement of your potential and talent because it is based on impressions of your past experiences rather than fact. The self image can be a deception not a description of reality.

Your past experiences started on the first day you began to play basketball. Naturally they included both successes and failures. When the mistakes and misses outnumbered the completions and hits, you started to believe your mistakes were standard behavior. Perhaps your parents, coaches, teammates or friends displayed negative reactions when you played poorly. A wrong glance, facial expression or put down further confirmed a growing feeling that you were not a natural athlete. To make matters worse, you foolishly compared yourself to your older brother, sister or the team's star.

How To Shape A Negative Shooting Self Image

When you first learned how to shoot a jump shot, you were enthusiastic and hopeful. You made and missed a lot of jumpers from all over. You noticed that each shot you made created a good feeling inside. You also noticed that when you dribbled and shot, you missed more shots than you converted, especially driving to the left (your weak hand). A feeling of disappointment after each miss discouraged you from making a commitment to work on that shot. It was easier and more rewarding to spot up and make it, than create a shot off the dribble, miss and feel bad. (The pain and pleasure principle in action.) By overreacting to the responses of your teammates and by avoiding offensive situations that required you to put the ball on the floor with your left hand, a negative self image was evolving. When you did drive and shoot with an unproductive outcome, you had further confirmation that you were permanently limited. When you occasionally finished a weak hand dribble drive, you labeled the success as pure luck. Once you've created a poor self image in any skill, it's almost impossible to improve your level of performance.

Take a look at the poor free throw shooting of some of those highly paid NBA stars who hit only 50% of their foul shots. They are afforded the best shooting instruction in the world, yet they can't shoot consistently from the line. Why? A poor self image is triggering a conditioned response of "no, you can't!" Unless the player's self image is changed for the better (that is, the way he anticipates himself shooting from the line), his shot will remain **successfully** inconsistent.

Self image pyschology also explains why even the power of positive thinking alone won't work with these poor performing athletes. When positive thinking is used but the body language and self talk aren't equally positive (nervous, jerky body language, tense facial expressions along with the wrong kind of self talk), the negative self image is still in charge. To improve the self image, positive thinking, body language and self talk must be congruent (aligned together). Without all three being up to the task, all the pep talks, positive thinking, expert coaching instruction or hoping will not help the athlete find the winner's shooting groove. Since it is the self image that is in control, it is the self image that must be improved.

How To Instantly Overcome A Negative Self Image

The car the two young brothers were working on was parked in the family driveway. With its front wheels removed, the Chevy Impala was precariously supported by three cinder blocks under its front axle. The younger brother was working underneath the front end of the car changing the oil when the car suddenly shifted and slid off the supporting blocks. 3,500 pounds of steel came crashing down on the younger brother, crushing the life from his body. The older brother, Tom, hearing the cry for help instantly realized what he had to do. Quickly Tom managed to lift the front bumper just long enough to enable his brother to safely roll out from beneath the car.

This amazing event occured in the fall of 1968, before the first championship season my high school basketball team would experience (there would be a string of eight more). To this day, I feel that this miraculous incident, more than any other, was responsible for our run of championship seasons. In fact, the development of Cybernetics Training and this book would never have materialized had Tom not found the sudden power to save his brother. Let me tell you why.

Tom was a student in my physical education class. When I tell you Tom could not complete ten push ups, climb the gym ropes or hand travel across the parallel bars, please believe me, he was not acting. Without exaggeration, physically, the 135-pound Tom was the **weakest of the meekest!** Then, all of a sudden, he had this capability to lift a full size car? Give me a break!

When Tom, the hero, came to school that next day, he told me that as he saw his brother being crushed to death, the power just came to him. He had no trouble lifting the front bumper of the car. The phenomenon of Tom's instant strength can be biologically explained as **the fight or flight syndrome.** Whenever we perceive a threat, our body automatically responds to the danger by preparing itself physiologically. During the emergency, Tom's endocrine system automatically excreted a chemical called adrenalin. This, in turn, excited his large muscles to perform beyond their normal limits. His circulatory system directed more blood to his arms and legs. He was ready for an emergency performance ... equipped by nature to perform this miraculous deed.

But the question bothering me was, why couldn't Tom tap this automatic system to work for him during physical education class? If all humans are endowed with this miraculous potential, why is it we can't tap into this source whenever we want? Being the eternal basketball coach, I also wondered why my players couldn't use their own inner power system for basketball exploits. If Tom could become an overachiever, why couldn't my players become overachievers too? (We were losing as many games as we were winning.) There was this question pulsating in my head. "Why can't we tell our body to do what we want it to do, when we want it to do it?" Was there a way to tell our body to perform all kinds of successful deeds in nonemergency situations, like grabbing a rebound, diving for a loose ball or converting a foul shot in prime time?

Was there such a process? I needed to know. I started by reading books on kinesiology, physiology, even way out books on Eastern philosophies. It wasn't until I read the self help books that I discovered one of the most important books I would ever read... *Psycho-Cybernetics.* I found what I'd been searching for!

Published in 1960 and written by a plastic surgeon, Dr. Maxwell Maltz, the book's general design was to help people get more living and enjoyment out of their lives. Dr. Maltz presented a scientific method that could help people achieve success in anything they really wanted. He evolved a technology of behavior drawing knowledge from both the science of self image psychology and the science of cybernetics. After reading a few chapters, I became excited about the possibilities it offered for getting my players to play more aggressively, more confidently and

16

more successfully. As I read this handbook for success, I had an explanation for Tom's instant heroism. More importantly, I had some answers to my coaching problems.

I realized that it was Tom's poor self image that prevented him from achieving in gym class. He never had a reason big enough to overcome his inadequate self image. When he was faced with the strong possibility of his brother's death and the massive pain he would experience if he didn't do something, his subconscious instantly provided his body with the power it needed. The old performance patterns (the product of a hopeless self image) were quickly rejected and replaced with the successful command of "Whatever it takes, I've got to save my brother!" In an instant, Tom overcame his negative self image and tapped his full potential.

Are you ready to overcome your patterns of negative thinking and replace them with empowering ones that can improve your self image? The process will require disciplining your imagination, changing the way you talk to yourself and move your body. Before you do, you've got to know about the great destroyer of dreams … .your comfort zone!

THE COMFORT ZONE

The comfort zone doesn't exist physically, but it's there psychologically determining the exact degree of your on the court success.

Incidentally, if you're looking for something to blame for not becoming the player you want to be … blame your comfort zone. You won't be wrong, because it's the permanent home for your self image! Unless the size and scope of your comfort zone are expanded, you can forget about reading the rest of this book. Your subconscious will be permanently incarcerated to a life of mediocrity. I can't say it more bluntly, "**A narrow comfort zone makes dream achieving impossible!**" The good news is that **you** control the size of your own comfort zone.

What is the comfort zone? As I said before, in basketball the comfort zone is all the habits you have repeated so many successful times that you feel comfortable doing them again. John-Roger and Peter McWilliams in their innovative book, *Do It!* explain the comfort zone this way:

"There is something we are trained to honor more than our dreams … it's the comfort zone. Whenever we do something new, it falls outside the barrier of the comfort zone. In contemplating a new action, we fear guilt, unworthiness, hurt feelings, anger … all those things we generally think of as uncomfortable."

Imagine your comfort zone as a circle of fear (losers consider it a wall of protection). Within that circle are your current basketball skills and attitudes which bring you the most success simply because you have done them so many times. The major problem with the comfort zone is that it prevents you from extending yourself and developing the basketball actions you need to live your basketball dream.

Overachievers in life operate out of an unlimited comfort zone. They are not afraid to work on new moves or to shoot from unaccustomed spots on the court. Mistakes are never permanent. Pain is no big deal, either. But what is important is the success that they expect to earn from working hard. That is why you'll always find them challenging themselves to do difficult things on the court, like dribbling with their weak hand, diving for loose balls or taking the charge. Instead of feeling threatened when playing a skill weakness into a strength, the uncertain course inspires them. Sure they feel the fear we all do, but they know how to play through their fear. They know how to **just do it**!

For most of us, the tendency is to respect our comfort zone and return to the same habits of **thinking and doing** that we've done so many times in the past. We use the same moves, shoot from the same spots, overuse the strong hand, make that unnecessary extra pass when we should step up and shoot. We spend the same amount of practice time, doing the same things . . . and somehow we expect better results. Is there a better definition for insanity? Unfortunately, many of the basketball tools needed to become the player you want to be, fall outside the parameters of your comfort zone.

By staying inside the comfort zone, regardless of the need to expand it, the past will always equal the future. Change will be impossible unless you break the chains of comfort that bind you and adopt new training strategies.

"To have what you have not, you must do what you have not done." This is a strategy that can broaden your comfort zone faster than any other. Every time you challenge yourself, by employing the untraditional tasks of CT, you'll be challenging your comfort zone, improving your self image and developing attitudes of the winner. You'll be forced to develop new thoughts about your capabilities including finding courage to take risks. Old habits, like anxiety, frustration, fatigue, injuries and fear that you've been hiding behind, will no longer be acceptable.

HOW TO EXPAND YOUR COMFORT ZONE

Here are nine major steps that can help you expand your comfort zone:

1. Value success over entertainment.
2. Set goals that challenge you.
3. Develop a feeling of certainty that success is inevitable.
4. Make it a habit to **do the thing that is hard to do.**
5. Feel the fear and do it anyway.
6. Learn to turn frustration into fascination.
7. Eliminate the word **try** from your playing vocabulary.
8. Strike procrastination from your life's game plan.
9. Use the Pain and Pleasure Principle to work for you (not against you).

Value success over entertainment: Think about the pleasure of success first. Make entertainment a distant second. Whenever you have a choice between entertainment (such as hanging out with your friends, watching TV, taking a power nap) or success (achieving a daily quota of 100 push ups, 100 sit ups, making 100 jump shots or dribbling the ball 10,000 times with your weak hand), find a reason to take action, put on your basketball shoes and go to work.

Set goals that challenge you: Be on the look out for training or performance goals that challenge you and take decisive action. Consider every goal as an extraordinary opportunity to develop a winning skill and expand your comfort zone. Leave this sign on that easy chair in front of the TV. "Sorry! I'm out expanding my comfort zone! Won't be back!"

Develop a feeling of certainty that success is inevitable: All overachievers have that feeling that success is waiting for them down the road if they stay with it. Because of this positive expectation that success is inevitable, setbacks are temporary, and never seem to discourage them. Learn their secret. They use the power of imagination to visualize what they want . . . not what they want to avoid.

Make it a habit to do the thing that is hard to do: Whenever you have an opportunity to choose between doing something that is easy or difficult . . . immediately do the thing that is hard to do. Follow this same game plan in life and you'll never have trouble finding the power to take the action. It will be there!

Feel the fear and do it anyway: When you experience any kind of pain such as fear, fatigue, boredom, embarrassment or a feeling of unworthiness, realize the benefits. This feeling of emotional and physical discomfort means that you have reached the outer limits of your comfort zone. This is good. Taking any kind of positive action has to expand your comfort zone. By the way, rename that feeling of fear you experience before games. Call it by its real name . . . **excitement!** It's only nature's way of preparing you for success!

Turn frustration into fascination: When you feel frustrated as a result of a setback or disappointment, turn it into fascination by asking yourself resourceful questions like "What's good about this?" or "What have I learned that will help me avoid repeating this situation again?" (See the section on Power Talk.) By asking smart questions, you activate your focusing device, the reticular activating system. Once it is activated, you will be provided with an unbelieveable source of energy, correct answers to your question and an expanded comfort zone.

Eliminate the word "try" from your playing vocabulary: Try is a three letter word for comfort zone effort. Is "I'll try" one of your pet expressions? I hope not. It qualifies you for an early **quit.**

Strike procrastination from your life's game plan: Stay away from the procrastinator's strategy of "I'll do it tomorrow." You ought to understand what **tomorrow** is before it's too late. "It's a road called **Someday** that leads to a town called **Nowhere!**" Although you'll never be alone traveling the easy road, it will always stop short of your true destiny . . . right at the edge of your comfort zone.

Use the Pain and Pleasure Principle to work for you (not against you): Motivate yourself by utilizing the pain and pleasure principle to your advantage. **No pain, no gain!** Don't consider pain punishment, but your admission ticket into the winner's circle. Make it a habit of projecting ahead, as winners do, to either the pleasure of success that awaits you or the feeling of regret you'll experience if you don't act.

THE COMFORT ZONE JUNKIE WITHIN

Beware of the **Comfort Zone Junkie** that lurks within all of us. The addiction is subtle. You never know when you've become one until it's too late and your career is over.

You ask, "How do you know that you've become a **Comfort Zone Junkie?**" There are two telltale signs. First, you're satisfied with the way you're playing. Second, your fear of making mistakes. You'll do anything to avoid making a mistake in games, including hiding from the ball when the game is on the line.

Watch out for these symptoms. You're addicted to your comfort zone when you. . .

C **Consider** weaknesses as permanent.
O **Overtry** in competition . . . but undertry in practice.
M **Make** security your #1 priority.
F **Frustrate** quickly.
O **Overconcern** yourself about results.
R **Remember** mistakes.
T **Try** with a comfort zone effort.

Z **Zero** in on what's wrong.
O **Overwhelm** yourself with too much thinking.
N **Negate** the positive.
E **Excuses** come quickly.

We all have a deep inner want to succeed. But for those of us who have been living too long within our narrow comfort zone, we tend to see life on the court as it is . . . rather than what it should be.

Congratulations! You're already on the road to recovery by recognizing the characteristics of a comfort zone junkie. By reaffirming your faith in your inner success system and trusting the CT process, you can make that final escape leap. Skepticism has never gotten anyone anywhere. For starters, stop doubting and start trusting yourself. Each day you spend on the court go for the pleasure of success and stop avoiding pain. Pain is good. It's the first sign that you are expanding your comfort zone. When you feel the pain, the unworthiness, the fear . . . do it anyway! Whenever you **do the thing that is hard to do**, consider the discomfort as a weakness leaving your body. Here are some addiction breaking tips:

C **Consider** playing weaknesses as opportunities to grow.
O **Overwork** in practice.
M **Make** success your #1 priority.
F **Free up** from frustration by refusing to get disappointed by your mistakes and missed shots.
O **Overtake** your concern with positive thinking.
R **Remember** to focus on what you do right, not what you do wrong.
T **Take Action until** . . . **you** get what you want.

Z **Zero** in on what's right.
O **Overlook** what overwhelms you.
N **Nurture** your self image with power thoughts, questions and words.
E **Excite** yourself with challenges that allow you to grow.

If you are willing to live these suggestions **one day at a time,** you'll do more than free yourself up from your comfort zone addiction. **You'll be fearless!**

STUDY THE WINNERS

Study the winners and you'll have proof that the list on page 18 is more than credible. Surely you must know a few overachievers that you can question on the validity of these nine steps. Let them tell you about the strategy that kept them motivated to take action. You'll have all the evidence you want.

What do you think motivated former Celtic great Larry Bird to seek out a junior high school gym to work out in the morning after playing over 40 minutes of bruising NBA basketball? So he could make more money, or hang another championship banner from the rafters of the Boston Garden? I don't think so. If you want an answer, review the list of how to expand your comfort zone. Pick one or a combination of any of them and you won't be wrong.

Now that you know about the physical and psychological components of your inner success system, there is one more stop you must make before I can tell you about the **FAST** formula of success. It's time you know about the power of self awareness.

The Importance Of Self Awareness

"Self-awareness comes from asking and answering hard questions."
Stephen Covey

Getting from here to there begins with understanding where **here** is on your basketball map. It's called self awareness.

Even with a road map in your hands, you can't intelligently ask for directions to anywhere unless you first know where **here** is. The same strategy applies to your basketball journey. You need to know **where you are** before you can move in the direction of **where you want to go**. Without knowing what your strengths and weakness are, intelligent goal setting is difficult.

A complete and accurate inventory of your strong and weak skills and attitudes is a good start. But self awareness also includes knowing the full potential of your inner resources, understanding the unlimited power of your imagination and, of course, acknowledging your greatest power … the power to choose your final destination.

You also need to be constantly alert to the force the **pain and pleasure** principle has on its traveling companions, your self image and your comfort zone. There is no force more powerful in determining your ultimate destination than the two basic needs of **avoiding pain and gaining pleasure.** Make most of your on court decisions based on the need to avoid pain and both your self image and comfort zone suffer excessive damage. Then the trouble begins. When your unsure self image and narrow comfort zone realize that you're dreaming an exciting journey, you are forced to respond: "It's too tough! I can't do this! I'm tired, give it a rest! Think of the embarrassment if I screw it up!"

A Self Image Check

The problem with traveling with an out-of-control, poor self image and a narrow comfort zone is that every time you have a tough decision to make on the court, you lower your goals and expectations. Your game strategy is to do only what you do best or take the safest route. Fear of failure and a feeling of unworthiness cause you to avoid those same weak skills you should be developing into strengths. You take few chances and, as a result, experience little change in your game.

You already know the good news. Since the self image is your creation, freeing yourself from the bondage of a poor self image can be your doing, too. Your human computer operates on the same principle as all mechanical computers function … input determines output. The task of expanding your self image and comfort zone require a great deal of positive thinking and doing. But first, let's examine your old way of thinking and doing so that you'll know exactly what you'll need to change.

This means being totally honest with yourself and defining your game objectively. Evaluating what you do well and what you don't. No exaggerations and no deceptions. Promise me that after you identify those weaknesses, you'll refuse to accept them as permanent, but rather as creative opportunities that will help you dramatically improve your game.

A QUESTION OF DEGREE

Once you understand that all skills, attitudes and emotions are neither good nor bad, but simply in various stages of growth and development, your self image will experience an immediate lift. There's a tendency in most athletes and coaches, especially when the self image is soft, to see things in black and white … good or bad. In reality, there are degrees of effectiveness.

Shakespeare said, "Nothing is either good or bad, but thinking makes it so." Solid advice worth considering now that you don't have to accept your weaknesses as permanent. What Shakespeare failed to mention was that changing the way you think can effectively be accomplished in small degrees!

An itemized list of your basketball assets with an attached degree of proficiency can help you establish exactly where you are as a player. Then you'll have a detailed map to accurately follow on your basketball journey confirming that you're moving in the right direction.

Additionally, a realistic inventory of your current skills and attitudes will give you a clear picture of every one of your self images! The psychological fact is that each one of your basketball skills has its very own self image mirroring it. For example if you see yourself as a perimeter player who rarely drives to the basket when faced with an open lane, you'll probably find a reason not to take advantage of the opening. In reality what's holding you back is a fear of failure produced by a soft self image. No matter how hard you practice aggressive offensive moves, unless you see yourself driving and finishing … the skill development won't stick! Neither will you find the personal power to persevere. It's not how well you can drive to the basket, it's how clearly you see yourself driving and finishing that is important.

Now, are you ready to look within from above? You'll find the view quite revealing.

A SELF AWARENESS INVENTORY: LOOKING WITHIN FROM ABOVE

Let's begin your self-evaluation at the defensive end of the court. Here is a list of defensive traits for self-appraisal. Score yourself using a scale of 1-10. A 1 represents a low self-estimation; a

10 signifies an extraordinary, super skill (or attitude) level. A score of 5 stands for a playable but not consistent skill; an 8 or 9 is a ready for prime time skill.

In order to objectively increase your self awareness level, use the following visualization procedure. Observe yourself competing from an aerial view. Normally you evaluate yourself (and the world) from an **inside-out** perspective. With an **outside-in** look, you'll be able judge your performance less personally … from above.

Do this: Visualize yourself leaving your body and feel yourself rising up to the ceiling. Now, imagine yourself looking down, but instead of seeing yourself reading this book, you have a bird's-eye view of a basketball court on which two teams are playing a hotly contested full court game. Zero in on the the game. There you are … right in the middle of the action … doing your thing. You're watching yourself playing defense—defending the opponent's best. Let's test all of your defensive self images. (Remember to rate from a 1 to 10 each skill or attitude ability you see yourself performing).

JUDGE YOUR DEFENSIVE ABILITY TO:

1. Control the dribbler. . . Are your feet moving quickly enough? Are you anticipating the offensive player's moves? Are you stopping the dribbler? _____

2. Defend the shot. . . Are you pressuring the shot? _____

3. Be aggressive. . . Are you forceful and physical? _____

4. Compete with intensity. . . Are you maintaining a high degree of desire? _____

5. Play with courage. . . Can you see yourself taking a charge, diving for a loose ball, or sacrificing your body for your team? _____

6. Enjoy playing defense. . . Do you see yourself excited, enthused and having fun? _____

7. Rebound. . . Are you boxing out? Is there second and third effort? Are you holding on to the rebound and quickly pitching it out? _____

8. Make a big defensive play. . . Do you see yourself turning a game around by making a key steal, deflection or stop? _____

9. Help and recover. . . Can you see yourself actively playing both ball and man? Are you a positive factor away from the ball? _____

10. Play post defense. . . Are you playing big? _____

11. Play deny defense. . . Are you unrelenting and determined? _____

12. **Endurance. . .**Are you staying strong? _____

The purpose of this test is to open an avenue of communication between you and your many self images. Notice that some of your self images are stronger than others. Later on, using the power of visualization, I'll show you how to increase your scores, inch by inch. At the same time you'll have an opportunity to reshape the controlling self image.

For now let's go back to the same aerial view, and evaluate your skills and attitudes on the offensive end of the court using the same 1-10 scale:

JUDGE YOUR OFFENSIVE ABILITY TO:

1. Hit the open jumper ____5____

2. Hit the jumper in a crowd ____3____

3. Create a shot for yourself with a decisive move ____7____

4. Drive hard and low to the basket and finish it off ____2____

5. Drive, draw and dish (drive, draw the defense and find the open teammate) ____7____

6. Rebound with quickness and power ____3____

7. Move without the ball ____7____

8. Set strong screens ____7____

9. Shoot the three ____5____

10. Handle the ball (dribble and pass) ____5____

What discoveries have you made? Any surprises? Now from above, imagine watching yourself running the court. Again appraise your performance in each situation with a 1 to 10 score:

JUDGE YOUR ABILITY TO RUN THE COURT:

1. Fill a lane ____8____

2. Pass and catch ____8____

3. Finish the break with a basket ____2____

4. Drive a lane ___6___

5. Run the court when fatigued ___4___

6. Run a defensive break (getting back) ___6___

   One final aerial look. Let's examine your inner character and attitudes (1 to 10):

1. Sportsmanship ___8___

2. Performance in the clutch ___3___

3. Determination ___7___

4. Rapport with teammates ___5___

5. Rapport with coaching staff _____

6. Optimism ___4___

7. Positive self talk ___4___

8. Ability to set realistic goals and achieve them ___5___

9. Honesty and integrity ___8___

10. Self-confidence ___5___

12. Concentration (pinpoint and peripheral) ___3___

13. Composure (control your emotions) ___7___

14. Competitiveness ___8___

15. Contribution to the team ___8___

17. Perseverance ___7___

18. Commitment ___6___

19. Courage ___7___

20. Ability to take on a challenge or risk ___6___

21. Resiliency _____6_____

22. Handle frustration _____7_____

This final visualization session will not be easy. Evaluating your attitude and character may require several tries. Recalling specific situations can help. Judge the inner skillls and character you displayed and grade yourself accordingly. With time and practice, you'll get better at this number game.

SCORE THE EVENTS OF YOUR DAY

Sharpen your self awareness ability at the end of each day by looking back at certain events that happened that day in practice, the game or the locker room. Close your eyes, recall the aerial view, peer down and numerically grade your response in those recently experienced situations (1-10). Before falling asleep at night is a good time to run these events through the mirror of your mind and score yourself. The habit of reviewing your daily performance and grading these events will help you make more profitable decisions in the future.

After games, feel free to update your inventory scores. Each time you do, you will be telling your self image that you are aware it's expanding and improving and that you appreciate the change. Not only will **knowing thyself** make you a better player ... you'll be a better person!

AVOID THE #10

Athletes coach themselves the way coaches coach. They **correct to perfect**. There's no easier way to abuse the self image then to strive for perfection. Don't get caught in the pressure trap of having to attain a 10 in order to feel good about yourself. If you're thinking you've got to be perfect to win, very few things you do on the court will be fun. In time, the only thing you'll achieve is **burnout**. I worry about a coach who says his team must play a **perfect** game in order to win. The pressure is immense. They rarely do ... and, hence, rarely win the **big** one.

VALUABLE SELF IMAGE INSIGHTS

If you're not satisfied with the outcome of your performance inventory, you've got two choices ... fix the blame or fix the problem. The easy way is to blame your genetic makeup (grandfather was a **hothead**, too). However if you want to be in control of your personal remote system and show some resourcefulness, here are some CT self image insights:

1. Realize that low self-description is self-defeating. "That's my nature, that's me. I can't help it," is unacceptable and untrue and prevents you from taking responsibility for your life.

2. Understand that all negative "I'ms" can be traced to the poor self image **which you have created.**

3. Before falling asleep, make it a habit to remind yourself of the positive contributions you made during the day.

4. Realize you have only winning skills and attitudes. However, some are in a stage of early development. Skills are never finished products. With a commitment to change, your skills will improve. Be patient and persistent.

5. As long as you continue to label yourself clumsy, you will have a built-in reason to avoid success and to be clumsy. Negative labeling becomes a self-fulfilling prophecy thanks to your RAS. Stop it!

6. Eliminate the "I'ms" that are negative and create positive "I'ms." "I'll try" is unacceptable because it's a comfort zone effort (losers try). "I'm enthusiastic, I'm aggressive, I'm capable" are the basis for new self talk conversations.

7. Understand that there is joy in a new way of thinking and doing. Not only does success come in "Cans," so does happiness.

8. It's time to realize that the power and freedom to choose which attitudes you want is in your hands (or should I say head). What you do with this power is totally up to you. **It's your responsibility. . . . so respond with ability!**

WHY YOU MUST VALUE YOURSELF

Since the beginning of time, there has never been a person exactly like you, and there will never be anyone like you until the end of time. When you consider your uniqueness, it's impossible to demean yourself.

For some reason you have been gifted with a miracle-producing inner success system and the freedom to choose how to use it. Find your real purpose and you will have more than you need to live an exciting and rewarding life. Maybe the philosopher was right when he said, "Life's purpose is to find a purpose." Is basketball yours? Only you can make that decision. Whether it is or isn't, I can tell you this: The lessons you learn along your basketball journey will help you develop the winning strategies and beliefs you'll need when you do find life's real purpose.

AND...VALUE YOUR TEAMMATES

You must accept and appreciate the uniqueness of your teammates, managers and coaches. They have been gifted with the same inner success system and power to choose. The belief and value systems of others are usually different. But team goals must be unified if a successful season is to be expected.

It is not necessary that every player on the team is likeable. What is important is that everybody on the team understands and likes one another. All you need to like someone is to look for good in that person. Do you look for good in your teammates and others you meet? You should. By looking for good in others you find good in yourself. The opposite is also true. Look for bad in others and you expose the bad in yourself.

There is a **looking for good** game that I play at airport terminals that is lots of fun. While waiting for my flight, I sit and watch the people that pass me. As they do, I identify one unique quality each of them has. It can be anything from the purposeful way they carry themselves, the uniqueness of their clothes, or some positive characteristic of their physical appearance. The game does more than pass the time of day, it puts me in an optimistic frame of mind for travel (and living).

Here's a **looking for good** exercise your team can play after workouts on the floor or in the locker room after games. It's called the **Circle For Giving And Forgiving.** We have a lot of fun with it at camp and it really helps the players respect and focus on the special efforts and abilities of their teammates. This is what we do: The team circles up as each player takes a turn recognizing a positive contribution that the teammate standing to his right made during the scrimmage or game. Even if a player didn't play well or didn't play at all, you can always find something good if you sincerely look for it.

The greatest waste of energy is focusing on what is wrong. Conversely, there is a synergistic benefit when all players on a team develop the habit of valuing each other. It's called success.

THE CHOICE IS YOURS

In closing this chapter on self awareness, I hope you'll be alert to your greatest power … your freedom to choose which goals excite you the most and in the long run will bring your the most happiness. Appreciate your personal power to choose from…

goal oriented or aimless.	alert or unobserving.
now person or procrastinator.	aggressive or timid.
courageous or fearful.	determined or a quitter.
worker or idler.	enthusiastic or indifferent.
creative or mechanical.	giver or taker.
relaxed or uptight.	winner or loser.

This, then, can be your ultimate awareness … the power to choose how you want to utilize your inner success system. Activating your power will require you to learn all you can about the art of effectively setting goals for your subconscious to act upon. The first key step in the **FAST** success formula of how to get what you want is **knowing what you want**. With the help of your self awareness inventory, let's examine the power of finding a goal and a reason why you want that goal.

FAST: The Ultimate Success Formula Of Cybernetics Training

"From the lowliest depth there is a path to the loftiest height."
Carlyle

Winners have a strategy worth remembering. Its called WIT, **whatever it takes**. Have you noticed that achievers seem to find a way to get the job done no matter what the adversity? This is the WIT part of the program ... the **how-to** of tapping your inner success system for best results.

There are four basic steps. Miss one of them and the cybernetic system breaks down. By using the acronym FAST, the success formula is clearly laid out in correct sequence.

Are you ready to challenge yourself and follow through on everyone of the CT methods you're about to learn? I hope so. Both your dream and your destiny are in the balance.

F...Find a goal and a reason why you want to achieve the goal.
Without a compelling reason, sticking to your game plan will be difficult.
A...Act as if.
You don't have to reinvent the wheel. Learn to model the winner's belief system, body language and self talk. It's the fastest way to condition your inner success system to produce that winning feeling.
S...See yourself having the winning skills and attitudes.
Winners have a habit of **seeing** what they want. Losers see what they want to avoid! Get smart and utilize the great power of mental visualization to develop self-confidence.
T...Take action until you get what you want.

FIND A GOAL, AND A REASON FOR WANTING IT!

"One person with a belief is equal to a force of ninety-nine who have only interest."
John Stewart Mills

It's time to take action. Goal setting is the first step in the **doing** process. Cybernetics is a Greek word meaning "the steersman". Goals require direction. Your success mechanism is constructed so that it will automatically steer you in the direction of your goal. It supplies you with the energy and know-how you'll need to achieve your goal.

The key question that you must ask yourself in setting goals is, "How important is it to me to achieve the goal?" Reasons come before results. Once you discover a reason big enough for wanting a goal, strong signals are sent to your subconscious announcing that you are not happy with the way things are and demanding a change.

Here's an example of the importance of first finding a strong reason before you can achieve a goal. At camp, I challenge the athletes to dribble a basketball 100,000 times before the end of camp. The dribbles don't have to be accomplished consecutively, but they must be weak hand dribbles. This task, I warn them, will cut into their free time and probably take a total of 14 hours to complete. Those who accomplish the 100,000 dribble challenge are rewarded. During the first few days, I notice a number of the campers dribbling with their weak hand, but by the second day, fewer campers apply themselves to the challenge. Why do they lose interest? Only a few have a big enough reason to persist. On the last day, when the two or three athletes who finish receive their award, I ask them why they were willing to spend all that time and effort monotonously dribbling a basketball. I always hear the same reply. It's not the award or even the skill improvement that motivated them. They applied themselves because of the challenge. Simply ... they wanted to see if they could do it. For the winner, loving the challenge is one of the most powerful reasons of all. If you want to achieve your goals, the first step after you determine what you want is why you want it!

Recently, I watched the University of Arkansas whip Duke for the 1994 NCAA Division I Basketball Championship. After Duke's semifinal win against the University of Florida, Grant Hill, the great Duke swingman, was interviewed and asked why it was important that his team beat Arkansas. He thought for a few seconds and said, "I guess I could brag to the other former Duke players at the beach this summer that I was on three National Championship teams." Even if he was trying to be glib, I still had the feeling that his motivation was not as compelling as the Arkansas players' motivation. To a man, they wanted to prove they could win the big one.

31

When you set and pursue a goal, you are doing what comes naturally. Your cybernetic device demands goals. Think of it, aren't you happiest when you're goal getting? For me, the saddest moment of a season was never the loss of a final playoff game. What saddened me the most was the reality that the season was over.

"The reason people love to jog is that running is the purest form of goal setting," explained running guru George Sheehan. During my own daily runs, I keep my subconscious busy and happy. Miss one day and I'm overwhelmed with a feeling of guilt. William Glasser in his book *Positive Addiction* explains that an addiction to positive goal setting activities can be developed. People who have to stay busy to be happy are in a sense addicted. I happen to be a charter member of this group.

SET REALISTIC GOALS

Wouldn't it be a simple matter for you to set some personal performance goals and then let the inner success system take over? But this is not the case. Setting realistic and challenging goals can be a real problem, especially with a restricting self awareness that a poor self image provides. I can recall a camper by the name of Matt whose unrealistic goal was to be an NBA player. Matt was slow and as if that wasn't enough of a handicap, he had a habit of not completing plays during camp games. He often "dead-ended" the play with a missed shot, bad pass, or fumbled reception. Without a realistic self image, a fictitious self can be created. This is what happened to Matt. He covered up an insecure and inferior self image by establishing superior and completely unreachable goals for himself. Because he had to impress others, he became a hot dog on the court, always making the easy play look difficult. Many of his mistakes were a result of overtrying. Although I never told him he wouldn't make the NBA, I did suggest that he start setting some self improvement goals that could help him contribute to his team's success. Matt had to accomplish the little things first, like being able to set a pivot foot, hitting the open teammate, converting a power lay-up and keeping an offensive opponent with the ball from getting around him.

For all of us there is a freedom to choose goals . . . to choose what is best. And in reality we never exhaust all of the possibilities and powers of our real potential. William James, the father of modern day pyschology, estimated we use only 10 percent of our natural mind capacity. He probably overestimated. Recent estimates state that less than 4 percent of our potential is actually tapped.

More often than not, I find that athletes underestimate the limits of their capacity. Those in the martial arts believe we use only a quarter of our real physical power, and they present visual evidence to prove their theories. Coaches of all sports know from their own firsthand experiences that there are too many athletes on their teams that have never come close to realizing their talents.

HOW TO USE YOUR INVENTORY TO ESTABLISH SMART GOALS

Before any realistic and significant goals can be set...you must come to **Know Thyself.** There is power in self awareness. That is why I have asked you to take an honest skill and attitude inventory. Let's take the results of the test you took in the chapter on self awareness and use it to help you create some realistic and challenging goals.

For starters, select one skill that will improve your game the most. Is it a better shot off the dribble? Let's say you gave yourself a 5 on the inventory. Close your eyes and focus in on the 5 for a few seconds. Now mentally increase that number by two points. Hold the 7 in your mind for thirty seconds. You have determined both a specific and reachable skill goal. Your mission is to improve your shooting ability off the dribble to a 7 level. Now think: What would you have to do on the court to increase your performance level for shooting off the dribble by just two more points? How much better would you have to shoot to attain the higher score? If you can't answer that question accurately, let me ask you, if there is someone you know who has a 7 level skill shooting off the dribble? I'm going to show you how to model that better shooter and achieve a higher score for yourself on the floor. But for now, all you'll need to do is:

1. Select two skills from each end of the court (offense and defense) and two important attitude habits.
2. Mentally establish a score two points higher for each one of these skills and attitudes.

Regarding the power of goal setting, here is a guideline list of nine powerful recommendations that I want you to follow.

1. Set goals that are high enough, so that they present a challenge, but are within reach.
2. A goal must be one that can be conceptualized ... mentally seen in the mind's eye as a **goal picture** or **end result picture**. You must believe there is a real possibility the goal can be reached. If the goal cannot be conceptualized, it certainly will not be realized. For instance, after Roger Bannister became the first runner in history to run a sub-four minute mile, other outstanding milers were suddenly running sub-four minute miles. This achievement was possible because others with the potential could finally conceptualize a successful sub-four minute mile.
3. Goal cards ... you must constantly remind yourself of your goals. Write them down in one, two or three words that create a positive word picture of what you want on a 3 x 5 inch card. Duplicate the cards. Put them in places where you can't avoid seeing them. For example: the wall of your room, on the mirror in your bedroom or bathroom, on the inside cover of your notebook, in your wallet, on your desk, or inside your school locker.
4. Sign the card on the bottom line as if it is a contract. It is! Consider it a personal commitment to the most important person you know in your life ... yourself.

5. Write these two words on the top line of the cards: "I CAN." (At camp, our goal cards are preprinted with these vital words.)

6. Fix a deadline next to the goal. This is the date you expect to achieve this goal. Deadlines offer the subconscious a more specific instruction.

7. The goal must be something you want ... not something that is imposed on you by your coaches, friends or family. The goal will lead to fulfillment of your own ambitions not someone else's. The best way to determine if you really want the goal is to ask yourself these two empowering questions:

   • **What will I gain if I achieve this goal ?**
   • **What will I lose if I don't take action to achieve this goal?**

   Honestly answer these two questions and you'll have all the firepower you'll need to move ahead to the culmination of your goal.

8. Establish one set of related goals at a time. Athletes who vacillate between goals or are always changing goals seldom realize any of their goals. Dropping goals and selecting new ones means learning how to quit. Careful judgements must be made to see if a goal is truly attainable. Only then should a new goal be substituted.

9. Goals should not be destructive in nature. The goal should not harm, intimidate, humiliate, or take advantage of another. Wanting to physically or mentally hurt someone or wish someone ill is wrong. These goals can be achieved, but you are using the marvelous power of the success mechanism for the wrong reasons. Hurting someone else will not benefit you.

There is tremendous power in goal setting. The most powerful electronic computer in the world has no power at all unless it's plugged in. Plug into a goal you want and your mental computer will have all the power it needs.

Now, for the second step in the CT success formula. By **acting as if** you will learn a short-cut method that can help you develop that feeling of certainty that winners enjoy. Discover for yourself the power of mirroring the beliefs, body language and self talk of successful others. It's easy and fun!

ACTING AS IF: MODELING THE BEST

"People seldom improve when they have no other model but themselves to copy after."
Goldsmith

Walk into the any **Yes, I Can! Basketball Camp** at the right time and you won't believe what you see and hear! There will be 250 screaming and growling campers, crouched over like wild animals, bellowing strange bear-like noises, bouncing around like uninhibited animals. No, they haven't gone insane. What they are achieving is an aggressive state of mind by radically changing their physiology. In essence, the body is telling the subconscious what the body wants the subconscious to do.

Acting as if, is one of the quickest ways there is to improve the self image, expand the comfort zone and control the focus of the RAS. When you physically pretend to be what you are not, and you do it with conviction, your subconscious will grasp what it is you want it to do. Am I suggesting if you pretend to be aggressive, combative, intense, confident and energized, that in time you will develop these virtues? **No, not in time…I'm telling you it will happen immediately.** Remember your subconscious absolutely cannot tell the difference between a real experience and one that is vividly imagined.

Changing your physiology is one of the most powerful tools you can employ to take charge of your game. The way you move your body, express your facial muscles, breathe and talk is instantly linked to the way you feel and think. If you don't believe me, try this:

Stand up straight, throw your shoulders back, head up, and take several deep breaths. With your eyes looking upward, put a great big smile on your face and rapidly slap your hands together (six times). With each powerful clap, shout the word "Great!"

Now, how do you feel? Feel any different than you felt before? If you did exactly as I suggested, you should feel more excited, energized and powerful. Your **motion created emotion,** thanks to the instruction signals that were sent to your subconscious via your body action.

You can create any state of mind you want by controlling your body motion, breathing, facial expression and tone of voice. Even your confidence level can instantly increase, if that's what you want. Follow these instructions and find out for yourself:

I want you to remember a game or a part of your game in which you played flawlessly. Remember how you felt … so confident, strong and unstoppable. Stand up and move your

The Bear-off Challenge

*You may not believe that aggressiveness and intensity can be developed overnight, but you'd think differently after several sessions of **Bear-offs**.*

body with the same excitement and assurance that you had in that game. Look now the way you looked then. Put that same unbeatable expression on your face that you had then. Breathe exactly the way you breathed then ... deep and strong. Can you remember what you said to yourself, or how you said it? Speak to yourself, right now, with that same feeling of certainty and tone in your voice.

Now how do you feel inside? You should be feeling more confident, upbeat and optimistic. When you duplicate the body language you experienced during any past moment of greatness, you duplicate the same confident state of mind. They are permanently linked together.

MODELING THE BEST

Do you want to play more aggressively and with more conviction? Most athletes do. Whenever you mirror someone's body language and mirror that person's attitude and beliefs, the process is called modeling. Find someone who is aggressive, model his strong body language, intense facial expressions, deep breathing rhythm and positive self talk, and you'll have his exact strategy of how to play aggressively. The **Bear-off** is the technique used at camp to induce athletes to play with more freedom, intensity, conviction and aggressiveness. This is how it is done:

- A proven aggressive player volunteers to be the **bear**.
- Next, another volunteer, who wants to learn how to play with more aggressiveness, steps up.
- The two athletes face off with one another in front of the campers.
- The aggressive player crouches down, with a wide stance, back straight, elbows out, hands out like a set of claws, and puts on the wildest, most intense facial expression he or she can create. The model begins to loudly growl and grunt and bounce all over the place, shouting "I'm a beast! I'm a beast!"
- Meanwhile the less aggressive player is told to carefully observe the wild performance of the **beast**, and when ready, to physically mirror the wild actions of the aggressive player. With equal abandonment, the unaggressive player must duplicate everything the aggressive player is doing, especially the strong body language, growling and grunting noises, and, of course, the screaming ... "I am a beast!"

You won't believe the chaotic scene in the gym when the rest of the campers demonstrate the **Bear-off** challenge. If the parents could see their handsome sons and lovely daughters grunting, growling and contorting their faces like wild animals, I wonder if they'd ever have sent them to the **Yes, I Can! Camp.** You may not believe that aggressiveness and intensity can be developed overnight, (How long did it take you to develop your unaggressiveness?), but you'd think differently after several sessions of **Bear-offs**. The competitive play is so fierce and intense, and the campers play with such freedom that the games have to be officiated very tightly, indeed. One girl who came to camp as a tentative and timid player, had an extraordinary transformation soon after the **Bear-offs** were introduced. Her high school coach, who was working camp, told me he couldn't believe how much her power game had improved since the beginning of camp. I had the pleasure of meeting her mother and father on the last day of camp. As they were leaving, the girl abruptly turned to me and, with a sparkle of freedom in her eyes, proceeded to scream at the top of her lungs ... "I am a Beast!" I will long remember that moment and the looks of astonishment on the faces of her startled parents.

Another effective modeling method is to study and mirror the actions of winners around you. This modeling technique considerably helped a former player of mine, Mitch Kupchak, recapture his aggressive style of play. At the time, Mitch was playing for the Los Angeles Lakers and had gone down with a major knee injury (followed by an operation). He returned after a year off, but unfortunately was having trouble regaining the same degree of abandonment that was his distinctive style of playing. I suggested that he get his hands on his old game videotapes from college and study his performance closely. As he watched the films, I asked him to imagine how he felt as he executed a strong baseline move, ripped a rebound, played tenacious one-on-one defense and ran the court tirelessly. By mentally mirroring what he saw in the tapes, Mitch soon recovered the same enthusiasm and drive he had before his injury.

There are unlimited resources that you can apply to the mirroring process. Just keep your eyes open. Beth Raptis, whose photograph is in this book, improved her point guard play immediately by modeling the confident, cocky attitude of an outstanding point guard she was playing with on an all star team. Beth's natural position is the shooting guard, but when she was told she would have to play some backup point, she simply paid attention to the starting point guard's body and facial language and emmulated exactly what she saw. Beth's game didn't miss a beat as she proceeded to play both guard positions with equal confidence.

HOW TO MODEL THE BEST: VAK!

To model someone's performance strategy for best results, you'll need to mirror three essential factors.

> 1. **What you see...Visual.**
> 2. **What you hear...Auditory.**
> 3. **What you feel...Kinesthetic.**

VAK is the acyronym the science of Neuro-Linguistic Programming uses to explain the mirroring process. This is the **how-to** part of the modeling process.

All programming input that enters your mental computer from the external world is received from your senses ... that is what you see, hear, feel, smell and taste. The three major senses you'll use to program new feed-in data enter through the senses of visual (sight), auditory (hearing), and kinesthetic (feel).

V... Before you can mirror a winner's performance strategy exactly, you'll need to find out what the action you wish to duplicate looks like. Keep this fact in mind ... your subconscious prefers pictures.

A... Involve the left side of your brain in the programming process. By employing words (or sounds), you can elicit the winner's internal strategy. Words allow you to lock into the same inner representations of success that your model experiences. When you associate the similar word or words to your action that the winner employs, or ask the same empowering questions to yourself that the winner asks, you usually elicit the same response. Words like **Yes!, Great!, Quick!, Now!, Slow Down!, Stay Cool!, Relax!, Do It!,** tend to produce the same conditioned responses that the winner produces.

K... Finally, you'll need to experience the same emotions and tactile sensations (sense of feeling) that the winner experiences. You'll need to know what it **feels like** to execute the winning skill. (Remember the **Bear-off!**)

In order to probe the winner's exact strategy, you must visually study the winner's action, listen to the winner's inner conversation and feel what the winner feels. In other words if you really want to program the same floppy disk the winner employs, you'll have to ... **see it** ... **hear it** ... and **feel it.** Once we get into the gym, I'll show you how to VAK the winner. Before we do that, let's discover more about **the power of words.** Their effect on your subconscious can range from delightful to devastating.

THE POWER OF SELF TALK

You can bet your last dollar on this one: **achievers do not talk to themselves the same way as underachievers do.**

As you read this book, one action you can immediately take to improve the quality of your game is to improve the quality of what you say to yourself. Learn to upgrade what you say, how you say it, and how often you say it and self talk becomes an empowering breakthrough tool that can quickly change your state of mind. If you are already in a power state of mind, positive self talk can help you lock in that feeling of success more permanently. By keeping the inner conversations of self talk positive, you provide invaluable road signs that keep you on course. However, should you wallow in the garbage self talk of negative thinking, you'll find that the road signs lead you in an opposite direction away from your most rewarding destiny.

Words have started and ended wars, moved us to tears, made us laugh, solved our problems and empowered us to live better lives on and off the court. It's time you understood the full impact words have on shaping your destiny. Do a little destiny shaping right now. Put the book down, sit up, throw your shoulders back and with a loud and clear voice say, **"My shot is incredibly great and my talent is awesome!"** Say it several times more. Even if your subconscious doesn't believe you (at this point), say it with conviction. In time, it will, especially when you repeat the affirmation to yourself after a successful on court experience. Your subconscious will take serious notice. When you speak positively, not only is your subconscious listening ... so is your destiny.

How To Kill A Tree

Have you heard the story about the witch doctor on a small island in the South Pacific who became famous for killing trees by yelling at them ? When a tree grew so big on that island that the natives couldn't cut it down with their primitive cutting implements, the witch doctor would do his thing. His bizarre method for downing a big tree was simple. He would sneak up behind a tree at midnight and for the next 30 days and 30 nights scream bloody murder at the tree. Though the witch doctor's technique was bizarre, he never failed to down a tree. The natives believed that by yelling at the tree, the witch doctor killed its spirit.

While you may not buy into this story, listen to this tragic event and you may have second thoughts about the validity of the witch doctor's method. Several years ago, I was asked to make a motivational speech to the students at a local high school. When I arrived at the assembly, I was surprised to find only a handful of students sitting in the auditorium. The principal explained that the previous day during lunch a tenth grade student walked across the school's deserted baseball diamond, climbed to the top of the baseball backstop and hung himself.

The student, I was told, was devastated as a result of breaking up with his girlfriend. In a clouded moment of depression, he had decided that death was the only viable solution. In essence, a temporary problem was permanently solved!

Can you imagine what he said to himself as he walked across the athletic field for the last time? Was his inner conversation optimistic, like "I'll get over it. Nothing is permanent!" Or did his inner voice whisper pathetically, "I'm fed up, and I'm not going to take it any more!" Whatever it was he said, it filtered down to his subconscious where it contributed to the last decision he would ever have to make.

If you shout angrily at a spirit, long and loud, whether it belongs to a tree or human, the spirit dies. The saddest of all facts is that the second leading killer of young people today is suicide. At camps, I ask the the athletes how many of them know someone who has committed suicide. I'm amazed that three-quarters of the hands usually are raised. I can remember talking to a **Yes,**

I Can! Camp in Maryland on this very same subject. That evening, a father came into camp to pick up his son and take him home. His mother had committed suicide earlier in the day. I later found out she was depressed by marital and financial problems and had more than once threatened to take her life.

I bring up the subject of suicide not to depress you, but to impress upon you the power of negative self talk. There is a phenomenon called partial suicide you ought to be aware of. Develop the habit of putting yourself down after every mistake and missed shot, and you'll kill your basketball dream. You'll shrink your comfort zone, destroy your self image to the point you'll just be going through the motions, afraid to make a mistake, frightened to take a risk and using only the skills you're sure of. Pile on enough "I can'ts" … "I won'ts" … "I better nots," and your basketball dream will be as dead as if the witch doctor worked you over for 30 days and 30 nights!

Now that you are aware of the destructive power of words, let me show you how to get your game into cruise control with the influence of **Power Talk.**

POWER TALK

This is what happens inside your mental computer when reciting a key word while performing a certain skill. The word and the successful action are stored together forming a cybernetic loop. They are literally linked and recorded as a unit in the memory bank of your brain.

> • Recall the experience and you recall the word.
> • Recall the word and you recall the experience.

Whenever you vividly recall an event, as far as your subconscious is concerned, you are also reliving the event. By employing a word during the training process, you involve both sides of your brain in the action. Not only is the left side, that deals with verbal expressions, activated, but the right side, that deals with controlling visual experiences, is equally employed. Take the specific action of catching a pass, for example. Should you repeatedly say the word "Ball!" (out loud) at the exact moment you receive a pass, two good things happen inside your inner computer:

1. The word "Ball!" and the experience of the catch are recorded as a unit forming a cybernetic connection or loop. The word "ball" and the catch become synonomous. Recall either one and you mentally experience the other.
2. The verbal side of your brain (the left brain) is kept busy from overthinking or producing negative thoughts. Thus a clear head is produced.

Here's the training advantage power words can give you: You can program your subconscious with imaginary experiences of catching a ball by just reciting the word "ball" over and over again. Say the word "ball" 50 times and your mental computer is simultaneously recording 50 successful receptions. Since your conscious mind can't entertain two thoughts at the same time, you'll also be developing the habit of clearing your mind of extraneous thoughts or doubts by busying your left brain. No, I'm not asking you recite a word each time you perform a skill in a game, but you can in drills. Then make it a habit to use that word to program a better skill. The additional advantage in games will be less thinking, worrying, doubting and analyzing. Hence, more completions.

At camp, key words are connected to shooting jumpers, free throws, power lay-ups, driving to the basket, quickening defensive feet, seeing the court, softening hands, eliminating frustration, and developing aggressiveness.

By allowing the left brain to get involved in the programming process, game skills can be programmed anywhere or any place … on the court or off, while watching sports on TV, riding in a bus, sitting in a study hall, eating a meal, sky diving or turning the pages of this book.

POWER WORDS AND MODELING

For extra programming effect, power words can be applied to the modeling process. If your hands are not as supple and soft as you want them to be, pay close attention to a teammate's confident hands in practice. At the moment the role model confidently catches a pass, recite the word "ball!" and imagine that it is you who is successfully receiving the ball.

Do power word modeling for a week and then judge for yourself whether your hands have improved. The results you're looking for will come in exact proportion to the time invested. "Repetition is the mother of skill," says Neuro-Linguistic guru Anthony Robbins. Coaches won't disagree. So stay with it.

POWER WORDS

Here is a list of Power Words you can use for programming various skills and attitudes. Feel free to create your own. Recite the power word to yourself at the exact moment that you are executing the action (or watching someone else performing the skill). During a break in the action make it a practice to recite the word slowly 25 to 50 times.

Ball! ....catching a pass and rebound.
See! ....seeing the entire floor; reading defense.
Quick!Quick!Quick! ....faster feet, especially on "D".
Sight! ....improving focus and concentration on the shot.
Feel! ....developing the confident sense of feel shooters
　　　　　　　　　　　　　　　experience while stroking the shot.
Yes! ....locking in the success feeling after a converted shot.
Clear! ....eliminating frustration of a missed shot or any mistake.
Stop! ....stopping negative self talk.
Big! ....playing bigger in the post or off the boards.
Low and Hard! ....executing strong, hard and low power drives to the basket.
High and Soft! ....shooting soft bankshots, especially off hard drive to
　　　　　　　　　　　　　　　the basket.
Next! ....changing goals.

POWER QUESTIONS

Winners know how to ask themselves the right kind of questions—questions that empower and keep them on track. On the other hand, underachievers know how to develop and maintain feelings of inadequacy, dependency and hopelessness by asking themselves stupid questions.

Your brain is the most efficient and powerful computer in the world. Push the right keys, and in seconds it can provide you with the firepower to face a challenge, solve a problem, upgrade your energy and produce the know-how you need to live your dream. By punching up better questions in your computer, your Reticular Activating System improves its focusing ability from a survival to a success setting.

STUPID QUESTIONS TO AVOID

You don't want to ask yourself these questions:
- Why does it always happen to me?
- Why can't I get better?
- What's the use?
- Why is my shot so lousy?
- Why was I born so slow?
- Why do I always fumble the pass?
- Why is life so unfair?
- Why is my talent so limited?
- What else could I be doing if I weren't spending all this time practicing?
- Will this ever work?
- Why does everybody dislike me?

Your impersonal mental computer serves you faithfully. Ask it stupid questions and it immediately goes to work to produce stupid answers like **"that's the way it is and that's the way it will always be!"** *The Bible* was right. "Seek and ye shall find." Seek resourceful questions that bring out your best. Every success story you've read about includes a struggle. Don't make your struggle permanent or personal by asking the wrong kind of questions.

Every successful athlete has faced self doubt at one time or another. The next time you are confronted with fear, a mistake, a tough call, a loss or a feeling of unworthiness, ask yourself a question that empowers you.

Try this list of successful questions on for size. After a series of setbacks, create a positive state change by asking:
- What have I learned?
- What must I do so this never happens again?
- How must I change to get the results I want?
- What must I do to become totally committed?
- Who do I know I can go to for help?
- What must I believe to be the best I can be?
- What is the ultimate reward for my efforts?
- What's great about what I'm doing?

- What's fun about what I'm doing?
- How can I turn the work into play?
- What am I excited about?
- What am I happy about?
- What did I learn today?
- What did I do great in practice or the game?
- Who have I helped today?
- What am I grateful about today?
- What am I proud about?
- What can I do so that my coach and my teammates like me?
- Who do I love?
- Who loves me?

By asking yourself empowering questions, you're directing your RAS to search out answers that empower you. Make asking yourself two empowering questions a daily habit. You'll enjoy the state change and the results it brings. Here are two of my favorites: "What am I going to accomplish today ... and have fun while I'm doing it?" After a mistake or an event that went wrong I ask myself, "What's good about it?"

Programming With Power Affirmations

You are now ready for power affirmations. The following positive statements will motivate you for peak performance. Repeated daily, they can help you reprogram your subconscious to achieve permanent change. Although your mind thinks best in terms of pictures, specifically selected words effectively create and transmit both pictures and feelings.

The affirmation process will help keep a positive mindset whenever you need a motivational pickup. There'll be times when things go wrong, or when negative thoughts and self talk appear. By getting into the habit of silently repeating to yourself your favorite affirmations, before or during a game or practice, destructive negative self talk will be eliminated. You'll find yourself in that winning groove once again, with a strong motivation to achieve remarkable results in competition.

As you begin this verbal reconditioning procedure, I want you to consider yourself as a computer programmer, feeding a new software program called **Power Talk** into your top-of-the-line IBM 100 billion bite computer. The data is in the form of specifically worded phrases that will direct your computer to produce confidence, poise and winning skills.

Before the new programming can take effect, you can expect the old programs to question the validity of the new input. With time, the new information will override the old, and you will start to experience the change you've been looking for. The first sign of new tapes being played may be as subtle as feeling less frustrated after failing to complete a play or missing a shot. With a positive mindset, you may become more aware of negative talk coming from your teammates or coach and recognize it for what it is. You may find yourself focusing better and thinking more optimistically in competition. Within a week, you should expect the first **on the court** breakthrough. You will notice you're playing more aggressively, taking more chances or executing offensive moves you have never tried before. Best of all, you'll be completing more plays. If you like, add the background affect of inspirational *Rocky* type music as you deliver the affirmations to yourself. A good idea is to record a list of affirmations on an audio cassette and play the tape back whenever you need a motivational pickup. Here's a list of my favorite affirmations. Create your own list. Personalize it to represent a certain skill or attitude you want to condition into your subconscious. What is it you want? Is it softer hands to catch a ball, a more accurate bank shot or an attitude of increased trust in your teammates and coach?

The Affirmations

1. My shot is incredibly great and my talent is awesome.
2. The drive and purpose of the winner flows through my body.
3. There is no limit to my strength, power and quickness. I have more than enough to win every game.
4. My potential is unlimited. I compete with the confidence of a champion, play after play, game after game.
5. Nothing bothers me in the heat of competition. I am poised and cool and always in control of my actions and reactions.
6. I let go of all past limitations and mistakes. They are gone forever.
7. My enthusiasm in practice pays off, and each day I play better in every way.

8.. My moves and reflexes are smooth, quick, and sure.
9. I am a winner each time I compete.
10. Overconcern and overtrying are unnecessary because I trust in the power of my subconscious.
11. I am free to take any risk to win.
12. I possess all the confidence, control and concentration necessary to play my best.
13. My mind's energy is clearly focused in the here and now. Nothing distracts me from completing the play.
14. A positive expectation, that winning feeling, is always with me.
15. I have the power and courage to successfully play the game I have imagined.
16. I work harder and practice and play smarter than my opponents. My quest is to be the best!
17. I am unstoppable. My drive to the basket is low and hard and I always finish it off with a score.
18. I am invincible!
19. Yes, I can!
20. I do the thing that is hard to do and the power will come!

HOW AN AFFIRMATION WORKED FOR ME

In 1987, I ran my first and only marathon. The event took place in Paris, France. In more ways than one, I'll never forget that day. It reaffirmed my belief in the power of affirmation ... especially this one: **"Do the thing that is hard to do and the power will come!"**

Here's the rest of the story: I run almost every day. Not far ... maybe three or four miles on a good day. Most days, a two mile slow jog is the full extent of my run. While visiting my daughter Carolyne in Paris, where she was studying at the Sorbonne, we decided to enjoy a leisurely jog together through the streets of Paris. On a beautiful spring day, we came upon several thousand runners who were preparing to embark on the world famous International Paris Marathon. Suddenly, we heard the starter's pistol and felt the rush of runners fly past us. Then, I made my first mistake. I stupidly told my daughter that running a marathon had always been a dream of mine. She looked at me and said, "It's time to live your dream. Let's do it!" She started to run along with the marathoners and I followed. Before I knew it I was making the turn at the Arc de Triomphe with the rest of the runners and living my dream.

All went fairly well until the 15-mile mark when my dream hit the proverbial wall. The pain was too much, so I stopped. I was ready to quit when I heard an inner voice say, **"Do the thing that is hard to do and the power will come!"** How many times had I used that advice to motivate athletes? The words helped me take a few steps. Soon I was talking to myself out loud. **"Do the thing that is hard to do and the power will come!"** I was repeating it louder and louder. My pace, surprisingly, was increasing. The words seem to be tapping a hidden energy source. After five hours and twenty minutes of painful running, I finished the marathon.

It was what happened at the finish line that really surprised me. Along with my daughter who had finished the race an hour earlier, there was a French marathon runner there to greet me. He gave me an enthusiastic hug, kissed me on the cheek, and said, "Merci beaucoup ... merci beaucoup." Realizing I was American, he explained in a strong French accent that he was about to quit the race at the 19-mile mark because of severe leg cramps when I passed him shouting "Do the thing that is hard to do ... !" He said he heard the words and started reciting them to himself in French, "Faites la chose qui est difficile a faire!" Without those words, he explained, he could not have finished the marathon.

There's a lesson to be learned, here. When life challenges you, don't give up. Instead of feeling sorry for yourself, employ the power of affirmations to help you fight through the tough times. It worked for me and for an appreciative Frenchman. It will work for you, too.

Now that you understand the F and the A parts of the FAST success plan for activating your inner success system, the next step—S—will show you how to harness the magnificent power of seeing the end result before it happens. The process is called mental visualization. What sets winners apart from losers is that feeling of certainty winners always seem to have. Their secret: they see what they want ... never what they want to avoid. Turn the page and find out how you can see into the future and develop that feeling of certainty winners enjoy.

An Affirmation Assignment

Will affirmations postively affect your performance? Prove it to yourself. I challenge you to complete this 10 day affirmation assignment and then check out how you feel and how you're playing. This is what you have to do: fill in the blank below with a skill or attitude you would like to improve. Then repeat the following affirmation a total of 100 times each day for 10 days. That is a total of 1,000 times you will instruct your subconscious to tell your body what you want it to do.

"EVERYDAY, MY _____ FEEL(S) BETTER IN EVERY WAY."

For now, fill in the blank with only one skill or attitude request. What is it you really want? A better jump shot, power move, freethrow, drive, rebounding or passing ability, softer hands, aggressiveness, poise or courage. Allow your faithful subconscious to experience 1,000 powerful and sincerely spoken commands. Then tell me if they work. Start counting right now!

Are you ready to run your sub-four-minute mile? Find a role model whose beliefs and strategies are already proven and model them. New opportunities for growth await you. Just keep your eyes open and play **follow the leader** with VAK.

SEEING WHAT YOU WANT

"Imagination is more important than knowledge."
Albert Einstein

HOW TO PAINT MENTAL PICTURES

How many windows are there on the front of your house? As you thought about an answer, did you see a mental picture of your house? The indisputable fact is, you think in pictures. Don't take this personally, but your mind operates no differently than that of primitive man ... we all think in mental pictures.

Because you think in images, it'll be the power of your creative imagination that will create your new playing future. Remember it was those shoddy inner images supplied by your self image to your subconscious that got your game into trouble in the first place. So let's get rid of them. They are only images! Once you do, and replace them with more successful ones ... new traits, attitudes and skills will appear.

POSITIVE MENTAL PICTURING: THE KEY TO YOUR SUCCESS MECHANISM

It was Shakespeare who wrote, "Assume a virtue if you have it not." Was he aware that the subconscious cannot tell the difference between a real and imagined experience? You're going to assume new playing virtues by mentally picturing yourself completing plays. As far as your subconscious is concerned, these synthetic pictures will be the same as an on the court experience. The degree of sameness depends upon the vividness and details of your mental pictures, but with a little practice, you'll get it right.

Don't tell me that you can't visualize. You certainly can. Look at any object in the room and memorize it. Close your eyes and tell me what color is it? Describe its shape, size and texture. See what I mean?

We don't all visualize with the same degree of clarity. Mental visualization can range from a big, bright, clear and colorful picture to just a feeling. With time and practice, visualization can become an emotional action sequence. But regardless of the size, scope and intensity of your current inner movies ... a subconscious effect is still registering.

The key to effective visualization is that you want your mental pictures to approximate the actual experience as much as possible. You want to be able to actually **feel** the experience and incorporate these feelings into your brain's memory bank and nervous systems. To become the basketball player you'd like to be, you'll need to create a series of clear mental pictures and feelings of the player you want to be. Hold these pictures long enough in your imagination, and your inner success system will have no choice but to accept them as true, especially when you begin to experience some on court success. The fundamental law of the mind is this: **Whatever you hold in your mind long enough grows and becomes real**. Think about those material things you've accumulated over the years which you consider valuable. Before you got them, didn't you think about them long and hard?

The key is to discipline your imagination with multiple layers of positive images. By visualizing the exact images that you want for yourself, over and over again, new mental microchips will be programmed and stored within the infinite capacity of your inner computer. It will be these recordings that instruct your subconscious mind to produce the conditioned responses called skills. No matter how brief a time you hold the mental pictures don't get discouraged. Eventually, you'll be able to fix and hold positive pictures as long as you want.

IMAGINATION: STRONGER THAN WILLPOWER

When willpower and imagination are in conflict, willpower rates a distant second. Want proof? Think about a skill weakness you have. Let's say you have trouble completing a dribble penetration with your weak hand. You and I both know that no amount of willpower is going to get that ball into the basket unless you have stored more green light images than red.

Willpower is an important force in my life as I'm sure it is in yours. But the fact is that I could not finish this book with willpower alone. It wasn't until I had spent hours imagining the completion of this book, that I found the know-how and willpower to get it done.

THE POWER OF IMAGINED PICTURES

Here's a mental exercise that illustrates the influence that mind pictures have over the subconscious.

Close your eyes. Imagine that you are holding a lemon. It's in your right hand. You can feel the coolness and waxy texture of its yellow skin. Try squeezing it a little. Can you feel its firmness? Smell the lemon. There's a unique odor to a lemon. Now, mentally cut the lemon with a knife (be careful). Bite deeply into the half-cut lemon and taste its tart and sour flavor. If you've used your imagination, by this time your mouth should be watering.

Did your mouth salivate? The chances are it did. You used **visual lies** to trick your subconscious into believing you were sucking on a sour lemon. Thanks to your creative imagination, you sent image signals to your subconscious. Instantly, your automatic robot told your salivary glands to get busy. Saliva was secreted to wash away the tart taste of the lemon juice ... an example of the power of suggested pictures.

This is the same power of mental imagery that produces your weak skills. There is a mental videotape orchestrated by your self image instructing your subconscious to tell your body to fumble the pass, miss the shot or allow your opponent to drive around you. Your reliable (and impersonal) subconscious has no recourse but to carry out the commands. Don't blame it!

Your subconscious does not know how to say no! So start picturing what you want. Your subconscious will do the rest. Trust it.

MY FIRST COACHING EXPERIENCE WITH MENTAL PROGRAMMING

I'll never forget the very first experience I had using visualization with one of my players. This was a historic moment for me. From it, I would learn how powerful the impact of visualization could be on improving the life of a player.

Ken was a classic underachiever. He was potentially one of the most talented players on my team, but he had one tiny flaw ... he managed to fumble the ball almost every time it was passed to him in the game. We drilled his large hands every day in practice, but in the game the results were always the same. He could not catch a pass when he was closely guarded. Since nothing seemed to help (nothing to lose and a ballplayer to gain), I asked Ken if he was interested in a different kind of training method requiring no extra sweat. He liked that idea! Having just finished reading Dr. Maltz's book, I was looking for a player to try out some cybernetic exercises. Ken would be my first experiment.

"What do you think about in the game just before a ball is thrown to you?" I asked Ken.

His reply interested me. "I see myself blowing the pass, Coach."

"That's your problem," I explained. "You're thinking the wrong thoughts. Keep thinking that way and you'll always fumble the pass. You've got to change your attitude about yourself. I want you to try this mental drill every day. See yourself catching passes ... mentally! That's right, all in your mind. Create a movie for yourself. You're the star. In this movie, I want you to see yourself catching one pass after another. High passes, low passes, hard passes, soft passes. In the end make sure you're always holding on to the ball, firmly, cleanly and decisively. I want you to see yourself becoming the player you've always wanted to be ... all in the movie in your mind. All day long, see yourself catching passes ... while you're sitting in the classroom, at home, in bed, even in the bathroom! I mean **EVERYWHERE!**"

I suggested that the mental visualization be as realistic and detailed as possible. He had to hear the roar of the crowd and even feel the texture of the ball as he caught it. "Imagine a lighted scoreboard with the score tied at 60 to 60 as you're catching the ball in a crowd, turning and scoring the go-ahead basket." But once in a real game, he was never to think about catching the ball.

Without exaggeration, the improvement in Ken's reflexes was so amazing he was actually catching the toughest of passes in each game's most crucial moments! Ken's overall self confidence, poise and reputation improved so dramatically that he was selected first team All-County and All-Long Island. My first experience with cybernetic training was an impressive success! Ken's inner journey certainly made his outer journey a lot more fun! And mine, too. Our team won its first county championship with Ken leading the way.

VISUALIZING: MORE THAN JUST IMAGINING

Ken's problem was that he was always expecting negative results. His worry and expectation to fail created a negative goal-picture that instructed his body to do just what it had to do to fumble the pass.

It has been said that, "What you can conceive your body can achieve." The task for Ken was to conceive a different picture ... a winning result. It was very important Ken visualize the positive thought rather than just imagine it. Visualizing means not just seeing it, but feeling it, using all of the body's senses as possible. The roar of the crowd (sound), the glitter of the scoreboard (sight), the texture of the ball (feel) were all factors that made the imagined experience acceptable instruction to Ken's subconscious. The purpose of telling Ken not to think about catching the ball in the actual game was to eliminate his fear of failure, a major inhibition for success.

THE TWO VISUALIZATION PROCEDURES: ALPHA AND BETA

There are two kinds of visualization procedures that can help you program your mind. One is called Alpha programming, a deeper level of visualization; and Beta, the conscious level of visualization. Use either one, and you upgrade your level of confidence.

The human brain actually radiates electrical impulse waves in different brain wave patterns. These waves can be measured by an electroencephalograph. The rhythms of this mental energy are measured in cycles per second. When you're awake and active, your rhythm runs between 14 to 21 cycles per second. This state of mind is called the Beta level.

A deeper level of mental activity is registered whenever a relaxed state of mind is achieved. The cycles per second drop between 7-14. This is called the Alpha level. It can be attained naturally while you're lying comfortably in bed awaiting sleep or immediately after awakening in the morning. These are excellent times to visualize positive mental pictures. The subconscious, at this deeper level of slow electrical activity, is more responsive to suggestion. The painting of mental pictures can be more vivid, clearer and more detailed when the mind is uncluttered and free of conscious distractions. The power of imagination is free to work its charm with your success mechanism.

Another good time for achieving the Alpha level is when you're sitting in a comfortable chair in a quiet room.

YOUR FIRST EXERCISE

Mentally visualize an official size basketball with your eyes closed. To help you develop a more realistic picture of the ball, place an actual basketball on your bed or desk in front of you before you start to visualize. Open and close your eyes until you can clearly see the basketball with your eyes closed.

As you visualize the ball on your inner mental screen, (on the inside of your eyelids) repeat slowly to yourself ... "ball, ball, ball," over and over again for a minute.

The next step is to produce a picture of a rim on the screen. Concentrate on this new image. Create the rim in detail, color and size. Repeat ..."rim, rim, rim," silently to yourself.

51

Your First Action Movie

Stare at this photograph of the ball dropping into the basket until you can feel the ball dropping through. Replay this movie 50 consecutive times. Each time you mentally experience the successful sequence of the ball dropping in, your mind and nervous system are recording a successful hit. 50 consecutive made baskets. Congratulations!

Once you develop clear and simple mental movies, it's time to graduate to more challenging and game-like movies. Are you ready to employ your greatest asset, your creative imagination to turn a weak skill into a strength and really live your dream? Let's see if **visual lies** can truly get your game out of first gear and into overdrive?

THE PROGRAMMING PROCESS: CHANGING BELIEFS

It's no secret that mental visualization has provided athletes of all sports with a proven short-cut for attaining peak performance. Disciplining creative imagination is a powerful tool being used today to cure cancer, overcome stress, increase salesmanship, dissipate fears and conquer migraine headaches, high blood pressure and obesity. Now it's your turn to take charge of your thoughts to get what you want. By focusing on the same kind of beliefs winners do, you'll be able to tap into the same kind of performance results winners experience.

Before you develop your visualization power, there are a few how-to procedures you'll need to learn. Whenever you visualize, I want you to think of yourself as a projectionist capable of slowing down, speeding up or even freezing a movie. Another critical factor will be to wrap the action with emotion and feeling so that the subconscious can respond to the picture commands as if they were real. There'll be times when you watch yourself perform, and times when you jump into the picture feeling the competitive event as a first person experience with all its glorious details.

Remember this: each time you participate in the imaging process, you actually will be improving your game performance a notch. By experiencing the mental workout you will be dealing directly with the automatic mechanism that controls your basketball success (or lack of it). No longer will your subconscious have to rely on your old subjective definitions of your past play for its input. Now, with the aid of visualization, you can store an unlimited amount of winning performances.

Remember your visualization may not be an image at all. It may take the form of a feeling you have or a statement you are saying to yourself. Regardless of its form, clarity or size, trust me . . . you've been visualizing.

For now, let go of all your doubts and cynicism. Make a sincere effort to keep an open mind. You don't have to fully believe that visualization will work for you, but you will need hope in your heart if you expect to get belief in your head. Has anything great ever been accomplished with a negative attitude? With a little advance trust . . . proof is on its way.

You can visualize any time or anywhere, but for best results a deep relaxation procedure is necessary. Once you remember the flow of action you created in the relaxed state, you can visualize while jogging, riding in a bus, waiting in line, sitting in study hall or watching TV. However, the very best time for mental visualization is while lying in bed before retiring or just before getting out of bed in the morning.

Before your first relaxation and visualization workout, I suggest that you either read through the following instructions several times or record the directions on an audio cassette and listen to your own voice lead you through the visualization exercise. Thousands of athletes have been guided through the visualization process by listening to the audio cassette *Living the Miracle*.

For information on ordering the cassette, write to *Living the Miracle* Audio Cassette, Box 134, East Setauket, New York, 11733 or call 516-751-3513. The cassette is available in 9 sports.

Let Your Inner Journey Begin

If you're ready ... sit back, fully relaxed, in a comfortable chair with both feet on the floor, uncrossed. Put your hands on your lap ... palms up. A deep relaxation response is required so your subconscious can be fully opened to accept the flow of positive impressions it's about to receive. When you finish the mental visualization experience, you will feel both energized and refreshed. If you are about to retire, you can lie on your back in bed, arms and legs fully extended, relaxed and uncrossed. Afterwards, you'll naturally fall off into a restful sleep. Let your inner journey begin.

The more you relax, let go and trust in the power of your subconscious, the sooner you'll experience the benefits. Close your eyes and begin to pay attention to your natural breathing rhythm. As you focus on each exhale, silently say to yourself the command, "Let-go."

Ready,

Let-go: Feel the air escaping through your nose and mouth.

Let-go: You are releasing all tension and doubt.

Let-go: You are becoming more and more relaxed as the air flows outward.

Let-go: Worry and tension are flowing from your body through your fingertips and toes.

Let-go: All concern and doubt are disappearing.

With each exhale you are becoming very deeply relaxed. All playing limitations and restrictions are permanently pouring out from your body.

Past mistakes and fears are disappearing forever.

A safe, trusting feeling fills your body.

You are now deeply relaxed.

Every command you hear will create a clear, detailed, positive mental picture.

The images will be indelibly recorded into the memory bank of your subconscious.

When needed, they will automatically provide your subconscious with the positive commands of the winner.

Your reliable power mechanism will accomplish the rest.

Continue to breathe evenly, but this time focus on the air filling your lungs.

Each time you inhale, feel the sensation of air filling every cell of your body with fresh confidence and energy.

Now,

Inhale: You are unbeatable!

Inhale: You are a winner!

Inhale: You are the best!

Inhale: You are great!

Inhale: You are unstoppable!

Now, imagine a large funnel at the top of your head.

As you breathe inwardly, feel a column of bright white energy pouring through the funnel into your head, down your neck and into your lungs.

With each inward breath, experience a sensation of power flowing through your veins into every muscle, every fiber, ever cell, and reaching deep into every atom of your body.

With each breath, feel a sense of radiating self-confidence and strength building up in the center of your body.

Feel free to draw upon this unlimited energy source anytime you need it during competition.

It will always be there to give you the power, trust and know-how to be all that you want to be in training and in competition.

You are now deeply relaxed, the ideal state to program your subconscious with positive commands.

To discover your true potential, it's time to decide on a specific playing weakness or attitude. A real problem in your game. One that if you could magically turn around into a strength would dramatically improve your game. Is it:

• A better shot, with a quicker release.
• Perhaps off a dribble.
• A clutch free throw.
• A decisive baseline power move.
• Quicker defensive feet to contain the offensive driver.
• More aggressiveness, second effort, or simply to play more freely, less uptight.

Once you've got a clear cut purpose for your subconscious to act upon, let's go to the video tape of your mind to direct a new script of images. You are about to discover that to do the impossible, you first must see the invisible.

With your eyes still closed, imagine that the insides of your eyelids have become a large silver video screen. Upon this screen you will visualize the action and moves you want. Each time you imagine yourself vividly shooting, driving, defensing or rebounding, your subconscious will receive new positive mental commands that will automatically guide your game. The visualization process, in order to give you optimal effect, will be in three progressive steps.

Initially, you will be only an observer, studying the confident movements of a star athlete; someone you admire, who possesses the skill or attitude you desire. Watch the role model perfectly performing—competing—finishing off the action successfully until you get a clear image of what it takes to perform that specific skill and play at your best.

In the second step, you'll enter the winner's body and go along for the ride. Here it will be a first person, slow motion sequence; so that you can feel the crucial, dramatic movements of the action. With repeated viewing, you'll soon sense a building of confidence—a feeling that you can do it all!

In the third and final phase of your video success story, abandon your role model. Now it's you playing at game speed, in game conditions. Visualize the opponent's best playing against you, hear the roar of the hostile or friendly crowd, feel the texture of the ball, hear the basketball shoes squeaking on the floor, sense your adrenalin pumping. Be sure to feel yourself always completing the action perfectly each time you rerun the video.

If you're ready, let the mental video tape roll! With your eyes closed, see the champion clearly before you performing decisively—in complete control, smoothly finishing off the perfect play.

Now replay the scene several times until you feel in total control of the movements.

It's time to jump inside the winner for the slow motion ride.

Allow your mind and body to enter the star's body.

You and your role model are one! This is a first person, here and now experience.

In perfect slow motion, feel the critical, decisive movements as you want them to happen.

Once again, clearly, vividly, always succeeding—repeat the slow motion winning sequence several times.

Now let's go at game speed. Quicken the action, add all the details, sense the excitement and the pressure of the moment. Add a score, a time factor. Is the score tied? Are you down a basket? What quarter is it?

Second, last?

If you are going one on one, make sure it's against the toughest opponent, and be certain to close off the play successfully.

You are now unstoppable, invincible, at your best, in perfect control.

Hear the crowd responding, and see your coach, teammates, friends acknowledging your outstanding performance.

The more often you repeat the video, seeing, hearing, and feeling the sure, confident action, the quicker your body will be conditioned to respond to your mental commands in competition.

Replay the video again and again, and you'll understand that it is true... **"You become what you think about!"**

HOW DO YOU FEEL?

Let me ask you the same question I ask the athletes at camp after their first mental workout.
- In step 1 ... Were you able to see the star?
- In step 2 ... Were you able to jump inside the star's body and feel the slow motion winning ride?
- In step 3 ... Were you able to abandon the winner and feel yourself achieve the successful action?

If the answer is "yes" to all three steps, you're not alone. Most campers experience little difficulty in seeing and feeling themselves getting it done. Although science cannot explain how we're capable of doing it, they know for certain that each time someone experiences an imagined event, the central nervous system accepts the unreal experience as real, especially if the imagined experience is vivid enough.

So now you know where the power switch for your inner success system is located. In your mind's eye! Winners have long used this power to help themselves get what they want. Don't you think it's time that you to do the same? Listen to what Mike Powell (the world record holder in the broad jump) said about the power of visualization:

"When I was a kid, I would run down the hallway of my house, plant my lead foot just outside of the kitchen, and jump through the dining room, into the den, over the green shag carpeting, and I would land somewhere in front of my mom's red leather easy chair. It was on these occasions, as I danced around the room, imagining that I had just broken the world record, that my Mom would usually point out that I had scratched on my take off, or that my jump was wind-aided. My Mom was a real comedian.

But then one day, I'm 27 years old and I'm in Tokyo, and the scoreboard tells me I'm in second place. So I take off down the runway, hit the board clean, and leave the ground. And I think about reindeer, and dunking from the free-throw line, and gliders, and slingshots, and Sir Isaac Newton, and air. And then everything gets really quiet. And as I stare at the horizon, at the peak of my jump, I think I see, just for a second, my mom's red leather easy chair at the end of the pit."

I received a letter from the mother of a nine-year-old boy by the name of Jonathan. He attended a **Yes, I Can!** Clinic, and while there, persuaded his mom to purchase the *Living the Miracle* audio cassette. Several weeks later his mom wrote:

*"Jonathan has been quite diligent about listening to your **Living The Miracle** audio tape. He recently won our city's Elks Club sponsored Hoop Shoot Competition for foul shooting with 25 out of 25 shots. He hit 24 out of 25 at the district competition. He practices and programs almost daily and his personal best is up to 93 (in a row). We've watched him mature and gain self confidence and poise on the court. Thanks to your tape, and the power of his imagination, he believes in himself. We honestly feel that the messages your tape sends him give him an edge over his competitors."*

Maybe Jonathan's story is not as dramatic a success story as Mike Powell's, but you better not tell that to Jonathan's mother. So, if the world's best and one of its youngest are visualizing … What's holding you back? Don't you have a victory tour of your own in mind?

INCH BY INCH, IT'S A CINCH

Maxwell Maltz wrote in his classic book, *Psycho Cybernetics*, "Once you give your subconscious a definite goal to achieve, you can depend upon your automatic mechanism to take you to that goal. But to accomplish this...you must think of the end result in terms of a present possibility. If you keep your positive goal in mind and picture it to yourself so vividly as to make it real and think of it in terms of an accomplished fact you will experience the self confidence, courage and faith you will need to achieve the goal."

Together, let's prove Maltz's concept was right. But rather than go for the whole ball of wax at one time and turn a specific skill from **a chump to a champ** level, let's do it gradually. An inch or two at a time will be easier to achieve. There will be less chance for jamming your success mechanism with overtrying.

Weightlifters start with gradual increments and so can you. The point is to determine a goal which you can attain without overtrying. I'm only asking you to lower your sights so that you can ease into the habit of success. If you agree … follow these steps.

1. Review the inventory you took in the chapter on Self Awareness. In the first step of the **FAST** formula on goal setting, I asked you to pick two offensive, defensive and attitude skills you wanted to improve, and numerically establish a reachable goal for each … up two.
2. Close your eyes and think about the particular score you gave yourself on a specific skill and raise it by two. Hold that number in your mind until you can answer this question: What would you have to do on the court to earn that higher score? How well would you have to play? If it's a 7 level of performance you want, you can help yourself by identifying

someone who consistently plays on that level. Think of how he or she performs to rate the higher score. Once you can conceptualize what you're looking for, your subconscious will know exactly what it has to do.

3. Imagine that you're observing the player performing the 7 skill you want. Is it a stronger drive to the basket? Keep visualizing and when you're ready, I want you to jump into the picture and make it a first person winning experience. Drive with the same speed, force and finish as your 7 role model. Repeat the inside-out visualization a dozen times.

4. Regarding this skill, evaluate your performance at the end of each practice or game. Don't be concerned that it's subjective. As soon as you achieve the higher score, then challenge yourself with an even higher score. Go for that eight.

You have a list of skills and attitudes you can work on. Inch by inch ... it'll be a cinch!

CLEAR! THE MASTER CLEARING TECHNIQUE

Wouldn't it be wonderful if you could simply push a control key on your own mental computer's keyboard to instantly erase the emotional residue of a past mistake? There would be no lasting anxiety, frustration or disppointment. You'd be free to compete with the same emotionally clear head of the winner. Well, there is a mental key you can push similar to the button on an electronic work processor. It's called CLEAR! Of course, you'll need to program the **clear!** response into your inner computer, but that won't take too long. Are you willing to spend a few minutes a day anchoring the word **clear!** until it sticks? If you are, I can promise you that in seconds you will be able to rid your mind of overconcern and overtrying after mistakes and misses.

HOW TO PROGRAM "CLEAR!"

1. Focus your eyes on any any plain white, uncluttered, clear surface such as a section of a white basketball backboard, a white wall or ceiling, or the back of a white T-shirt and memorize what you see.
2. As you concentrate on the surface, say the word **clear!** either out loud or to yourself.
3. Next, close your eyes and imagine the same clear, white surface on the inside of your eyelids. As you do, again anchor the word **clear!** either out loud or to yourself.
4. Alternate opening and closing your eyelids for one minute. As you focus on the white surface with your eyelids opened, anchor the word **clear!** and repeat **clear!** as you imagine the same clear, white surface on the inside of your closed eyelids.

Once you can mentally visualize the white surface with your eyes closed, let's test the clearing process. Close your eyes and recall a recent shot or mistake you made in your last game (or workout). Can you recapture the frustration of the moment? With your eyes still closed, say the word **clear!** What happened? Were you able to imagine a clear surface? Did the emotional response of the mistake disappear? If it did, congratulations. The clearing process was effectively programmed. If you were not able to picture the clear surface on the first try, you are not alone. Only about twenty percent of our campers clear on the initial go-around. Return to the four step programming procedure until you can successfully clear after an imagined mistake.

TESTING "CLEAR!" ON THE COURT

The next time you miss a shot or make a mistake, calmly recite the anchor word **clear!** Repeat the anchor on every miss and mistake you make until you achieve a clearing of your mind. Continue to sharpen your clearing ability away from the court for a few minutes a day and you'll love the outcome.

THE ART OF REFRAMING

Everybody makes mistakes. Basketball is a game of mistakes. Yet, have you noticed how some athletes keep making the same mistakes over and over again? Then there are others who make a mistake, learn from it and move on. Which group do you belong to? Learn the art of reframing and your mistakes won't become a series of self-fulfilling prophecies for making more mistakes.

Reframing is the art of changing a mistake or an unfavorable experience into a productive learning experience. By improving the way you look at the experience, you can turn any negative event to your advantage. I said it more than once, (but I love this attitude and so should you), "There are no mistakes ... only learning experiences."

Ask yourself what have you have learned from a negative experience and your answer will help you avoid the mistake in the future. Let your imagination guide your Reticular Activating System to produce fewer mistakes. It will if you learn how to reframe bothersome miscues that have a habit of reoccurring.

The best time to reframe a stubborn mistake is to get to a quiet place, away from the action and...

1. Close your eyes, relax and imagine yourself making a stupid playing mistake.
2. Ask yourself what skill or attitude you must develop so this mistake doesn't happen again.
3. Identify someone you know who performs this skill with ease.
4. Imagine him or her performing the skill in competition.
5. Jump inside the mental movie and in slow motion feel yourself inside the star performing the successful action.
6. Now abandon the star. Feel yourself performing the skill in the game at competitive speed, finishing off the play perfectly.

Winners instinctively reframe. You should too ... before it's too late and you become your mistakes!

THE ERASURE TECHNIQUE

There'll be times when a stubborn skill, weakness or attitude cannot be easily reprogrammed. Although, you faithfully follow each step of the act as if, power talk and visualization procedures, the losing skill or attitude does not disappear. Try the **erasure technique.** Anthony Robbins used this method to help NBA shooting star, Byron Scott (then with the Los Angeles Lakers) recapture his shooting groove. Buried in a prolonged shooting slump, Byron was in a tense state of mind every time he took a shot. In minutes, Robbins was able to change Byron's state of mind from frustration to fascination while shooting. He asked Byron to:

• Pretend that you are watching memories of some of your biggest mistakes. Imagine in this movie you are seeing yourself miss one shot after another.
• Mentally see yourself miss shots for several minutes.
• Now start at the end of those bad memories and run the movies backwards at triple the

speed. In other words, see everything going in reverse. The ball is coming off the rim backwards and is sucking back to your hand. While you see everything happening in reverse, I want you to simultaneously hear amusing sounds like nickelodeon or circus music playing in the background. Music that would make you happy, and I want you to see all the action in your favorite color, too.

• Now, run the movie forward at super speed and imagine that Mickey Mouse ears are growing out of the head of the other players. Imagine their noses getting longer. Imagine you're slam dunking the ball. Hear the humorous music and keep running this memory backward and foward, faster and faster, until every time you think about shooting and missing under these conditions, you smile or laugh."

What Byron Scott did was destroy his old mental tapes of how he felt about his inconsistent shooting. Instead of feeling frustrated, disappointed and depressed everytime he shot and missed, he attained a fascinated mindset. Rather than feeling uptight, a mindset in which he would not achieve peak performance, he created a more resourceful and optimistic state of mind. Anthony Robbins compares the erasure process to scratching an old record over and over again until you don't want to hear it any longer.

Before experiencing the erasure technique, Byron Scott was converting one out of every two jumpers he shot. Afterwards, he drilled twenty-five in a row from beyond the arc. Why not employ the erasure technique on a major glitch in your game. All you'll need to do is scratch it until your computer won't access it anymore. Now it's your turn:

Sit up and feel strong and powerful. Close your eyes and imagine that terrible weakness you have as a movie that you are watching. Let's say you get really steamed every time you make a mistake or get a bad official's call. See the mistake happening and see yourself getting hot under the collar. Run the memory to the end and now run it backwards at triple the speed. Add the circus music and see everything in the color pink! Now imagine all the players in clowns' costumes and circus makeup, including yourself. Imagine a big red nose attached to the middle of your face. Imagine big, floppy clown's shoes on your feet. From the beginning, run the memory forward, faster and faster to the end and then, reverse the action. See yourself getting frustrated ... moving backwards! When you get to the beginning of the memory, run it forward again. Keep running the movie backwards and forwards until it gets so silly that you find yourself laughing at the absurdity of the memory of losing control of your emotions in a game! Congratulations, you've erased the negative memory by linking a new response and feeling to making a mistake. Test it. Imagine yourself making a unforced turnover in a game.How do you feel?

TEAM REFRAMING: THE CIRCLE OF "WHOOSH!"

Are you ready for the mother of all weird programming techniques ... **Whoosh!**

Walk into our **Yes, I Can!** Camp at the end of a game, and you will observe both teams circled up, vigorously applauding their mistakes! No, they haven't lost their mind ... only trying to regain control of it. They're reframing as a unit. This is the step-by-step team whooshing procedure:

1. The team circles up. Each player thinks about one frustrating mistake he made during the game and starts applauding (all applaud at the same time).
2. On the command of "ready," they stop clapping, make two fists and open their hands toward the floor as if they were purging the emotions of the mistake from their body. As they do this they all shout ... **whoosh!**
3. After the **whoosh!** they take a quiet moment and reframe the mistake. They imagine seeing themselves successfully executing the skill they had performed poorly in the game. First slow motion ... outside in. Then inside out (first person experience) at game speed.
4. They finish by applauding their imagined success as a team.

If you're a coach reading this, I know the method sounds wacky, but team whooshing offers players a great opportunity for a quick state change as well as an opportunity to visualize together. After scrimmages, try team whooshing for a week and you may just notice your players competing with an increased level of freedom.

For the athlete, I would recommend you individually whoosh at home. Think about a mistake, applaud it, whoosh it and reframe it. Just make sure the door is tightly closed behind you.

Someone once said, "If wishes were horses ... beggars would ride!" I agree. Wishes won't make it happen. **Whooshing can!**

THE "SWISH!" METHOD

No, not the sound of the ball passing into the basket. **Swish!** is an inner game method for eliminating your most persistent playing problems . Originally the swish pattern was developed by Richard Bandler as a key NLP (Neuro-Linguistic Programming) technique for overcoming negative habits such as procrastination. The first time I introduced **swish!** was to a player habitually experiencing a problem common to many players ... a loss of confidence as soon as his coach started yelling at him. He was having trouble maintaining his composure any time his coach laid into him during a game. The coach's disappointed facial expression or angry tone of voice unhinged him. The player's concern was, "I feel that I have to play perfectly to stay in the game." Since his soft self image was doing the talking, his faithful subconscious was doing the overtrying.

The player was putting needless pressure on himself. Instead of playing with the aggressive, creative state of mind he intended to at the start of the game, his play was tentative and tight. The wrong kind of thinking was making his life miserable and his game inconsistent.

This is what I asked the athlete to do:

1. Can you remember the last time you felt frustrated after the coach responded in a way that upset you? Close your eyes and relive that scene. Make that mental image big and bright and see it directly in front of you, in your mind's eye, until you can recapture exactly how bad you felt.
2. With your eyes still closed, I want you to imagine placing the picture (tightening up in competition) you want to change into the palm of your left hand. That's right, mentally put it into the palm of your left hand and imagine it staying there.

3. Now with your eyes still closed, I want you to create a movie of the person you'd really like to be under pressure. The ideal you. The player you truly want to become. Can you remember a time when you were brimming with confidence, when you did everything right on the court? Nothing could bother you. You were strong, unstoppable and decisive. I don't care how brief that moment was or who you were playing against ... just remember the powerful state of mind you were enjoying at that precise moment.
4. Make that picture even bigger and more vivid than the first one, but now I want you to imagine it shrinking and becoming a tight, compact, small ball of energy. Place it into the palm of your right hand. Squeeze that hand into a clenched fist and feel the imaginary ball there within your fist. It's the ideal person you want to be ... rolled into a tight ball.
5. Next, with your eyes still closed, yell the sound **swish!** as you punch the fist of your right hand that is holding the image of the **ideal you** into the palm of your left hand which is holding the image of the **old you**. At the moment of contact, feel the new picture shatter the old picture into a thousand small pieces. All that is left is the big, bright picture of the **new you**.

Repeat the **swish!** pattern a half dozen times in rapid succession. Get excited and shout **swish!** each time you punch your fist into the palm. Feel the new image busting through the old image destroying it into tiny bits and pieces and then replacing it. Don't stop! Keep doing it ... again and again. Repetition and speed are important. Feel the breakthrough. Envision the image of the ideal you in your mind's eye. Feel the triumph and the victory.

"Great job," I told the player. "Now it's time to see if your reconditioned thinking has collapsed the old negative anchor you've associated to your coach's behavior. Let's see if **swish!** has really created the confident state you want." So I asked him to...

1. Think about your coach reacting strongly to a mistake you made in a recent game.
2. Say **swish!** to yourself, simultaneously driving the fist of your right hand into the open palm of your left hand. (If you're lefty let your dominant hand be the fist).
3 Repeat the action several times until you feel the state change.

I asked the player how he felt? With a big grin across his face he said, "I feel tremendous...fantastic! The second I thought about my coach, I felt a surge of power in my body." The real test would be in his next game. "But until then," I added, "keep reinforcing the **swish!** anchor whenever you experience a tightening feeling for whatever reason. Being as inconspicuous as you can, just drive your fist into your palm and think **swish!**"

HOW TO PROGRAM BETTER GRADES (AND HIGHER COLLEGE BOARDS SCORES!)

You should select and obtain academic goals, too. Obviously, achievement in the classroom is important in itself, but poor work habits and attitudes in school work often carry over as poor work habits and attitudes on the court. A student-athlete who is irresponsible in the classroom is usually unreliable on the court. This is especially true when conditions are threatening. The athlete reverts to his old thinking and doing habits. When challenged in the gym the athlete who is unmotivated and failing in school applies the same comfort zone defense mechanisms he uses in the classroom.

"I just don't like school,"(which means I don't like to work in school) in the gym becomes "Defense isn't my thing." "I'm not smart enough," converts to "I'm not good enough," in the gym. Classroom values such as laziness, forgetfulness, procrastination, projection, rationalization and disinterest spill over on to the basketball floor. Underachieving students can easily become permanent losers in the gym by applying these same negative classroom habits of thinking and doing. Short range daily goals aren't met, assignments are late, chapters aren't read, projects are seldom completed, preparation for exams is minimal. Performance on the court can be similarly unacceptable, especially when the challenge is threatening.

A common reason for a negative attitude, lack of enthusiasm, and other failure type characteristics is a fear of failure. Fear controls your expectations in turn controlling your destiny in the classroom and in the gym. Of course, at the source of the problem is an inadequate self image (haven't you heard that before?). It's important to set realistic, achieveable, short range goals that provide the underachieving student athlete with a series of small wins. Coupled with constant self-reinforcement through repetitive visualization, modeling and positive self talk, the athlete's self image and comfort zone both grow.

Are you an underachiever in the classroom or on tests (including college entrance exams)? Here are the CT techniques to guide you towards a more fulfilling destiny in school (and subsequently in the gym):

1. **Goal Card.** Write an exact numerical grade you want on a goal card for each one of your subjects or a test you are about to take. For example: 85 on a test or in a course, or 800 on your boards. Duplicate the card so that it can be placed in several places—in your wallet, on your desk or the best place possible, the inside cover of your course notebook.

2. **Time Limit.** Establish a deadline by which you will attain this grade or achieve this test score. Put it on your goal card. Will it come on the next unit test, chapter, or report? The more immediate, the better.

3. **Sign the card.** Sign the card and put the words **"I CAN"** on the top line. Place the card where you can see it conveniently.

4. **Visualize the grade.** Program your subconscious for achievement with the power of visualization. Awaiting sleep or upon awakening while lying in bed are excellent opportunities to program yourself. Before you begin your visualization session, take a moment and think about what you'll gain should your grade or test score increase. Also think about what you'll lose if you don't increase your scores. That should provide the leverage you'll need to remain persistent and to do what I'm about to ask you. Visualize the following scene on a large imagined screen approximately six feet in front of you.

Mentally picture the academic goal you desire. Visualize it as an accomplished fact. Vividly see yourself on this screen receiving the specified grade, handing in the project, reading the assignment or passing the College Boards with the scores that you need. Successfully experience that good feeling of achievement. In the movie, you see your friends, coaches or parents congratulating you on a job well done. Stay with this movie as long as you can. Don't forget to actually picture the grade or goal you need to obtain. Flash it on and off like a neon sign.

Now, take one step backward in time. See yourself walking into the classroom about to take the test. Notice how confident you are as you walk in and sit down. You're sitting exactly like the smartest student in the room is sitting. Your facial expression and body language are identical to your super smart role model. Take another step backwards in time. In your mind envision yourself working on the assignment or preparing for your college board test. You are enthused, hard working, and enjoying the work. Your work ethic is the same as your smart model. Envision yourself enjoying the academic challenge as she or he does. Hold this movie as long as you can in your imagination until you feel the confidence growing inside. Repeat the movie several times. Let it become more real, vivid, and detailed each time you run it.

5. **Act As If.** As you're taking the test, think of yourself as that good student you modeled in your visualization exercise. Walk into the classroom as if you are this person. Sit up the way he or she sits when taking a test. Talk to yourself the way you think he talks to himself when he's taking a test. Move, look and feel as if you are this person. Give your best effort preparing for the test, visualizing the best result. Then, relax and let it happen. Replicate the bright student's body language, self talk and strategy, and just do it. Don't waste a second worrying about the results. If you can't achieve this loose state of mind, that's OK . . . just act as if you can.

This method has helped many struggling athletes achieve higher scores on tests. I know it can work for you if you give it your best shot. I am not suggesting that you substitute this programming process in place of hard work and study . . . use it along with it.

The captain of the ship is the master of his fate as long as he keeps his destination in mind. Like that captain, you'll need to keep a clear picture of your final destination in mind. Don't be discouraged whenever an academic goal isn't attained immediately. Anything that is worthwhile takes time. A plane flying from New York to Los Angeles is off course 90% of the time, yet it still gets there. The plane's directional system, cybernetic in nature, is programmed to land at LAX.

So set your cybernetic operating subconscious for a correct landing, and don't quit on yourself or your mission. **One step short of success is failure.** Don't quit on the programming process either. Success is just within reach.

There you have it . . . the power of visualization; words and physiology all working together to change your self image and comfort zone. Now for the final step of the FAST formula for success. **T . . . taking action.** Without getting yourself to take immediate and decisive action, you'll never be able to live your basketball dream. All great people have one thing in common. No, it's not their talent. It's their ability to take action.

TAKING ACTION

"To hope is to risk pain. To try is to risk failure. But risk must be taken, because the greatest hazard in life is to risk nothing. The person who risks nothing does nothing, has nothing, and is nothing. He may avoid suffering and sorrow, but he simply cannot learn, feel, change, grow, live, or love. Chained by his addictions , he's a slave. He has forfeited his greatest trait, and that is his individual freedom. Only the person who risks is free."

Leo Buscaglia

Without a decision to take persistent and decisive action, you can forget about your basketball dream. Your vision of success will remain nothing more than a series of hopes, wishes and fanciful thoughts. Action must be taken. You must learn to do the thing that is hard to do in training and games. "Action is eloquence," wrote Shakespeare. To take persistent action until you get what you want is the commodity of the winner. The opposite of taking action is avoidance and you already know that road leads nowhere near where winners travel.

But if action is so essential, why don't we all take action? What attitude separates the winners (overachievers) from the losers (underachievers). The answer lies in their fear of consequences. Losers are afraid of failing. Their fear of pain, embarrassment, guilt and feelings of unworthiness forces them to ride in the slow lane of life. They activate their inner focusing device, the Reticular Activating System, to search out reasons why they shouldn't take action. Winners on the other hand, aren't overconcerned about screwing it up. They have no trouble identifying reasons that empower them to pay any price necessary for achieving success.

Developing the winner's action habit can be as easy as asking smarter questions of yourself. Here are the two questions I ask myself whenever I'm faced with an opportunity to take action or play it safe:

"What will I gain if I decide to take action?"
"What will I lose if I don't take action?"

Winners leverage themselves to do the thing that is hard to do by honestly searching for answers to these two questions. Losers on the other hand know how to ask the mother of all disempowering questions, "What will I lose if I take action and fail?"

THE CRYSTAL BALL METHOD

Here is a method we use at camp to encourage athletes to find the commitment to take immediate action to turn a playing weakness into a strength. Once they find the reasons why they must act, it's no surprise they simultaneously find the needed courage and commitment. Use the **Crystal Ball Method,** right now, to find the inner power to take the action you've been avoiding. Follow these steps:

Think about a weak game skill holding you back from becoming the player you want to be. Something you should have been working on long ago. Sit back in a comfortable chair. Relax and close your eyes. Imagine a big, misty crystal ball in front of you, one with magical powers that can predict the future. Look into it. See the mist within the ball clearing. Imagine yourself performing a weak skill that you never turned into a strength. Of course, you screw it up. Look closely into the crystal ball and tell me what your teammates, coach and friends are saying about you behind your back? See yourself in the crystal ball. How do you look and feel? Is that a happy face staring back at you?

Now, time travel two years into the future. Because you never took the time or expended the energy to turn that weak skill around, you're still saddled with it. Look into the crystal ball and tell me what you see. What are your teammates and coach saying about your game? How many opportunities have been lost because of this terrible weakness in your game? Now that another season has passed with a litany of unfulfilled games, how do you appear in that crystal ball? Are you strong and confident or can you see pain and frustration in your face? Not a great scene is it?

Let's project much farther into the future. Your playing days are now over and you're looking back upon your playing career. What do you see in the crystal ball? Are you seeing yourself fulfilled, happy, satisfied? As a result of never improving the weak skill, what do you see? Is it an unhappy, depressed and unfulfilled image looking back at you?

Now let me ask you, what if you decided to commit to turning that weakness around? Let's say you did everything I recommended in this book, plus you worked hard in practice, and played that flaw in games until it gradually became an incredible asset. Look into the crystal ball and tell me what you see.

It's next season. Imagine yourself with the ball in your hands in a game winning situation. Since you turned the weakness into an extraordinary strength ... what do you see yourself doing in a game? What are your teammates, coach and friends now saying about your game? See your own reflection in the crystal ball. Are you wearing a happy and proud expression on your face?

Project two years into the future. Think about all the games you contributed to because you developed that ready for prime-time skill. How do your parents and teammates feel about your ability to step-up and perform in the clutch? Find yourself in that crystal ball and tell me what you see. Notice the confidence and inner strength that you're exuding now.

Let's take the final step far into the future. Your playing career is over. Look back at your accomplishments. Think about all the games you were able to impact because you were willing to do the thing that was hard to do and work on that playing weakness.

So there you have the **Crystal Ball Method**. You've taken both a painful and joyful ride into the future. Which one did you prefer? Do you feel compelled to take immediate action? Now that you are back to the present, what are your plans? Time flies! Do you feel encouraged to take action or are you locked into the past? The choice is yours.

What Would You Attempt To Do If You Couldn't Fail?

What a great concept! What creative offensive moves would you try in your next game...what shots would you attempt ... what chances would you be willing to take on defense, if you couldn't fail? The fact is you **can't** fail, if you really think about it! The worst scenario is you end up with a valuable learning experience, which you can reframe. Consider that the next time you are walking on the court to play your best game ever.

Start asking yourself this question when you're challenged. "What's the worst thing that can happen to me?" This is a question I often ask myself when I'm faced with a "should I" or "shouldn't I" situation. Let me give you two examples in my life. In one I took creative action and in the other I cowered back into my own comfort zone and avoided the risk involved.

Several years ago after finishing a camp in Colorado, my wife and I decided to experience white water rafting. There were twelve of us in a large gray rubber raft enjoying the adventure of our lives. As we glided down the Colorado River anticipating the white water rapids that lay ahead, little did I realize that my adventure would be different than the rest. I was located in the front of the raft with a paddle in my hands. My main responsibility was to keep us in the middle of the river.

A hundred yards ahead of us in the white water, I noticed nine small individually operated kayaks skillfully being maneuvered in various patterns and formations. As they came out of a figure eight formation, the kayakers joined hands and formed a single circle. With the front of the kayaks facing inside (tails out), the circle of kayaks gracefully slid over the churning white water.

What happened next was truly amazing. One of the paddlers sprung out of his kayak and proceeded to jump from the rear of one kayak to another, around the circle of kayaks until he safely returned to his own kayak. This dangerous action was followed by a second man who emerged from his kayak. Inconceivably, he was juggling three tennis balls in his hands as he completed his dance around the outer edge of the circle of kayaks! I couldn't believe what I was witnessing! Then a third kayaker, a courageous woman, successfully took her turn. This was all happening while the unit of kayaks in this star formation rode the unpredictable rapids.

"What a thrill they are having," I thought to myself. Then suddenly, our raft collided with the circle of kayaks. Before I could think twice, I found myself stepping out of my raft and leaping onto the circle of kayaks. Incredibly, I was prancing from one kayak to another! My wife couldn't believe it. Our guide couldn't believe it. The kayakers couldn't believe it. And I couldn't believe what I was doing! I made no conscious decision to take action. I just did it. As our raft converged with the kayaks, I remember thinking this was a rare opportunity to have some fun and if I didn't take action, it would quickly pass. Completing that jaunt around the circle of kayaks will always remain as one of my greatest memories of all time.

The second event I want to share with you did not produce the same pride as the kayak experience. Still it offers an equally important lesson that I will long remember. The year after my unforgettable trip down the Colorado River, my wife and I vacationed in Mexico. While there, we visited the Mayan Temples in El Castillo.

Climbing the staircase to the top of the ancient pyramid is a challenge only the more courageous take. There is a steep rise between each step. To climb to the top of the temple you must climb at least 125 steps. If you aren't in love with heights, (and I'm not), the climb is not an easy task.

I was about to take the risk, when our guide leader warned me to be careful. Earlier in the year, he said a teenager was killed when he lost his footing and toppled down the staircase to his death. That's all my subconscious had to hear. After climbing a dozen stairs, I froze. Clinging to the stairs, I sheepishly returned to ground level.

I never did climb those steps and to this day, I regret not taking advantage of the challenge it presented. Instead of mastering my fear, as I should have done, my fear mastered me. In the kayak experience, I didn't have time to visualize failure. I knew the worst possible outcome would be a swim in the cold waters of the Colorado River. I was wearing a life vest and I'm a strong swimmer, so I knew I could handle that scene. At the foot of the Mayan Temple, I envisioned the worst outcome and I couldn't handle it.

I did get a chance to redeem myself and climb an equally steep stairway on Diamond Head in Hawaii, a year later. This time, I did not allow my fear to control my destiny. I asked the right questions of myself and received the right answers. While I was climbing, I kept mentally picturing what I wanted to do rather than what I wanted to avoid. I imagined myself safely standing on the top of Diamond Head, enjoying the panoramic view of Honolulu and the magnificent cystal blue waters of the Pacific Ocean. This time, nothing was going to stop me from getting to the top. While climbing I started to experience a queasy feeling. Recalling that feeling of regret that I experienced in Mexico, I reminded myself ... "Yes, I can!" and kept climbing.

As I stood at the top of Diamond Head, the view was sensational. But not as sensational as the feeling I had inside of me.

Incidentally, two hours after the climb up the side of that Hawaiian volcano, I personally met Dr. Robert Shuller, the author who coined the expression, "What would you attempt to do if you could not fail?" (Was it coincidental or serendipitous?)

FINDING THE POWER TO TAKE ACTION

Here are some additional steps for learning how to take action:
- **Set specific, daily goals and achieve them.** Determine short range goals that challenge you. They must be specific and reachable. Your subconscious responds best with clear cut specific requests. Is it a daily challenge of a total of 100 pushups, 100 situps or 50 baseline drives you want to complete after practice? Whatever short range goals you set, stay with each one of them until finished.
- **Use the power of your imagination.** Develop a feeling of certainty that success is inevitable by vividly imagining the successful outcome in advance. See it, think it, feel it, and let nothing stop you from doing it!
- **Anchor for power.** There is no better or quicker way to tap your inner resources for prime time action and risk taking than anchoring into a powerful state of mind. Make it a habit to anchor your great moments of strength, courage and confidence whenever you are on a roll. Employ a key word (like **Great!**) and a unique hand action (like slapping your hands together) while you're in an intense state of confidence. The power state is now deposited for future use. The key to opening your emotional vault is the sound and touch of your

anchor. Then, should you need an emotional pick-up to take action, rapidly fire off several success anchors. Will it work? I cannot count the number of times I've used my energy anchor to empower me through the long summer of one camp after another (or empower me to take action to write this book).

* Anchoring is explained in detail in the next chapter.

"CARPE DIEM!"

If all else fails ... just do it! Feel the pain, the fear, the unworthiness and the guilt ... and take action anyway. **Life is short** is a reality factor you cannot ignore. Before you know it, your basket-ball playing opportunites will pass as they have for the great ones and the not so great ones. Time does not stand still or wait, but it does run out for all of us. You can't put time into rewind and relive what you've lost (except for a little reframing). You have a responsibility to yourself to live each day to the fullest. A coaching friend, gave me this unforgettable quotation, **"Today I gave the best I had. For what I've kept I've lost forever!"** Don't let a day go by without taking some action to improve your game. Give it everything you have and you'll never have to say the saddest of all words, "I coulda ... woulda ... shoulda!"

Did you see the movie *Dead Poets Society*? There is an unforgettable scene where Robin Williams' character, an odd ball English professor at a boys prep school in New England, is teaching the concept of fully living each moment of life. To dramatize the lesson, he takes his students into the lobby outside his classroom where trophies and photographs of past championship teams are gathering dust in the trophy case. "I want you to look carefully at those photographs, boys. You may have taken them for granted." He continues, "Some of these teams competed over a hundred years ago. Get closer and study the faces of these athletes. They look just like you, boys. Do you know what these athletes are now? They are fertilizer for dandelions!"

Cupping one hand to his ear, he continues, "Can you hear their voices? Listen to what they are telling you? Hear their legacy before it's too late and you become a forgotten photograph lost in a trophy case."

He pauses and then whispers in a ghostly voice, **"Carpe ... Carpe ... Carpe Diem ... seize the day, boys! That is what their ghosts are telling you to do! Listen to them begging you ... seize each moment you have and live an extraordinary life!"**

Are you ready to seize the moment and live an extraordinary life before it's over? It's the ultimate challenge! Take action, now, before it's too late.

This then completes the four basic steps of the FAST formula.

F ... **find** a goal you want.

A ... **act as if** you have the same beliefs, body language and self talk of the winner.

S ... **see** yourself succeeding.

T ... **take** action until you achieve what you want.

To win the inner battle, you'll still need to know everything you can about developing the inner skills of concentration and composure. Along with confidence, they comprise the ultimate state of mind ... **the Power State.**

PART TWO

THE BATTLE WITHIN...

"When I got cut from the varsity team as a sophomore in high school, I learned something. I knew I never wanted to feel that bad again. I never wanted to have that taste in my mouth, that hole in my stomach. So I set a goal of becoming a starter on the varsity."

Michael Jordan

THE POWER STATE: Discovering Your Best

*"The key to peak performance, is to learn how to access and maintain
your most resourceful state of mind...the Power State"*

Stan Kellner

Some call it **The Zone**, **Flow**, **Peak Performance**, **Optimal Experience**, **Wired,** or **On Automatic**. You can call it what you want; but unless you can consistently achieve this resourceful state of mind, you'll never tap the greatest quality of your inner resources. Athletes, coaches and sports psychologists are constantly searching for ways to access this peak performance state of mind. This chapter is about how you can both capture and maintain what I call ... the **Power State**.

Let's examine what you have learned so far. The first inner rule of performance is that your beliefs, self talk and body language control your state of mind. The second key rule is that your state of mind controls the level of your performance. For instance, when you feel confident, focused and composed, you finish plays. Feel unsure, distracted and over-excited (or under-excited) and you major in below par performance. These positive and negative feelings are not only associated to your state of mind, they're interchangeable. Change one and you change the other.

The secret of Cybernetics Training is to put consistency into your game by teaching you how to control the three essential winning states of mind ... namely **confidence**, **concentration** and **composure**. Access all three states and you access the winning feeling you need to play your best.

The irony is that you already know how to experience the **Power State**. Go into rewind and think about a time when you played at your best. Recall how you felt and you'll know exactly how the **Power State** feels. Let me help you. Didn't you feel unstoppable with a tremendous feeling of certainty? Weren't your mind and body in perfect harmony? Weren't you totally absorbed in the here and now? **You were in a Power State**. There was no indecisiveness, second guessing, overtrying or frustration. Nothing could distract you. Aware of what was important and what wasn't, you were able to make the right decisions play after play. It also helped that the game action seemed to be traveling at a slower speed. Your play was quick but unrushed. You had achieved the three sub-states of the **Power State**: confidence, concentration and composure.

TAPPING IN

There is no substitute for correct skill technique. I hope you understand that. Success in any endeavor requires skill preparation and repetition. However, you can learn and practice the proper shooting technique all day long, but momentarily lose your confidence, focus or composure, and even your most reliable jump shot from your favorite spot will find a way to rim the basket. Your **Power State** becomes the **Stopper State**!

Thanks to the science of Neuro-Linguistic Programming, there is a way to automatically trigger these resourceful inner states that support your peak performance. The name of the NLP process is **Anchoring**. I briefly talked about anchoring in **Taking Action**, but let me further explain its power.

THE POWER OF ANCHORING

Since you started playing basketball you've had all kinds of experiences. Some good, some bad, and some even great! Each and every basketball experience you've had, regardless of the outcome, has been stored in your biocomputer. Recorded along with these experiences was the state of mind you were in at the time. Thus the experience and the state of mind are indelibly linked together.

Does this mean if you retrieve the memory of one of your great basketball moments, you also recall the associated state of mind? Yes! And you can bet your destiny on it, too! Think of the possibilities you have here. By using the NLP method of anchoring, you'll be able to generate any state of mind you want ... when you want it. Fumble a pass, miss your first shot, or blow a free throw and instead of your mind telling you what it wants you to do ... you'll be telling it what you want it to do!

ANCHORS AWAY!

Anchoring is the process of reaching back in time to your past experiences and feelings of success—and making those same positive feelings permanently available to your subconscious—allowing you to play as well, now, as you did then.

An anchor is any unique sight, sound or feel that is associated with an experience. An anchor can originate internally or externally, or be verbal or nonverbal. Anthony Robbins describes it this way: "Anytime you are in an intense emotional state, anything that occurs around you on a consistent basis, while you are in that state becomes linked (anchored) to that state."

The fact is you're always anchoring. Any time you play your favorite upbeat music in the locker room ... you're anchoring. Even the commercials you watch on TV base their effectiveness on the anchoring process. Advertisers spend millions creating unforgettable jingles or tunes and enlisting celebrities so that each time you hear the music or see the face of the celebrity, you're automatically conditioned to think of their product.

Anchor associations can be either positive or negative. For example, whenever you are in an intense negative state of mind—such as frustration because you just blew an easy lay-in, fumbled the ball, or threw a pass into the stands—anything you're doing, seeing and feeling differently at the time will become anchored to the state. Repeat these unique responses each time you get frustrated, and you reinforce the anchor. Specific facial, body and verbal expressions (even your habit of breathing a certain way), all become permanently linked to the state you're in.

Now all you have to do to achieve a state of frustration is fire off several of your anchors linked to frustration and you will enjoy a conditioned response of frustration. Try this now while you're not frustrated and see for yourself. Just breathe the way you'd be breathing if you were frustrated; stand or sit the way you'd be standing or sitting if you were frustrated; whisper to yourself the same self-deprecating expressions you normally recite whenever frustrated, and presto ... you've successfully achieved a state of frustration!

ANCHORING FOR WINNING PERFORMANCE

Do you remember Pavlov's dogs? Pavlov wasn't a coach but he could have been. He knew how to train. If you remember your high school psychology, he was the scientist who conditioned dogs to salivate by ringing a bell. What he did was pure anchoring and great coaching! Every time he fed his dogs, he rang a bell. Then, the scientist rang the bell without giving the unsuspecting canines a drop of food, but the dogs salivated as if they were about to enjoy their favorite bowl of chow. Because the food was anchored to the sound of the bell, when the dogs heard the bell the dogs' nervous systems were programmed to expect food.

Apply this same anchoring formula to your game and you will be able to experience a powerful state change any time you need one. All you have to do is fire off several word or hand action anchors and you will experience the state change you want ... just like Pavlov's dogs did!

Here's how to do it.

1. Find a quiet place and a comfortable chair to sit in. Close your eyes and think back to a time where you were in the specific state of mind you want to anchor. If it's more confidence you're looking for, remember a game where you were unstoppable and incredibly confident. If it's concentration, think of a game where your mind and body were totally focused into the here and now. If it's more composure, think of a time when you felt poised and under complete control.

2. Step into the picture and reexperience the way you were feeling at the time of your success. At the peak of feeling confidence, shout the word "Great!" as you slap your hands together. Enthusiastically fire off three powerful anchors one right after another in rapid succession. Make sure to coordinate the verbal ("Great!")and nonverbal (hands slap) action ... simultaneously.

3. Stack the anchor. Collect a bunch of them by recalling a series of winning moments and

relive each one. At the very peak of feeling good, employ the same word and hand action anchor three times consecutively. It's essential to upgrade your movie by projecting yourself inside the mental experience making it a first person event. Remember the way everything looked to you, how you felt and talked to yourself. Feel the intensity of the game and then anchor it all.

4. Time to test the positive anchor to see if you conditioned it into your mental computer. Get into a lousy frame of mind. Think about a game where you were screwing it up big time. Recall several of your key miscues. Feel the embarrassment and sinking feeling you had at that unforgiving moment. Now fire off the positive anchor you just installed and test the conditioned response. Shout the word "Great!" (three times) as you forcefully slap your hands together. If you followed the anchoring procedures correctly, the anchor was effective. If it wasn't, review the process and start over. More reconditioning time is needed. Here's your anchoring checklist again:

> • **Were you in an intense state?**
> • **Did you anchor at the peak moment?**
> • **Was the anchor unique?**
> • **Did you stack the anchor often enough?**

STEPPING INSIDE THAT PROUD MOMENT

If you have trouble remembering a peak game in which you achieved a specific state you want anchored, I'm sure there was a time no matter how brief or where it was (in the backyard playing against your kid brother or sister), when you performed aggressively, or displayed exceptional poise, or couldn't miss a shot. Relive any of these memorable moments and anchor it. The best way to access this **proud moment** is follow a three step process.

1. First, imagine the event as if you are observing it from a close camera angle.
2. Now, jump inside the picture and retrieve the rewarding moment from a first person experience ... with one exception. Put all the action into a slow motion time frame. In this way, you'll be able to **feel** the intensity of each crucial step of the successful action.
3. Finally, let your imagination go at game speed. Still in the first person, feel yourself performing the peak experience with the same pace of action as the original. Emphasize the intense **feel** of the emotions you had at the time. Can you also retrieve the state of joy and satisfaction at the finish? Anchor it right now!

Just a word of caution. Effective anchors need to be enhanced and nurtured. Even if you can create a strong positive anchoring response, I want you to make it a habit to anchor the state at least 10 times a day for 10 days. The best rule I know for permanent anchoring is—the more the better.

SPECIFIC ANCHORS

Here are some of the specific anchors we use at camp to lock in various states:

- **State of Confidence:**
  For Shooting Success
  Verbal anchor . . . ."Yes!"
  Nonverbal . . . . .Snap fingers (one or both hands)
  Play Success
  Verbal anchor . . . ."Great!"
  Nonverbal . . . . .Slap hands together

- **State of Concentration:**
  Pinpoint focus
  Verbal anchor . . . ."Sight!" or "Ball!"
  Nonverbal . . . . .Touch finger to right eye
  Peripheral focus
  Verbal anchor . . . ."See!"
  Nonverbal . . . . .Touch both eyes

- **State of Composure:**
  Aggressiveness
  Verbal anchor . . . ."Beast!" or "Big!"
  Nonverbal . . . . .Fists of both hands extended below waist
  Toughness
  Verbal anchor . . . ."Tough!"
  Nonverbal . . . . .Right fist across chest
  Courage
  Verbal anchor . . . ."Guts!"
  Nonverbal . . . . .Extend both fists over head
  Calmness, Coolness, Poise
  Verbal anchor . . . ."Ice!" or "Clear!"
  Nonverbal . . . . .Press thumb against the second finger of
  the same hand (both hands)
  Smooth Play
  Verbal anchor . . . ."Oil!"
  Nonverbal . . . . .Squeeze both hands into a fist and release
  Optimism
  Verbal anchor . . . ."Trust!"
  Nonverbal . . . . .Slap right hand on right thigh

Feel free to create your own verbal and nonverbal anchors. Remember, the more unique the better. Attach them to a state of mind which best supports the skills you're looking to develop and enjoy the state change. Your opponents won't!

ANCHOR BY MODELING

You can stack all kinds of anchors by modeling others. Observe the success of others in practice, games or on TV, and anchor their winning moments.

1. Find someone who is performing well.
2. Using your sense of sight, sound and feel, go inside the winner and see, hear and feel the internal emotions that are supporting the performance.
3. Intensify the internal state by firing off a strong anchor.
4. Anchoring winning performances must be practiced often.

Make it a habit to stay with one specific state by piling up at least a dozen similar anchoring experiences. For instance, if it's shooting confidence you're after, study a shooter on a roll and verbally anchor the shooter's inner emotions with the word "Yes!"

ANCHORING YOUR OWN BEST MOMENTS

Take advantage of your own great plays. Lock into the intense **Power State** you're in by immediately engaging a dramatic anchor. Then, when you need an emotional lift of confidence, concentration or composure (after a "screw-up" or before a game), fire off that anchor.

Watch any Olympic event and you'll see the world's best athletes anchor themselves physically and verbally before and after their performance. Find a quiet way to anchor before, during or after competition. The embarassment you might feel by openly slapping your hands together and mumbling a word or two does not carry the same emotional discomfort as the rotten feeling you experience when playing poorly.

So start today creating those anchors that produce a **Power State** of mind. I can't tell you the number of times that I've used anchors in my life. I've overcome the disabling effects of fatigue, fear of speaking in front of large groups of people, brain lock (in writing this book), and even a paralyzing fear of flying with the help of anchoring.

If you're ever on a plane that is experiencing rough weather, and you notice a smiling man furiously slapping his hands together and shouting the word "Great!" ... come on over and say hello.

Now let's take a close look at the master inner skill of concentration. It's the centerpiece of the Power State.

CONCENTRATION: The Master Skill

"We have the power in any moment, by a simple act of attention to release the illusions of the past and future, and simply handle what is in front of us—now, and now, and now."

Dan Millman

Your Focusing Device

The better you concentrate, the better you'll play. Underachievers show little control over their ablilty to focus attention on what is important and what isn't. Winners have learned to control and direct their attention skills. Without mastering this inner skill of concentration, success in any skill or activity is unlikely.

A key to athletic excellence is the ability of the prime time athlete to put all of his or her powers of thought and desire on to a single task . . . to commit all energy to one act. It's also true that any outside element can distract the underachieving athlete. The focusing mechanism, your **Reticular Activating System**, must be conditioned to work for you and not against you. If you have trouble focusing in games, practice or the classroom, this chapter is for you. It's time to master the master skill of concentration.

What Concentration Isn't

Concentration is not pushing out thoughts; it is not analysis; it is not contemplation. It is not thinking about the past or the future. Concentration isn't straining or trying hard to pay attention; it isn't gritting your teeth and tensing your muscles and using will power.

Try too hard when shooting a free throw, and you unintentionally increase muscle tension. Determination, or straining effort decreases concentration and increases tension. Saying "I will concentrate. I must concentrate," only makes it harder for you to prepare your body for optimal performance.

WHAT CONCENTRATION IS

Concentration is the art of focusing attention on to a task, an object, an experience, or a goal. Concentration is a natural and effortless fundamental of the mind. Concentration means living in the present ... in the here and now.

The past and future do not exist for athletes who have mastered this integral skill. For most athletes, unfortunately, the quality of concentration is all too brief.

DEVELOPING THE MASTER SKILL

There is no better way to improve your concentration than through the disciplined use of imagination. In all of the visualization exercises you've been asked to perform daily, you're sharpening the master inner skill of the mind. In each exercise, you are focusing your mental powers on an object, skill or attitude.

Staying with a mental picture is the same as staying on the rim or ball or opponent in the game. The transition is natural. The systematic use of imagination will benefit you in so many other ways, as well. You will remember plays and become more aware of the entire court (peripheral vision). You will see the ball clearer and bigger. You will be able to listen to your coach's instructions during time outs. Internal or external elements will not distract you easily. You'll generally perform and learn more effectively because you will be playing in the here and now.

Imagine what the effectiveness of a flashlight would be if there were no aluminum reflector inside its head. The light would diffuse in all directions. When you fail to concentrate, your mental power is weakened in the same way.

THE TWO KINDS OF CONCENTRATION

To be successful you need to develop two forms of concentration:
1. Pinpoint (or narrow) Concentration
2. Broad (or wide range) Concentration, also called peripheral vision
Both forms can be equally sharpened through the programming methods of CT.

1. PINPOINT CONCENTRATION

When you focus attention completely on the rim while shooting, you are exercising pinpoint concentration. When you center your attention on the ball as you rebound, you are using pinpoint concentration. When you defensively stay with your assignment, credit your ability to fine tune your pinpoint concentration. Pinpoint concentration prevents your mind from occupying two purposes or goals at the same time.

Your chances for success are minimized when your focus wanders during competition. For example, when you are on the foul line ready to shoot a crucial free throw, you are in trouble if your eyes and mind momentarily stray from the rim. There are many distractions that diffuse shooting concentration: thinking about your last missed free throw; thinking about the importance of the shot after looking up at the scoreboard; becoming aware of the crowd or being engrossed in the actions of teammates, coaches, opponents or officials. If you seriously want to become a prime time player, you need to eliminate interference and totally center the powers of your mind on the task at hand.

DEVELOPING PINPOINT CONCENTRATION

A simple way to increase your ability to concentrate is to see how long you can hold on to a single thought in your mind . . . any thought. This can be done any place and any time. Right now, for instance, see how long you can hold on to the thought running through your mind. Or else, think of the number one. Hold on to the image of the number one as long as you can. At the beginning you will be able to stay with the image for only a few seconds. Practice this simple routine a few times a day and you will be surprised how quickly you can increase your ability to concentrate. Whenever your mind begins to wander away from your thought, gently bring your mind back to it. Remember not to force your concentration. Unhurriedly return your attention to the original thought.

To continue practicing concentration you simply need an object on which to center your attention. A ball or a rim is as good an object as any. Concentrate on these images on your silver screen in bed each night and in the morning when awakening. Remember to vividly detail the rim and ball for a few minutes. Gently focus your complete attention on the images of the ball and then the rim, becoming totally engrossed in them. Develop a fascination, even a love for these objects. Observe their natural beauty. Begin to feel that you are becoming one with the ball . . . one with the rim . . . you and these objects are the same. The ball is an extension of your hand; the rim is part of your body. As you are observing the ball, say to yourself, "ball, ball, ball." As you hold this picture in your mind, you are seeing, feeling, experiencing and recording these objects into the memory banks of the mind. You are developing the power of concentration.

Develop your concentration on the defensive end of the court by picturing an opponent on your mental screen. Focus on a small imaginary red irridescent dot in the area of the belly button (the opponent's center of gravity). He or she can't go anywhere unless the center of gravity also moves. Learn to stay with the red dot, and you learn how to stay with your assignment.

2. PERIPHERAL CONCENTRATION

Peripheral vision is total court awareness. Your ability to look straight ahead while at the same time observing your movements of opponents and teammates to your left, right and even behind you is essential to your offensive game. When on defense, if you pay strict attention to your opponent, you will be vulnerable to picks and screens. If you look directly at your teammate when passing (telegraphing your passes), most of your passes will be picked off. If you want to be an effective passer, developing your peripheral vision is a prerequisite. Pinpoint concentration develops tunnel vision, which is great for shooting or catching, but it handicaps your ability to pass, play team defense, run the court and move smartly on offense.

Here's a peripheral vision drill that is both fun to do and can help you see the court better. In John McPhee's book, *A Sense of Where You Are,* (A Profile of Bill Bradley), Bill Bradley explains how he developed the ability to stare at the floor while awaiting lobbed passes. Known for his pinpoint passing, the former NBA star, Rhodes Scholar, and now Senator from the State of New Jersey describes a unique mental exercise. He credits the development of his reputation to see out of the back of his head to this one exercise.

Bill felt he expanded his peripheral vision as a small boy, walking down Main Street gazing straight ahead, trying to identify objects in the windows of stores he was passing.

If you're tipping your passes off, try this peripheral vision exercise the next time you're walking in a mall, in school or in town. Without looking directly at the passing people, identify the color and style of the clothes they're wearing. The practice of looking away from your friends may temporarily hurt your social life, but with your improved passing ability, you'll develop a more lasting relationship with your teammates.

ALTERNATING CONCENTRATION

There's something you should know that can dramatically improve the level of your play. **The quality of your game depends on your ability to effectively change between one form of concentration and another.**

In the continuing action of a basketball game, your focus bounces back and forth hundreds of times between pinpoint and peripheral vision. Take for example a fast break and you'll see how many times one player employs instant changes of concentration. The player rebounds (pinpoint); reads defense and locates an outlet (peripheral); pitches out (pinpoint); fills an open lane (peripheral); catches a return pass (pinpoint); dribbles (peripheral); elevates for a jump shot (pinpoint); then jump passes to an open teammate under the basket (peripheral).

Want to enjoy more completions? Improve your skill to shift concentration gears and you will. What if I could show you how to **see out of your ears?** Would that help?

SEEING OUT OF YOUR EARS!

Oh! You can't see out of your ears? That's too bad. Because if you could, you would be able to handle the ball on offense more effectively. Think of it. You could read the defense with your eyes and see your teammates with your ears!

Who knows, maybe you can! Do this:

- Look straight ahead and place your hands behind your head.
- Focusing on any object directly in front of you, start moving you hands, with one finger up, around towards the front of your head.
- As soon as you can see (peripherally) the extended finger on each hand, stop the movement of your hands. Remember your eyes are staring straight ahead.

- Your hands should be somewhere near your ears. Imagine that your ears are doing the identifying, not your eyes. Wiggle different fingers and identify your moving fingers, using your ears only.

See, I told you … you can see out of your ears.

SQUARE-UP DRILL

Try this pinpoint-peripheral alternating exercise with three of your friends. Employed daily at camp, the Square-up drill opens up the court for the narrow focused player.

- The drill requires four players to form a circle and join hands. They drop hands and take two big steps backward forming a square. Each athlete faces a partner standing directly opposite him or her.
- Each player is flanked by an athlete to his immediate right and left.
- On the command of **"pinpoint"** each athlete in the square focuses on the right eye of the player directly in front of him for several seconds.
- On the command "peripheral" each athlete raises one hand high over his head.

- Still looking straight ahead (with a softer stare), all players must identify which hand is being raised by the player to both sides.
- The identification process must be accomplished without looking to the right or left. **The ears are doing the peripheral seeing.** The eyes of the four athletes must remain centered straight ahead during the entire drill.
- The drill continues back and forth between the pinpoint and peripheral commands until the players are able to comfortably recognize the upraised hands **seeing only with their ears.**

With practice and a little imagination, ears are conditioned to see with 20/20 vision!
The next step is to use two basketballs in the drill.

- The head couple has a ball which they pass back and forth to each other and the side couple has theirs which they pass to each other.
- Using a mix of two-hand bounce and chest passes, the purpose of the drill is to see how long the four players can pass their ball across to their partner without the two balls colliding.
- Eyes are used to pass and catch, and ears are used to read the action of the side couple.

With time, the players are suprised at their pinpoint and peripheral vision ability in games. They're no longer telegraphing or fumbling their passes, or getting picked off on defense. Their shooting off the dribble also improves. Credit their ears for helping out.

AN ON-THE-COURT FAST BREAK DRILL: 3 ON 2, 2 ON 1

Your coach has probably used this drill in one form or another in practice. It is a nonstop full court fast break drill which involves five players.

- Three offensive players fast break against two defensive players (3 on 2).
- After the attack is completed (or incompleted) and without taking the ball out of bounds, the two defensive players return a fast break towards the other basket (2 on 1) against the offensive player who last touched the ball.
- After the 2 on 1 break is completed (or incompleted), again without taking the ball out of bounds, the 3 players join forces and form a three lane return fast break.
- The three players attack the two remaining players at the other end of the court ... 3 on 2.
- The drill continues back and forth without a stop.

This drill is effective for developing peripheral vision (passing and playing defense) and pinpoint vision (shooting and catching). When passing, the offensive players are instructed to make it a habit to look straight ahead at the defense and to locate their teammates with their ears! The key passing tip is not to throw to the offense, but away from the defense. In this way, the defense will be unable to read the passing lanes resulting in fewer interceptions. The defensive players are instructed to be aggressive (making it tough for the offense by faking up and back). The defensive players are told to see the ball with their eyes and be aware where the offensive wings are by peripherally seeing them with their ears! With a little help from Cybernetics Training, your ears are seeing with perfect vision!

HOW TO DEVELOP BROAD AND NARROW CONCENTRATION AT HOME

It's easy. Select three different objects in the room in which you are sitting—a bookshelf is excellent for this exercise. Use the middle book and the two end books as the three objects upon which to center your attention. Focus on the middle book. Select a distinguishing mark on this book and fine center your attention on it for a few seconds. Now change your focus from narrow to broad. While staring at the middle book see if you can become visually aware of the two books placed at each end of the shelf. Repeat this alternating exercise many times.

Now that you understand the value of concentration and how to increase it, go to work. Nothing great has ever been accomplished without concentration.

COMPOSURE: THE ART OF LETTING IT HAPPEN AND MAKING IT HAPPEN

"The big lie involves the notion that it is only through struggle and extra effort that you achieve anything."
Wayne Dyer

Without the proper mixture of aggressive effort and poise, playing at your best is difficult, if not impossible. At the defensive end of the court, play should be hard and spirited—a make it happen mindset. On the offensive end, however, optimal performance depends on a less intense and more trusting mindset. A let it happen relaxed frame of mind produces a more consistent shot and a more efficient, less rushed style of play. You're about to learn how to regulate your intensity level so it serves you best at both ends of the court and when the game is on the line. Success requires controlling the composure meter of your mind and body. When it comes time to play, the athlete who masters his emotions, feelings and arousal effort more often ends up in the winner's locker room.

PLAYING UPTIGHT

Playing uptight can be caused by many factors, most of which you can regulate. Let's examine the principle reasons for tight performance. Then, we'll offer you some CT solutions.

1. **You try too hard**. There's too much effort. You perform under the impression that the harder you struggle, the better you'll do. How wrong you are!
2. **You worry about making mistakes**. The fear of making a mistake inhibits your performance. Muscles are tighter. Your play is mechanical and tentative.
3. **You are overconcerned** about the outcome of the game or the outcome of the play. The result is careful, anxious and mechanical play.

4. **You are overaroused and overexcited.** You forgot that your best game was spontaneous and natural. Overarousal strains the success mechanism. You feel that every action is a life and death struggle. You become so anxious to do the right thing, so conscious of every move, that your performance is tense.

Unfortunately, most coaches have no systematic approach for training their players in the art of hanging loose in games. In fact, these are the same coaches who unwittingly produce uptight players for big games by being uptight and overaroused themselves.

I have made a study of various mind/body relaxation techniques and exercises. Depending upon the athlete, some work better than others. What applies for one, can be quickly rejected by another. You can decide which methods and exercises you feel most comfortable trying. (If you're a coach who shouts, **"Relax! Relax!"** before your players shoot a freethrow, please read this chapter more than once.)

How To Overcome A Lack Of Confidence And Too Much Effort

Stop trying so hard. You don't have to go at full speed to perform at top speed. You don't have to kill yourself to be a winner. When you try too hard, you upset the balance between the doing and thinking, and between your success mechanism and your body. In the end, muscle fights muscle. Every time you exert extra effort while executing a skill, speed and agility are lost.

Physically, this is what happens: Each time there is precision body motion, there is coordination between two sets of muscles. Since muscles can only pull a bone in one direction (by the force of contraction), the muscles that are designed to pull the bone in the opposite direction (called the antagonistic muscles) have to relax and let go. Whenever you try too hard, the protagonistic muscles responsible for pulling the bone function perfectly, but the antagonistic muscles have difficulty relaxing, since they are tense from the over effort. The resulting action is muscle tying up muscle.

When you try too hard when dribbling, don't you find the dribble to be hard, noisy and erratic? Fingers lose their quick reflexes. If you try too hard to catch a ball or shoot a jump shot, you'll find your hands lacking the necessary suppleness and control. Also, too often, the pass is fumbled and the shot is released with a flat, hard trajectory. You may notice your arm follow through is not smooth and complete, and has a habit of pulling back after the ball is released.

The Importance Of Reducing Over Effort

Try this: Clench your hands as many times as you can within five seconds. Have someone else time the five seconds for you. Score a point for each clench. Make every clench intense and full. You're going for the World Hand Clenching Championship Trophy, so get excited and really pump out those clenches. 100% effort ... ready count!

1 second ... 2 seconds ... 3 seconds ... 4 seconds ... 5 seconds ... Stop!

Remember your count? Now I want you try it again, but this time reduce the intense effort just a bit. Be quicker if you can, but don't try so hard. Ready ... count!

1 second ... 2 seconds ... 3 seconds ... 4 seconds ... 5 seconds ... Stop!

Got your new score? Was it higher on the second try? Most athletes at camp, score higher when they employ less effort. Why? Blame your faithful subconscious. When you overtry, your subconscious takes you at your word and sends instructions to too many muscles. Muscles that should be relaxing are contracting, resulting in muscle fighting muscle. Both antagonistic and protagonistic muscles are contracting at the same time producing less speed and more fatigue.

Athletes score higher when they reduce their effort because there is no muscle tie up. The antagonistic muscles are allowed to relax and the protagonistic muscles are allowed to do their job. It's a concept you must understand and accept, because your overtrying effort is killing your game ... and your basketball dream.

A Master Concept For Controlling Your Composure: Playing At Speeds

At camp, this is how we teach the athletes the importance of performing at various effort levels. The athletes line up for full court sprints. They are asked to run from baseline to baseline at full speed. They are to run as hard as they can and give it everything they have. We clock them and inform them of their time. This, we tell them, is their 10 speed.

For their second sprint, they are to run at half speed 5 speed. On the third sprint we ask them to run at 9 speed. Run fast, but don't try as hard. Relax and take off a little of that extra effort. They surprisingly discover that the 9 speed time is often faster than their 10 speed time. The lesson learned is that extra effort holds them back.

They continue the sprints at various predetermined speeds. The coach calls out a speed (6, 7, 8 or 9), and they are to execute that speed in a sprint. The 6 speed should be a notch faster than half speed. After a while, they can reliably regulate their speed to the coach's request.

There are court situations where a 9 speed is needed (filling fast break lanes, getting back on defense or overtaking an opponent). There are times when a 6 or 7 speed is more appropriate for optimal performance (catching, throwing or shooting on the move, getting ready to stop, moving in a crowd of players, or changing speeds on a dribble). If you're working too hard (forcing your offense, for example), simply reduce your speed effort to a 7 or 8. Or perhaps you're not putting out on the defensive end of the court with the intensity that you should (foul trouble, fatigue, or you missed your last three shots). Increase your intensity level to a 9.

After a few days of drilling, the athletes react naturally and easily to our number game. So will you. Think of it. You'll have a composure control knob for speed, intensity and poise.

Learn to Trust Yourself

When it's time to play, it is totally up to you to trust yourself and remain composed. For the athlete who understands the laws of cybernetics, trusting yourself means trusting your **God-given** creative success mechanism. **Letting it happen** means the same as letting it work. Attempting to make your subconscious operate as a success mechanism by extra effort only strains your mechanism. An overtrying effort is self-defeating. The words **trust** and **let** are synonymous with maximum performance.

Since your creative mechanism operates below the conscious level, it is essential that you always place a positive demand upon it. The best way you can do that is by developing an expectancy to do well ... **a winning feeling.**

Whenever you experience that winning feeling, your internal machinery is automatically set for success. There is no need for worry, fear or anxiety about the outcome of the next play or the game. When that winning feeling is strong, you're in a power state. Your shot is in an incredible groove; you feel stronger and quicker. You can do no wrong. Your play is creative, spontaneous and free. Performance is automatic, natural and effortless.

How do you attain that magical winning feeling? Again, the CT secret is simply to recapture in memory the feeling of success and confidence from a past peak experience. Every athlete at one time has had a peak game or part of a game when he or she could do no wrong. Can you remember yours?

I recall the point guard on the college team I was coaching struggling in a terrible shooting slump in the first half of an important game. He was 1 for 9 from the field and 0 for 3 from the line. He also had several unforced turnovers. At half time, I told him to sit by himself in the locker room and do some heavy visualizing. This was before I discovered the power of anchoring. I asked, "Do you have a favorite game that you played in ... a game where you could do no wrong? A game in which you were on automatic and your shot was in a fantastic groove. A game where you were in charge and in total control of your team's offense. I want you to relive that game and when you do, it's going to help you enjoy the best half of basketball you've ever had."

When I finished talking to the rest of the team, my point guard bellowed out, "I got it back! I got it back, coach! I'm ready to go! I feel great!" His play in the second half was as flawless as it was flawed in the first half. Shooting 8 for 8 from the floor and 4 for 5 from the line, he led our team to victory. The win was reward enough, but I'll never forget his grateful hug at the end of the game and the whisper of "Thanks coach ... it worked."

I have also seen this powerful expectancy factor affect our opponent's performance, in a reverse way. Over a span of six consecutive years the high school team I was coaching lost a total of one game on its home floor. I strongly believe that a contributing factor to this impressive record was our opponent's negative expectation before the game. Being aware of our record (their coach may have foolishly reminded them) may have started them off with a feeling that victory was only possible if they played a perfect game with a super effort. Little did they realize this mindset of perfection was contributing to their downfall. Their inner machinery , instead of being prepared for a winning feeling, was tightly set for the impossible game and inevitable failure. Many times, good shooting teams came into our gym unable to buy a basket. Was it our defense, or was it because they were trying too hard? We always felt that their super effort was our super edge.

GETTING LOOSE BEFORE THE GAME

It's been my habit to approach games (away games, too) marching to the tune of a different drummer. Here are several guidelines I employed to keep my players loose before games.

1. **Winning was never mentioned as an overt goal.** (Winning is the benefit of playing your hardest.) We talked about the game as an opportunity to learn and grow. We reminded the players that the fun is in the process of preparing and playing. There are many difficult challenges and responsibilities in this world; playing in a basketball game is not one of them. Today's game is tomorrow's trivia, we reminded them. The importance of the game is an illusion whose outcome will be quickly forgotten. The effort they expend to be the best they can . . . is real!

2. **We never over or underestimated our opponents.** Their strengths and weaknesses were described in detail. Our defensive strategy has always been to shut out the opponent's number one or two offensive player(s). Our opposition may win the game, but the star player wasn't going to contribute. Our basic defensive strategy was to deny their best player from getting the ball. If the star had the ball, he was immediately overplayed and forced into defensive help. We wanted to force their other players to have to win the game.

3. **It's important that the players trust themselves, trust each other and trust me.** Belief in all three is necessary for successful results. Everything that was done in practice was designed to develop and perpetuate this trust. I've observed other teams who win summer league championships fail miserably during the regular season because they didn't believe in their coach's ability. (I must stress: No matter what . . . start believing in your coach's ability.)

4. **Every pregame locker room session would end this way.** Each player (coaches and managers included) stood up and described to the team a good deed that they had performed that day for someone other than a teammate. The rule was that it had to be an unselfish and helpful act that contributed to improving the life of someone (parents, teachers, friends, even a passer-by)— anything from cleaning the kitchen, washing dad's car, helping someone do their homework, running an errand for mom or a teacher. As the season progressed, the good deed stories became more generous and noble. One of my goals in coaching was to teach the bigger picture: the value of giving and sharing both on and off the court. The act of selfishness is one of life's most disempowering emotions, contrasted with the act of contribution as life's most rewarding. There are too many self-serving people of all ages living their lives with the habit of taking . . . without discovering the reward of giving. Occasionally, our warm up time had to be shortened as we stayed in the locker room too long listening to stories of contribution.

Have you done a good deed today? What was it?

89

HANGING LOOSE THE NIGHT BEFORE THE GAME

1. The night before your next game try this at home: Sit down in a comfortable chair (or lie down in bed), and go to the movies in your mind. Defense first: Visualize yourself successfully executing your assignments for the approaching game. If your responsibility is to defend the opponent's star, watch yourself confidently acting out your assignment by denying your opponent the ball, shutting off the driving lanes, forcing the offensive player to use the weak hand or to defensive help. See yourself cleanly stopping the player with the ball on the baseline and changing the trajectory of every one of your opponent's shots. Then jump into the movie and feel yourself performing these same outstanding actions.

2. If your opponents use a full-court press, picture your team destroying the press and controlling the tempo of the game with crisp passing, catching, and shooting layups with poise and confidence. Now take the movie to the next step and jump into the action. Feel yourself executing the specific assignment that your coach expects from you. Remember ... you'll get what you expect.

3. I always asked my players, managers and assistant to vividly visualize this scene the night before a game: They were to see themselves, after the upcoming game, strolling over to shake the hands of our opponents ... who we had just defeated!

4. So that I could get into an equally confident winning frame of mind myself, I programmed (in great detail) my own mental computer the night before the game. I saw myself calling the correct plays, switching defenses effectively, and making smart substitutions at the perfect time. And of course, I saw myself shaking the hand of the losing coach.

No, we didn't win every game. But we were ready to. My goal was to prepare our team to be physically and mentally peaked. What more would you want?

HANGING LOOSE DURING THE GAMES

Should you be performing poorly or feel you need a mental uplift, use the confidence inducing anchors you've been developing ... and fire a couple off. During an unobtrusive break in the action, you can combine the anchoring with a short stint of visualization. For example, you suddenly lose your shooting touch. Wait for a break in the action and get back into a confident groove by sinking a dozen imaginary shots. Link your particular shooting anchor word ("Yes!") and hand action (snapping your fingers) with each mental score.

Anchoring is one of the most powerful techniques for changing states. Be smart and use anchors.

Here are various mind and body relaxation training procedures all of which I've used from time to time. These exercises, practiced on a daily basis, are designed to reduce tension, unclutter your mind from extraneous and disturbing thoughts, increase concentration and eliminate the growing feeling of anxiety before or during the game.

1. The quickest and simplest of muscle relaxing methods is called the **breathing technique.**

This technique can be used at any time ... even on the foul line before taking a shot. It takes only a few seconds. Natural breathing is a universal rhythm. By listening to the air pass evenly through your mouth and nose, relaxation can be quickly obtained. Silently repeat, "Let go," on each exhalation. Letting go, implies the releasing of muscle tension.

2. The second relaxation exercise is based on Dr. Edmund Jacobson's famous method for decreasing tension before sleep. Used before games, it will decrease tension. Lying in bed or sitting in a chair, slowly count to ten, increasing (not decreasing) your entire body's tension on each upward count. After reaching ten, start counting backwards gradually decreasing your body's tension. All tension is fully released by the count of one. If you don't feel completely relaxed at the count of one, repeat the exercise again. While counting forward, squeeze your toes, buttocks, clench your fists and grit your teeth tighter on each count. As you count backwards, allow these same parts to go limp and loose.

3. The deflating basketball technique is a quickie that can be used in the locker room or on the bench. Close your eyes, take a deep breath, and slowly exhale. Begin to visualize yourself as an inflated basketball gradually losing its air. As the air escapes from your mouth (the valve!), let your body go slack, wiggle your neck and allow your head to limply hang on your chest. In less than ten seconds, you've become a deflated ball.

4. The light-gray cloud technique helped one of the worst hotheads I have ever coached stay cool in the game. Jim was one of our better players, but once an official's call went against him, he would become enraged and useless to our team. Nothing his teammates or I could say would calm him down. He tried visualization techniques, but nothing helped. What finally worked for him was the light-gray cloud technique. If you qualify for a hothead award, try this the next time life treats you unfairly.

   Imagine the official blowing his whistle and making a horrible call against you. Instead of getting upset and feeling smoke emanating from every orifice of your body, imagine a cool light gray cloud protecting your body. The bothersome call cannot penetrate your cool gray shield and upset you. You're totally insulated! You are free to stay calm, cool and collected. Press your thumb and second finger together to anchor this great feeling of control. Now, when you are confronted with a "bad call," quickly place these two fingers together for instant recall of your light gray cloud.

5. The quiet room technique will aid you in quieting your mind, while at the same time, relaxing your body. Quieting the mind requires slowing down the thinking process. Before the game, it's a good idea to still your mind for a brief two minute break.

   Build a little mental quiet room in your imagination. Paint the walls of this perfect, peaceful and comfortable room in your favorite color. Mentally construct the walls with thought-proof and sound-proof materials. In the middle of the room, imagine your favorite easy chair. Whenever you feel pre-game tension mounting, mentally retire into this quiet center to relax and clear your mind. Visualize yourself sitting down in your chair, totally at ease and feeling secure.

   Escaping into your quiet room has the effect of clearing your creative mechanism. Just as an electronic adding machine can be cleared of previous computations with the pressing of a key, you can clear your mental machinery from life's unwanted computations by escaping to your quiet room.

6. The blackboard technique attacks those concerns that in reality you can't do anything about. It can be anything from a lack of rapport with your point guard who refuses to appreciate your talents on the fast break, or a coach who doesn't see the best in you. Every time you think about them (and it's too often), a feeling of hopelessness sets in.

Would you like to regain control of your thoughts and stop wasting good energy? Do this:

Feel yourself sitting in your mental quiet room. There is a chalkboard in front of you. Picture the numbers 1, 2 and 3 boldly written on the board. Look at the board and notice that your three most energy absorbing concerns are clearly written out next to the numbers. Next to the number one is your most important concern. Become part of this movie and feel yourself getting up from the chair and walking over to the board. Pick up the eraser on the runner below the board and erase the number one concern. Wipe it off cleanly. There, it's gone forever. You've eliminated it from your mind. Do you feel the relief? You realize that the bothersome thought can only bother you if it's in your mind. You put it there and now you erased it. That was easy. Return to your chair and stare at the second concern until you grow tired looking at it. It's brought you enough pain. What are you going to do? You can't resolve it, but you can eliminate it from draining your energy. You know what you have to do. The eraser is still in your hand. Stand up and purposefully walk over to the board. Erase your second concern permanently and completely. Now, it, too, is gone. Nice job! Return to your chair and think about your final concern on the board. Hasn't it brought you enough grief? Let's get rid of it ... now! Walk over and erase it from your life.

Hey! Congratualations! There are no concerns left ... unless you want to put them back on your mental chalkboard. That is your privilege. Whenever you want something to bother you, just jot it down on your inner chalkboard (in bold print) and keep thinking about it. Do you really want to waste energy worrying about a circle of concern that you can't do anything about except worry? I don't think you do.

You know what has to be done. Use that mental eraser and get on with your life and your season.

7. Garbage in ... garbage out! So keep your self talk positive. Remember, when you talk, your automatic pilot is listening. Here are some affirmative action expressions that will help you stay in the groove.

Hang tough...
Let go...
Stay loose...
Relax...
Let it happen (on offense)...
Make it happen (on defense)...
Forget it...

Trust is a must...
Tomorrow's another day...
Just do it...

8. From Olympians to professional athletes, a growing number of athletes have been using a mental procedure called Transcendental Meditation (TM) to quiet their minds and energize their bodies. They claim it makes them think, feel relaxed, and perform better.

Dr. Herbert Benson has written a book called **The Relaxation Response**. This best-seller prescribes a simple meditation technique that is based on the TM procedure. It's easy to learn and results in a deeper level of relaxation (compared to our other relaxation techniques).

Judge for yourself. All you'll have to do is close your eyes, pay attention to your breathing and silently repeat a meaningless one syllable word or sound to yourself. Follow these instructions:

- Sit quietly in a comfortable chair.
- Close your eyes.
- Deeply relax all muscles, beginning at your feet and progressing up to your face.
- Breathe through your nose and become aware of your breathing rhythm. As you do, repeat the word "one" each time you exhale.
- Continue for 10 to 20 minutes.
- When you're finished, sit quietly for several minutes at first with your eyes closed, then with your eyes open. When distracting thoughts occur, ignore them, not through effort, but by repeating the sound "one." Practice the technique once or twice daily. Dr. Benson believes that this method will help the individual cope with the pressures of society and competition. Try it yourself and observe the outcome.

GETTING A GOOD NIGHT'S SLEEP

I have often been asked, "Is there a method of mentally training an athlete to fall asleep?" Coaches realize the importance of getting a good night's rest for their players and themselves in order to be in top shape for practice or a game. A sleepless night robs you of your energy. Counting sheep seems to be the only solution coaches offer their players to solve the problem of a sleepless night. A common cause of sleeplessness usually is an overactive mind... worry, excitement and anxiety. Try this **let it happen** exercise to quiet the mind, relax the body, and give you a good night's sleep. My habit is to slow down all the action of the people in my thoughts to a slow motion time frame. All conversation and body movement, including my own, are reduced to a crawl. Words are slurred. People are tired and yawning. Sleep soon arrives.

Here's another method: Next time you have trouble sleeping, get into a comfortable position in bed. Close your eyes and concentrate on your breathing. Every time you exhale, feel the air pass through the space below your nose. Pay gentle attention to the air as it passes through this space for several minutes. Now, look upward behind your closed lids at the top of your head. Hold this eye position for as long as you can. When your eyes become tired, let them drop to their natural position. Again, return to the rhythm of your breathing. This time, silently say to yourself,

93

"Relax" on each exhalation. Starting with your toes, feel the tension release from each part of your body, progressing upward. Think of the muscle, then the joint above it. Continue upwards. Consider all parts of your body ... even teeth, nose, eyes, eyebrows, temple, scalp, and finally hair. Sleep will arrive sooner than you think. If you find yourself still awake, repeat the cycle, starting from the feet again.

By centering your mind on your breathing rhythm, your mind is pacified. Two thoughts cannot occupy the mind at the same time. By listening to your rhythmic breathing, you will find yourself drifting away from your active thoughts. Your body will lose its tension, and a deeper level of body comfort will be experienced ... followed by a natural and rewarding sleep.

Employ one method or employ them all. Knowing how to relax, clear your mind and concentrate are the keys to a better game. Use whichever method suits your need, but train not explain these methods to yourself. Remember that relaxation and concentration cannot be achieved through positive commands and will power. You cannot instruct yourself to relax and concentrate unless you sincerely train these responses into your biocomputer.

Never forget that the three major principles for uptight performance are a lack of: (1) self confidence, (2) concentration, and (3) composure (resulting from trying too hard).

The principles of the mind/body relationship for peak performance have long been acknowledged. The irrevocable fact is when muscle tension is reduced, athletic performance is increased. Trust and let it happen, are my final CT words for you. Master the meaning of these words and you will be finally cut free from the mental and physical disabilities that have been plaguing your game.

CT's Greatest Achievement

One of the most incredible achievements of personal freedom and glory I've witnessed in over twenty-five years of coaching occurred to a young man who mastered the inner game and then triumphed in the outer game even beyond my own expectations. There have been countless athletes who have dramatically profited from CT, but none with the miraculous improvement experienced by a shy and timid athlete by the name of Bob Schreiber. By far, he was CT's most dramatic accomplishment! In one year's time, Bob transformed his self-conscious, unaggressive personality and body into the most intense, motivated, competitive and self-confident athlete I have ever coached. And I've coached quite a few.

Initially, Bob came out for the team as a junior. I first noticed him while he was playing chess in the library. It was in the fall of his junior year. Knowing I had no size coming up, I was on the lookout for anybody over six feet two. Bob, who was six feet five, told me he had played some church ball, and when asked if he was interested in coming out for the team, said he'd think about it. I was surprised when he did. Wearing a pair of spanking new canvas tennis shoes, white tennis shorts and a perfectly ironed white T-shirt (with no printing!), he looked as if he'd just come from choir practice! Overweight and poorly conditioned, Bob Schreiber had the most unathletic looking legs you could imagine. Unable to run the court freely due to his heavy thighs, (they had a habit of rubbing together), he was forced to waddle like a duck up and down the court. To his credit, he seemed to be sincerely interested in becoming a player, so I put him on the junior varsity even though he was a junior. That first year, he played inconspicuously on the JV team. In the spring, I put him on an off-season running program, a weight-lifting program, and for his self image, a CT program.

I asked him to spend 30 minutes each evening sitting in his favorite easy chair where he was to relax, close his eyes and imagine himself before a large motion picture screen on which he was playing basketball with great determination and aggressiveness.

Each week we gave him a new role to play in his mind. The first week he was to see himself running the court with strong and quick strides. The next week he had to visualize himself ruggedly rebounding and blocking shots. Another week he was to focus in on playing tough defense. Hard and low unrelenting drives to the basket were his next assignment. Above all, he was to always see himself completing plays and having fun while he was playing.

When his senior season began, he continued his daily visualization sessions. Additionally, we worked on his body language and self talk. Every day in practice, I would have Bob scream at the top of his lungs while rebounding or posting up for the ball. At the beginning, the only noise that emanated from his body was a high pitched squeal! With time and the help of his teammates, who demonstrated the proper technique of producing deep, harsh, angry grunting noises, Bob's timid nature was changing. After practice I could hear the growls and grunts of a dozen angry beasts whooping it up from the locker room.

The change in Bob was gradual but surprisingly steady. In time, I was watching him sprint up and down the court, decisively driving to the basket, rebounding and shooting his patent turn-around jumper. I realized what was happening in front of my eyes was a miracle of major proportions. Look at the numbers he put on the board in the only season he played for me. Our team's dynamic center was averaging 23 points, 11 rebounds and 4 blocked shots a game. Bob became the third leading scorer in the county, and more importantly, led our team, not expected to achieve a winning record, to a divisional championship.

Here's the rest of the Bob Schreiber story ... he completed four years at Colgate University, where he received a number of impressive playing honors, including being elected team captain and NCAA Eastern Division Player of the Week more than once.

If you ever find yourself near Colgate University, check out their athletic trophy case. You'll find Bob Schreiber's uniform jersey. He's been inducted into the University's Hall of Fame. Not a bad accomplishment for a shy young man whose legs had a tendency of rubbing together when he ran.

YOUR MIND IN THE GAME

"Behold the turtle. It makes progress only when it sticks its neck out."
James B. Conant

Once competition begins, your automatic mind takes over. There is little conscious thinking involved. Usually, your actions are not thought out while you perform. Calculation and visualization take place in practice, in the locker room, on the bench or at home, but rarely in the game. Think too much while playing and your play is mechanical and tentative. Successful play is automatic, flowing and spontaneous. **The play is the thing**. The athlete who thinks while doing is interfering with the doing. In competition you have to learn to. . .

- let go
- let it happen
- stop trying so hard
- stop thinking
- relax
- go with the flow
- just do it. . .

And trust your automatic success mechanism.

It's the successful athlete who has learned not to jam the creative machinery while playing. Think back. Weren't your best games automatic, uninhibited and unthinking? Ask the best basketball player you know what he or she thinks about in the game. "I don't know!" or "Nothing!" will probably be the answer. It's the underachiever who does the thinking in the game.

You don't need the advice of a sport psychologist (or Yogi Berra telling you "You can't think and hit at the same time.") to tell you that once the game begins highly complex motor skills such as shooting, dribbling or passing are performed automatically. Because they are actions that are classified as overlearned skills, they are handled on the subconscious (automatic) level.

YOUR MIND STAYS AHEAD OF THE ACTION

Largely because of the speed of action and a kaleidoscopic flow of changing situations, your mind has to stay ahead of your body action. Any skill that has to be thought about is destined to fail. The skill that has to be deliberated upon is not ready for competitive use.

You perform with less certainty when you have to consciously think about the position of your elbow on your shot or which foot is forward on the defensive stance. Skill in any performance arena, whether in sports, playing the piano, or typing is directed by your habit maker ... the subconscious mind.

SEARCHING FOR PLAYING CLUES

What would happen to the performance level of a skilled typist if he or she suddenly became aware of the specific movements of her fingers as she typed? She'd probably make more mistakes than usual and type more slowly. The typist's mind, like the athletes's mind, has to be ahead of body actions so that she can continually pick up words from her dictation pad. Likewise, the basketball player's mind has to be focused ahead searching for the cues and clues of the on-going action of the game.

When you are on an offensive fastbreak, you don't look at the ball as you you dribble or think "time for a change of direction dribble." Your mind is well ahead of the action, searching for the critical playing clues, such as an open teammate, a driving lane, position and movement of the defense or an opportunity to shoot. All good players, have the ability to catch or pass the ball, and at the same time spontaneously analyze the fast forming playing cues that are essential while deleting those that aren't. Without a clear mind, you will not be able to play good basketball.

AN EXAMPLE OF OVERTHINKING

When my son played Little League baseball, I recall listening to his two adult coaches preparing him for a crucial turn at bat (bases loaded, two outs).

"Choke up on the bat."
"Don't swing too hard."
"Take a short step with your front foot."
"Take one strike before you swing."
"Don't go for the homerun."
"Use a lighter bat."

I could see the mental wheels moving as he strode to the plate. After a called strike and a few unnatural swings, he was soon putting on his catching equipment. Overloaded with instructions, he had struck out! He successfully executed every one of his coach's instructions. Too bad their instructions didn't include:

"Relax."
"See the ball."
"Hit the ball."

Do you overburden your inner success system with too much thinking? Achievers don't.

PROOF THAT TOO MUCH THINKING STINKS

Your responsibility is to keep your game on automatic control during competition. Try this demonstration with a friend who is a great shooter. Ask him to shoot 10 shots from his favorite spot. Then ask him to explain his shooting secrets. "Is it your full follow through and relaxed wrist action?" Ask him to tell you which foot he prefers to set before the shot. Keep pumping him with questions. After he reveals his secrets, ask him to take 10 more shots. More often than not, you'll find his shooting percentage will decrease. Why? With your guidance, you moved his shooting skill from an unthinking, automatic level to a thinking, conscious level.

You could also compliment the opponents' best shooter (during an appropriate break in the action) and see what happens. Pay your respects to his perfect stroke, his quick release, his ability to create his own shot. Your acclaim will probably get him to think about his great shooting form and in the process change an automatic skill into manual control. If he falls for it, you've got him!

YOUR BOWL OF LIGHT

Whenever I am in Hawaii, I take the opportunity to talk to the young men incarcerated at the Koolau Youth Correctional Facility situated on the windward side of the Island of Oahu. The visit to the facility is as rewarding as it is painful. In stark contrast to the island paradise with its majestic mountains, dancing blue waters and proud and joyous Hawaiian people, the jail is filled to capacity with defeated teenagers gone astray because of the wrong kind of thinking and doing. I was saddened to discover over 80 percent of them will repeat their incarceration.

Why is this so? In spite of the pain of imprisonment attached to their past behavior, they are still not ready to change their strategy of living, nor change the disempowering beliefs responsible for getting them there in the first place. A teacher at the facility told me that one of their problems is that they never learned how to develop problem solving skills. They can't handle their emotions when things go wrong.

On my last trip to Hawaii, I met an altruistic man by the name of Umar Rahsaan. He is a fifth grade teacher at a small elementary school on the other side of the island, away from the jail. While visiting his classroom, I was instantly filled with fascination and excitement. The colorful mural walls of the classroom were in complete contrast to the depressing gray surroundings of the jail. The vivid, pastel illustrations on the walls of Umar's classroom were entirely created by his gifted students and produced a feeling of adventure, purpose and discovery. Throughout the room there were projects depicting the history of the people of the world at work and play. As I stepped into this sanctuary of learning, I felt I was in a special place full of love and appreciation.

It was there in that room, I found an ancient Hawaiian saying scripted on a plain piece of brown paper centrally placed on an old wooden table for everyone to see. The table sat next to a window overlooking a mountain (very similar to the mountain that borders the correctional facility). Rich with optimism, its simple advice expressed a message of hope that I only wished could be memorized as a code of behavior by the young inmates at the Correctional Facility at Koolau.

The next time you get overwhelmed with frustration, anger and disappointment read this untitled Hawaiian saying:

"Each child born has, at birth, a bowl of perfect light. If he tends to his light, it will grow in strength and he can do all things. Swim with the sharks, fly with the birds, know and understand all things. If, however, he becomes envious, jealous, angry, or fearful, he drops a stone into his bowl of light and some of the light goes out. Light and the stone cannot hold the same space. If he continues to put stones in the bowl of light, the light will go out and he will become a stone, himself. A stone does not grow, nor does it move. If at any time, he tires of being a stone all he needs to do is turn the bowl upside down and the stones will fall away and the light will grow once more." Ancient Hawaiian Saying

The very next time I returned to Koolau, I brought a large wooden bowl and some lava rocks of different sizes. I asked the young men to think about who they hated or were angry at the most. I asked them to pick the size of a rock that closely represented their feelings regarding this person. "Now, drop the rock into the bowl," I said. After a half a dozen rocks were placed in the bowl, I passed the heavy bowl around the room for all of them to hold. Then I said to the last one who held the bowl, "turn it over." As the rocks poured out of the bowl, I asked him to evaluate how the bowl felt now that it was free of the burden of the rocks. The young men passed the empty bowl around the room as I read them a copy of the Ancient Saying.

Why don't you try this same exercise? Find a large empty bowl and a dozen rocks. Think about your last game and put a rock into the bowl for every incident that created frustration, disappointment, anger or fear. Judge the heaviness of the rock-filled bowl and you tell me . . . do you want to carry that bowl up and down that court as you play (or live life)?

The next time you put a rock into your bowl of light because you're frustrated, make a decision. Turn your bowl over and let the rocks fall out. Then notice how quickly your bowl fills up with perfect light.

WHOOSH AWAY FRUSTRATION

You can **whoosh** away frustration in an instant. Imagine all of your frustration turning into two heavy rocks . . . one in each fisted hand. Exclaim out loud . . . "Whoosh!" and throw the rocks toward the floor as far away from you as you can. There . . . the frustration is gone. Now with a bowl full of light anything is possible!

STOP WASTING ENERGY

One early spring day, I struck up a conversation with a remarkable man while riding on a bus in New York City. He offered advice about living that I will long remember. He was eighty-eight years old but looked to be in his sixties. I couldn't help noticing him. On a very cool day, he boarded the bus wearing only a pair of shorts, a T-shirt, tennis shoes and carrying a handball racquet. I was so impressed with the youthful manner and the graceful way he carried himself that

99

I felt compelled to talk to him. He told me that he was returning from two hours of racquetball. Playing racquetball was his addiction. "If you've never played racquetball at two in the morning, you haven't lived," he said.

I asked him if he had a secret for his youthful appearance. He responded without hesitation. "Don't waste energy!" He continued, "I don't get angry or frustrated or upset. They are a waste of energy. I don't constrain or force myself not to be upset, I just mentally walk away from these wasteful emotions. They are useless as far as I'm concerned. I've got better things to do with my energy."

So next time you get caught up in wasting energy . . . remind yourself, as I often do, "Stop wasting energy." Then think about how great you'll look when you're eighty-eight years young.

There you have it . . . . everything you needed to know about the inner game, but didn't know who to ask. Now that you know all about your **Inner Success System**, how to activate it with the **Ultimate Success Formula** and how to achieve the **Power State**, it's time to turn inspiration into perspiration and take action on the court! If you're ready . . . let's go to work, or should I say play. This is the fun part of Cybernetics Training.

PART THREE

ON THE COURT....

"I can't stand a ballplayer who plays in fear. Anybody who has a good shot has got to take it and keep taking it. So he misses. . . so what?"

Red Auerbach

DRAMATIC PROOF: GETTING THE RIM

"Look within. Within is the fountain of good and it will bubble up, if thou will ever dig."
Marcus Aurelius

Let's walk our talk! Time to test the power of your subconscious and confirm that our **FAST** formula for activating your inner success system works. One of the most anticipated events at camp is the **Getting the Rim** challenge.

"Close your eyes," the youngster was told. "Relax by using the breathing exercise that we talked about. Now, picture yourself clearly touching the rim. After you've formed this picture vividly in your mind and you feel ready, go ahead and do it . . . get the rim!"

The player stood there and thought for endless seconds. Slowly he ran to the basket and jumped. Not only did he touch the rim for the first time in his life, he had an inch or two to spare. The six-footer had never come closer than three or four inches. Jim Harley (camp director) called the demonstration "amazing." Some campers nearly fell to the floor. Their eyeballs were as big as saucers. There was no magic, no mirrors, no tricks. It was just one example of mind control, the results of a forty-five minute lecture on Basketball Cybernetics by Stan Kellner, basketball coach from Brentwood High School (Brentwood, New York) at Harley's Basketball School at Eckard College in Florida.*

---

*As it appeared in the sports pages of the St. Petersburg Evening Independent—Florida—in June, 1976.

By now, you should know how and where this athlete suddenly found the hidden capacity to explode and get the rim for the first time in his life.

Most athletes have the potential for jumping higher. The only requirements for getting the rim are that you must want to jump higher, not be afraid to fail, and be only two to three inches short of the rim on your best jump. We use the rim as a target because it establishes dramatic visual proof of success.

If you've already reached the rim, here's an alternate plan. Run and jump at the rim until you establish your best jump. Using a magic marker, draw a line on the part of your hand or arm that touched the rim. Draw another line two inches above that mark. Now use this second mark as your visual target. Your goal is to touch that higher mark to the rim. If your best jump is just below the net or backboard, use the bottom of the net or backboard as your goal.

When you consider the time and effort it normally takes to improve your strength, quickness and jumping ability, this inner game jumping procedure is going to be easy. The traditional methods of "no pain ... no gain" will not be employed here. This short cut CT method involves five basic steps after you establish your best jump and a 2-inch higher achievement goal.

1. Mentally picture the rim.
2. Quiet your mind and body.
3. Utilize the power of visualization to provide your subconscious with a new empowering belief.
4. Create a **power state** by centering all of your mental powers on an end-result picture of success.
5. Stay with your goal until you achieve it.

The demonstration procedure is simple. Establish your best jump from a running start near the top of the circle or from the hash marks near midcourt. Jump as many times as you want at the rim (or backboard or net) until you feel confident that you have established your highest jump. Again, inches short of your target is perfect. (Or, use the magic marker.) Ready to go for it? Now do this:

1. Stand two steps in front of the rim in line with the angle of your run. Focus steadily at the rim until you memorize the rim in all of its detail (orange color, cold steel loops, white nylon net, etc.). Next, close your eyes and vividly imagine the rim in your mind's eye. If you have trouble seeing the rim with your eyes closed, open and close your eyes until you can imagine the rim with your eyes closed.
2. With your eyes closed, quiet your mind and body by paying close attention to your breathing rhythm. On each exhale (as you feel the air escaping through your nose and mouth), say to yourself "let-go." Feel the tension flowing out from your finger tips. Feel the pressure of the moment flowing out of your body. You are feeling very relaxed and comfortable. Imagine all the limiting beliefs of how high you can jump are flowing from your body. You should feel very, very comfortable and relaxed.
3. Now, begin to pay attention to each inward breath passing through your nose and mouth. As the air fills your lungs, feel yourself becoming lighter and stronger. Imagine there is a magic mixure in the air you're breathing making you actually feel lighter and stronger. A sensational source of power is filling your lungs. On each inhale, say "light and strong."

Sense the large muscles of your legs absorbing the energy flow from the air you're inhaling. Can you feel your body becoming lighter and stronger with each inhale as you repeat "light and strong"?

Now, imagine a large funnel above your head. Visualize a powerful column of bright, white energy coming from high above you—flowing through this funnel—and into the top of your head. Feel this column of cosmic energy pouring through your head, down your neck and into your chest cavity charging your body with incredible energy.   Especially feel your legs becoming more powerful and energized, like two powerful springs. Each muscle fiber, each cell, each molecule, each atom in the muscles of your legs is becoming electrically charged by the white energy flowing through your body. Can you feel how strong, energized and light you are?

4. With your eyes still closed, return to the mental image of the rim. Now, mentally lower the rim exactly two inches. In your mind, you can do anything you want. Create an image of your hand touching the rim. At first, make it a still picture. Hold the image several seconds in your mind until it becomes so big and clear you can actually feel the cold steel of the rim on your hand. If your objective is to jump higher than the rim, imagine the second line you drew on your hand with the magic marker ... touching the rim.

Now imagine watching yourself running at the rim, exploding and touching the rim. See yourself getting the rim several times. Now, make it a first person experience. Step inside the movie and feel yourself running, jumping and touching the rim. Sense the infinite power of your jump, experience the exultation of the successful jump.

5. You're locked into a resourceful power state. Go ahead and do it! The power is there. Keep jumping until you achieve your goal.

CHANGING PHYSIOLOGY

When a demonstrator has trouble achieving his goal, I quickly empower him or her by simply changing the demonstrator's physiology.

- I ask the jumper to stand in front of me (two steps away).
- I get into a power state myself, by thinking that I have just gotten the rim.
- "Mirror me!" I tell the athlete. "I want you to copy everything that you see from the way I am standing, holding my shoulders and back, breathing deeply, my facial expression and the intense look in my eyes. Whatever you see ... duplicate exactly."

After about 30 seconds of this nonverbal modeling, I say, "You're empowered! Go ahead and do it ... get the rim!" When the athlete suddenly reaches his goal, the doubters in the gym become believers.

WHAT'S NEXT

The jumping event is not supernatural or mysterious. It is natural and scientific. You have simply reprogrammed a new belief into your automatic success system. The belief supplied the know-how. So, what's next on your wish list? What is it that you really want? Which skills and attitudes will best help you live your dream?

1. More intensity on defense.
2. Improved freethrow and field goal shooting.
3. Increased strength, endurance and speed.
4. Stepping up as a prime time performer.
5. Freedom to make mistakes.
6. Winning attitudes such as courage, aggressiveness, second effort, poise and self-confidence.
7. More fun playing basketball.

With the **FAST** formula in hand and your inner success system in your head, turn the page and discover the impact of Cybernetic Training on the court.

THE EVIDENCE PROCEDURE:
THE ACHIEVEMENT CARD

"With goals you can create the future in advance."
Anthony Robbins

The proof in the pudding is in the **seeing**. Coaches and athletes are no exception. They love results they can measure.

So, in the first hour of camp, each athlete is given a ball and a 5x8 **Achievement Card**. The card lists 15 different skill challenges that measure the athlete's ability. Additionally, the card:

1. Monitors the athlete's skill improvement during the week of camp (this includes floor and foul line shooting accuracy, quickness, agility, dexterity, dribbling and passing ability).
2. Provides documented proof that the program's inside-out methods work.
3. And, clearly provides evidence that each athlete is endowed with a success mechanism.

The evidence process works this way. Athletes are tested before and after they employ one of our CT techniques. For most of the tests, there is a 30 or 60 second time factor or a consecutive best factor (how many baskets the shooter can make in a row). For all of the tests, a score is recorded.

<table>
<tr><td colspan="2" align="center"><u>30 Second Challenges</u></td><td><u>60 Second Challenges</u></td></tr>
<tr><td>Side Step</td><td>"Mikan" Drill</td><td>Jump Shots (no dribble)</td></tr>
<tr><td>Passing</td><td>Weak Hand Lay-in</td><td>Jump Shots (with dribble)</td></tr>
<tr><td>Dribbling</td><td>Strong Hand Lay-in</td><td>Jump Shots (banked)</td></tr>
</table>

<u>Total Amount of Seconds</u>
Power Series (total seconds needed to complete 6 Power Lay-ins)

"YES I CAN!" BASKETBALL CAMP ACHIEVEMENT CARD

Name . . . .

	1	2	3	4	5	±
MIKAN (30 sec.)						
PASSING (30 sec.)						
SIDE STEP (30 sec.)						
DRIBBLING (30 sec.)						
WEAK HAND LAYUPS STRONG HAND (30 sec.) (Equal Score add 10 pts.)						
JUMP SHOTS NO DRIBBLE (60 sec.)						
JUMP SHOTS WITH DRIBBLE (60 sec.)						
JUMP SHOTS BANKED (60 sec.)						
HOT SHOT (60 sec.)						
10 FREE THROWS						
POWER MOVE SERIES (Timed)						
PERSONAL BEST JUMP SHOTS — NO DRIBBLES						
PERSONAL BEST JUMP SHOTS — 2 DRIBBLES						
"BEAT THE PRO"						
TOTAL						

<u>Personal Best Jump Shots</u> (consecutive baskets made)
　　No Dribble
　　2 Dribbles

<u>10 Free Throws</u>

<u>Beat The Pro Games</u> (total daily amount)

The first challenge is the **side step** foot-quickness drill. The procedure is to test each athlete's defensive side step quickness (in 30 seconds), record the results on their achievement card and then introduce them to the VAK modeling method**.**

SIDE STEP QUICKNESS TEST

Athletes pair off. One athlete scores the results while the other performs a side step shuffle back and forth in the 3-second lane (for 30 seconds). There are 3 lines involved in the test (two real lane lines and an imaginary middle line). For each line the athlete side steps over (or on), he receives a point. The athlete's goal is to side step over as many lines as possible in 30 seconds. His partner counts the lines then takes his turn.

Next, I introduce the VAK mind training method. Afterwards (with no additional physical practice), the athletes' side step quickness is retested, scored and recorded on their card. By comparing the before and after scores, athletes have first hand proof of what the power of the mind can do when harnessed.

Almost all of our campers improve their score.

MODELING WITH VAK

After the entire camp is scored on the initial side step test, the six campers with the highest scores are selected to act as models. The models side step again in the 3-second lane as the rest watch and program:

V for Visual: As the **quickest feet in the gym** perform, I say to the onlookers (programmers): "Imagine that your eyes are a video camera permanently recording the action. Focus on the quick feet as they glide across the lane. Observe the quick change of direction. Notice the power, decisiveness and determination of the legs. Can you close your eyes and still see the action of the quick feet? If you can't, open and close your eyes until you can commit to memory the winning action. Next, visualize the swift feet with your eyes closed."

A for Audio: After a brief rest, the models side step again. The campers' focus is now audio. "Listen carefully to the quick feet attacking the lane lines. With each step say 'quick, quick, quick' to yourself."

K for Kinesthetic: The volunteers rest for a few seconds more before they side step one last time. And I say: "Imagine what it would **feel** like if your feet were wearing those incredibly quick basketball shoes. Mentally jump inside the winner's shoes. **Act as if** your feet are inside of those incredibly quick shoes. **Feel** the amazing quickness."

SET A HIGHER SCORE BY TWO

Before the rest of the campers are retested, they:
1. Repeat the commands "quick, quick, quick" to themselves for 30 seconds.
2. Establish a new goal for themselves (and their subconscious).

A score of 48 becomes 50. By looking up at the gym's scoreboard and imagining their first score has already increased by two they are telling their subconscious ... **see this** ... **do this! This is what I want you to accomplish!** I also remind the athletes to repeat the "quick, quick, quick" commands as they perform the side steps.

The outcome is astonishing. Most reach their goal. In fact, it's not uncommon to see campers improve their scores by ten or more. I've even seen scores increase by over twenty lines.

Try the Side Step challenge with several friends. Follow the process exactly. Score each other. VAK the best. Set a higher goal by two and go for it.

Now that you have dramatic proof of the existence of your marvelous subconscious and the impact of VAK ... check out the rest of the challenges on the Achievement Card and have some fun.

MORE 30 SECOND TESTS: THE MIKAN RIGHTY-LEFTY LAYUP DRILL

You're under the basket with a basketball. You have 30 seconds to convert as many layups as you can (no dribble). Alternate layups from both sides of the basket. Score the total amount of baskets made (not consecutive baskets). When shooting from the right side, shoot with your right hand and step off of your left foot. When shooting from the left side, shoot with your left hand and step off of your right foot. Always keep the ball above your shoulders while shooting and pivoting.

VAK the Best. Model someone who is a skilled shooter. (At camp, the highest scorer with the best form becomes the role model).

V ... visual: Study the shooter's form and the high and soft trajectory of his shot off the board (for at least a dozen shots).

A ... auditory: Repeat the words **"High and soft!"** on each shot. Add the word **"Yes!"** only after a made basket. (I'll tell you why in the shooting chapter). Link these three words in a very confident tone. (12 times)

K ... kinesthetic: Mentally jump inside the good shooter and imagine what it would **feel** like to shoot layups with the same grace and efficiency as your model. Feel the texture of the ball in your hands. Feel the successful finish. (12 times)

Retest: Before you go for another Mikan, repeat the **"High and soft! Yes!"** commands (to yourself) for 30 seconds. If your righty-lefty coordination isn't what it should be, execute 30 seconds of Mikan-ups against a wall (using an imaginary ball). Don't forget the verbal commands. Next, establish a higher score (by two), look up on the scoreboard and imagine your higher score has already been achieved.

After the second test, compare the number of baskets to the first test. If you haven't improved, repeat the modeling procedure one more time and retest again.

THE DRIBBLE CHALLENGE

Pair off. You'll need a partner to keep time and count the same 3 lines you crossed in the side step drill. This time you will be dribbling a basketball. Instead of a side step shuffle, you'll sprint back and forth (crossing your legs) as you dribble across the lane. Face in the direction that you're dribbling. Your back should never face the basket. Dribble low and hard with the hand further away from the basket. As you step on or beyond the lane line, quickly reverse direction. For a good score, your change of direction dribble must be sharp and decisive. Your partner counts the total amount of lines you cross in 30 seconds.

Now, model the best.

V ... visual: Watch the best (and quickest) dribbler in the group dribble back and forth across the lane. Pay special attention to the **pull-back** change of direction dribble. Notice the ball is protected by the dribbler's body and off-hand.

A ... auditory: Listen to the soft rat-tat-tat sound of the ball hitting the floor. Memorize the sound. Start to say **"Low and quick!"** as you watch the dribbling rhythm of the star swiftly driving back and forth across the lane. Say **"Low and quick ... low and quick ... low and quick."**

K ... kinesthetic: Next, mentally jump inside the dribbler for the winner's ride. Can you feel the ball as you control it with your outside hand? Can you feel the same confidence and quickness?

Retest: Practice your **"Low and quick!"** verbal commands for 30 seconds. Before retesting, set a goal. Add a plus 2 score. If your first score was 32 ... go for 34. Imagine "34" lighting up on the scoreboard as if it has already happened. It's important to repeat the words **"Low and quick!"** as you dribble. Afterwards, compare the score with your first effort.

THE PASSING (AND CATCHING) CHALLENGE

Pair off. Once again you'll need a partner to count the 3 lane lines and to pass the ball back to you. (Two-handed chest passes only.) Begin the drill by standing on the right elbow holding a basketball at chest level with two hands. (The elbow is the spot on the court where the foul line intersects the foul lane line at right angles.) Your partner is standing near midcourt, approximately 5 full steps away from you. The 30 second test starts when you pass the ball to your teammate and sprint to the other elbow, 12 feet away. Your partner immediately tosses the ball back with a proper lead. The object of this drill is to run back and forth, passing and catching the ball, crossing as many lines as you can. Each of the 3 lines once again represents a point. Remember to count the imaginary middle line. The total number of lines crossed in 30 seconds constitutes the player's score. **Go for it!**

As before, VAK the best at this drill.

V ... visual: Select the most adroit passer on the team (or the player with the top score) as the model. Observe the winner's smooth supple hands. When he catches the ball, pay special attention to how soft and accepting they are. See how quickly his thumbs meet behind the ball on each clean reception. Do you see how relaxed, poised and straight his hands and arms follow-through on every pass?

A ... auditory: On each reception, associate the word **"Ball!"** Link the word **"quick"** on each quick step the model takes across the lane, interrupted only by the power command **"Ball!"** on the reception. **"Quick, quick, quick ... Ball! Quick, quick, quick ... Ball!"**

K ... kinesthetic: Ready to jump inside the winner? I want you to **act as if** and feel each successful pass, feel each confident catch, feel the quick and skillful feet of the winner sprinting across the lane...scoring point after point.

Spend 30 seconds repeating the words, "Quick, quick, quick ... Ball!" Set a higher goal and imagine it lit up on the scoreboard. Then, go for it!.

THE STRONG HAND AND WEAK HAND LAY-IN CHALLENGES

These drills are designed to make your weak hand equally effective as your strong hand in competition.

First, let's test the dribbling and shooting efficiency of both hands. You'll need someone to keep time and score. The object of this drill is to make as many lay-in baskets as you can in 30 seconds, driving to the basket from the elbow. Let's test your strong hand first, and then your weak hand.

Strong hand: If you're right handed, stand on the right elbow and drive to the basket using your right hand. Lay the shot off the board (hand behind the ball ... no finger rolls).

Scoring: If you make the shot, you get a point (no points if you miss and no putbacks). After the shot, grab the ball before it hits the floor and dribble rapidly back to the same elbow using your left hand. At the elbow, quickly reverse and dribble back to the basket using your right hand for another lay-in. Remember, no second chances if you miss. This drill is to see how many baskets you can make in 30 seconds … first with your strong hand, then with your weak hand. The ultimate goal is to consistently score the same amount of points employing your weak hand as you did with your strong hand. Compare the strong and weak hand scores. If your strong hand score isn't higher, repeat the strong hand test until you're sure you've achieved your best possible strong hand score.

Weak hand: Same rules apply except from the opposite elbow. If your left hand is your weak hand, stand on the left elbow and drive using your left hand. On the shot, you must take off from your right foot, and then, dribble back to the elbow using your right hand. No put-backs allowed.

Now, model the skill of an athlete whose strong hand is your weak hand. (For example, you're a strong righty, so your model should be a strong lefty.)

V … visual: Memorize the image of the model driving and converting one basket after another. Can you see the winner excel making one basket after another with your eyes closed? Open and close your eyes several times until you can.

A … Auditory: Connect these words to the action. **"Low and hard!"** on the drive, and **"High and soft!"** on each shot. Add the word **"Yes!"** after each made shot.

K … kinesthetic: Jump inside for the winner's ride. Make it a first person experience. As you watch him, feel as if you're inside the body of the star. Experience the same confidence and control on every drive and shot. Recite the words **"Low and hard!"** on the drive, and **"High and soft! Yes!"** on each made shot.

Before you retest your **other hand** (you won't call it your weak hand anymore), imagine yourself driving and shooting **other hand** lay-ins. With each mental drive recite **"Low and hard! … High and soft! Yes!"**. Repeat this imagery session at least 12 times.

Retest and score the proficiency of your **other hand**. Did you get the outcome you wanted? Nice going! There are more shooting drills coming up in the next chapter.

VAK technology will improve your game. Continue using it. Wherever there's a winner, there's a role model for you to follow.

Next … the Ultimate Shooting Method. Trust it and discover the great shooter inside of you.

THE ULTIMATE SHOOTING METHOD: BECOMING A PRIME TIME SHOOTER

"I know that once I get a good rhythm and a good feel, no one can stop me."
John Starks, New York Knicks

Can the good shooter's rhythm and feel be taught? And if lost—as often happens during the season—can rhythm and feel be reacquired? Ask coaches whether they've been successful in teaching rhythm and feel, and if they're honest, their answer is not encouraging.

Coaches are quick to offer the shooter in a slump advice like "keep the elbow straight" ... "take good shots" ... "get more leg into your shot" and the most common suggestion, "keep shooting!" Let's face it, most coaches are not experts on rhythm and feel as much as they are on shooting form and hope. Coaches believe that timing and completions are up to the players themselves.

With the **Ultimate Shooting Method**, I'll prove that rhythm and feel can be taught and even recaptured when temporarily lost. But first, you'll need to master three essential inner shooting skills.

SUNNY SKIES AHEAD WITH THE ULTIMATE SHOOTING METHOD

Basketball teams are invariably made up of good shooters and bad shooters, with the majority somewhere in between. For the good ones, it's Blue Skies. For the bad ones (and their coaches), it's Stormy Weather.

Bad shooters usually make life unhappy for their coaches. No matter how much teaching and practice go into the effort, the coach usually winds up convinced that the particular player just doesn't have the talent to shoot.

Of course, the coach could be right. But knowing what I know about cybernetics and human potential, I don't buy it. Neither should you. The wise athlete, after fruitlessly checking all the obvious causes for poor shooting such as balance, hand and elbow position, and focus should ask, "Could the problem lie in my head?"

Yes! I believe that many players shoot poorly because of the wrong kind of thinking, not because of bad form. Ever notice how, after a coach has worked on a player's shot, the ball doesn't drop as consistently as it did before?

With that premise in mind, I have developed and refined a specific mental approach to shooting that strategically involves both sides of your brain. The secret of the **Ultimate Shooting Method** is it fully utilizes the verbal ability of the left side of your brain and the visual abiltity of the right in a team effort. Working together, they'll help you lock into an extraordinary shooting groove in a very short period of time. If this right brain-left brain stuff sounds too technical, let me first cite the three mental components of shooting as I see it.

1. **The quality of your focus.**
2. **What you feel during the shot.**
3. **Your response to a make or a miss.**

THE PERSONAL BEST GAME

Before I introduce you to **The Method**, let's test your current shooting accuracy with a game called **Personal Best**. It's important to know exactly how good your shot is at this moment, so you can measure your improvement using The Method. **The object of the Personal Best Game is to determine how many consecutive jump shots you can make in 10 minutes.**

Pick up a basketball and set up in the 3-second lane with your back to the basket, about two or three steps from the hoop. Toss the ball away from the basket, step toward it and catch it on the first bounce. As you pivot to face the basket, immediately shoot a short jumper.

Rules: Shoot all shots within a radius of two to five steps from the basket, no further out. No dribbling. No bank shots. Once you miss, begin a new count. You don't have to rush your shots. Try to make as many shots in a row as possible. Remember your best string.

THE THREE INNER ESSENTIALS OF THE ULTIMATE SHOOTING METHOD

Here are the three inner essentials of the shot that need to be mastered. And in this exact order only:

1. **Sighting Your Target**. You must begin by picking a spot on the basket to focus on. It could be the front or back of the rim, the sliver of space within the rim, or the nearest forward loops which hold up the net (in direct line with your shot). The target you pick is not important. What is important is having quality eye contact with that specific target. It's not how long you hold the focus … only how well.

2. **Feel**. What you want to feel while shooting is not so much the feel of a ball in your hands, but the inner sense of confidence that the ball will travel straight, true and drop cleanly into the basket. That's the mental picture you want. This feeling is critical since it acts as a homing device guiding the line, trajectory (arc), and finish of your shot.

3 **Combining focus and feel**. Successful shooting is no different from opening a combination lock. Unless you click the numbers in correct order, the lock won't open. And unless you apply sight and feel in the correct sequence and rhythm, you can ruin your shot. Too many shooters look and shoot at the same time, and wind up rushing their shot. You must apply focus and feel with a smooth, flowing, rhythmic cadence.

The **Ultimate Shooting Method** will:

1. Sharpen your focusing ability.
2. Combine the two inner skills in a smooth, unrushed, confident shooting sequence … creating the good shooting rhythm you're looking for.
3. Permanently lock in that **I can't miss** feeling of success, producing a reliable shooting groove and a solid base of confidence. You'll also eliminate that frustrated feeling after a miss.

LEARNING TO SUCCESSFULLY MISS A SHOT!

If you are serious about becoming a prime time shooter, you must learn how to **successfully miss a shot.** To achieve shooting consistency it is essential that you never let a missed shot cause doubt and concern. This interferes with the confident feeling good shooters have.

The prime time shooter maintains a clear, uncluttered mind before, during and after shooting regardless of the make or miss outcome. Hoping, wishing or wondering whether the shot will go in are not part of his mindset. Neither does the good shooter try to make a shot. The money player takes all shots with the clear, confident mindset of **let it happen.**

THE METHOD

From now on, each time you play the Personal Best game, you will be expected to call out loud three key command words as you shoot the ball: They are **Sight!**, **Feel!** and **Yes!** (if you make the shot) or **Clear!** (if you miss). **Clear** will erase the negative emotion of the miss.

> **Sight!** is coordinated with the sighting of the target.
> **Feel!** is coordinated with the act of shooting (stroking the ball).
> **Yes!** is added when you make the shot.
> **Clear!** is substituted for Yes! when you miss.

Once you learn to call out these terms loudly and positively, they will become an automatic part of your shooting. Call out the words only in Personal Best games. In actual game competition, **just do it**—shoot without talking or thinking.

STEP 1: HOW TO DEVELOP THE POWER OF FOCUS

Focus is important because it allows you to stay with what you want to do . . . rather than what you don't want to do!

Start by returning to your Personal Best game. As you toss the ball and pivot to face the basket focusing on your specific target, call out loud the word, **Sight!**—bringing the ball up over your shooting shoulder as you pivot and square up to the rim.

Do not shoot—stop everything as soon as you call **Sight!** This will help you hold the quality of your focus and prevent you from thinking about anything else.

To sharpen your focus, each time you pivot and face the basket, hold eye contact with your target for several seconds after you recite the word **Sight!**.

> *Tip: Good shooters have a habit of sighting their target sooner than poor shooters. Be sure to turn your head (face-up) as early as you can, so that you can sight your target during the pivot.*

Repeat the **Sighting** exercise for several minutes, changing your position on the floor after every two pivots.

STEP 2: HOW TO DEVELOP THE CONFIDENT FEELING

Stand a half step in front of the rim and shoot the ball easily over the rim into the basket. At the exact moment you see the ball behind the front rim dropping into the basket, call out the command word, **Feel!**. Be certain to say **Feel!** in a confident tone.

Note: If the shot is missed, do not say anything. Associate the word **Feel!** only with a score—

118

PROGRAMMING WITH THE SHOOTING PICTURE

Exercise One: *Study the picture of the ball sequencing into the basket and say...*
SIGHT!...as you spot your target.
FEEL!...observe the ball dropping into the basket.
YES!...focus on the ball in basket.
100 repetitions daily, if motivated; 50 reps, if involved; 25 reps, if interested.
You decide how badly you want that great shot.
Exercise Two: *Practice your shooting stroke at picture without a ball.*
How many reps? How motivated are you?

119

a correct flight and a successful shot.

Continue shooting very short shots (one step away from the basket) for several minutes, changing shooting angles after every two hits. Continue to anchor the word **Feel!** to each successful shot. (No bank shots.)

STEP 3: COMBINING SIGHT! AND FEEL!

Now move two or three steps away from the basket and face the hoop with a ball in your hands, ready to shoot. If you are right handed, set your left foot forward (reverse foot positions if you are left handed).

Say **Sight!**, squaring up to the rim as you bring your back foot forward (slightly ahead of your pivot foot), and focus on your target. Then, as soon as your back foot hits the floor and you begin to elevate on your shot, say the word **Feel!**

Important: Feel! is now part of the entire stroke, not just linked to the end result of a successful shot. The word **Feel!** helps guide your arm and hand smoothly to a correct finish of the shot.

Note: There should be no hesitation between **Sight!** and **Feel!,** and no pause in the shooting action. Words and actions should flow rhythmically together like a two syllable word … "Sight-Feel."

Add as many **eeee**'s as you want to stretch the word **Feel** (F-e-e-e-l) throughout the entire follow through of the arm. If your shot is too flat, add a few more **eeee**'s to **Feel!** This will induce a higher and softer trajectory for your shot.

Change shooting angles after every two made shots.

Note: You can save time and get more practice in by getting a feeder to pass you the ball.

Caution: Before receiving the pass, make certain to have your left foot forward (for right handers). Then bring your right foot slightly forward of the left foot on the reception.

STEP 4: HOW TO LOCK IN THAT CONFIDENT FEELING

Now, add the final word **Yes!** to the **Sight! Feel!** verbal sequence. By doing this you're pushing the final key on the keyboard of your internal computer. Once the shot has dropped and spreading the net, call out loud the anchor word, **Yes!** This completes the verbal programming sequence, more permanently locking in that feeling of success after a basket.

Drill: Return to the Personal Best game and coordinate **Sight! Feel! Yes!** with the pivot, shot and finish. Do not say anything after a miss—only **Yes!** after a hit.

Now compare your new score with your original (pre-Method) score. Any difference?

EVALUATING RESULTS

Normally, about 9 out of 10 shooters improve immediately after learning The Method. Some will double their scores; others may even triple them.

But why do some shooters experience little or no improvement at all? Consider these reasons:

1. They take their misses too seriously. They're not frustrated because they missed a shot—they missed the shot because they're easily frustrated. Any degree of frustration will interfere with the right feeling you're looking to develop. Once you learn how to clear away the emotional backwash of a missed shot, you'll be surprised how many fewer misses you'll experience.

2. They continue to miss shots because of a vague visual target. A more specific focal point is needed.

Let me show you how easy it is to rid yourself of the destructive habit of feeling bad after a miss.

USE THE CLEAR TECHNIQUE YOU'VE LEARNED

By now, I hope you've been routinely using the anchor word **Clear!** after frustrating mistakes in competition. I cannot stress enough the importance of clearing your inner machinery and playing free of negative emotions. You can practice shooting from dawn to dusk, but unless you eliminate the emotional debris of a miss, you'll always be just a streak shooter.

Use the command **Clear!** after each miss while playing Personal Best and see what happens to your shooting consistency. Get rid of those negative feelings that lead to overtry ... once and for all!

> **Sight! ... Feel! ... Yes!** for a score.
> **Sight! ... Feel! ... Clear!** for a miss.

Keep your eyes open while saying **Clear!**.

Play Personal Best for another 10 minutes, then compare your best run with your previous best. How much improvement was there? It is helpful to know that your shot is developing. With time and repetition, **Clear!** will pay big dividends.

FINE TUNING THE FOCUS

The quality of your shot will improve in exact proportion to the quality of your focus. You may need a more specific target upon which to focus. The nearest steel loops underneath the rim (supporting the net) offer a natural target.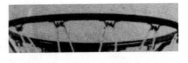

Stand with a ball over your shooting shoulder, two steps in front of the basket in direct line with one of the front loops.

Focus on the loop, and say the word **Sight!** out loud. Center your attention even more intensely. Draw your focus into the space within the loop, and repeat the key word for concentration ... **Sight!**

Now, align with another loop repeating the word **Sight!** as you pinpoint the inner space of each loop for several seconds (nearest forward loop).

By identifying the inner detail of the loop, you slow the sighting process. This will help you develop the shooter's rhythm by slowing down the tendency to rush the shot.

Next, without a basketball, look for the loops and physically go through the motion of shooting a ball. Emphasize the follow through and be certain to feel as if your shooting hand is directly over the nearest loop facing you.

Key Shooting Tip: On the follow through, direct the index finger of your shooting hand straight over the middle loop of your rim target. This will help you shoot on a straighter trajectory.

Return to the Personal Best game for another 10 minutes using the loops as your visual target. Remember to look for the loops in game competition. At times it may be impossible to set up in direct line with a loop during a game. Position yourself between the two nearest loops centering your attention on the two inches of steel rim between the loops. Make this small section of rim your visual target (over which you will shoot the basketball).

PERSONAL BEST OFF THE DRIBBLE

Since you won't always be shooting standing still, developing your shot off the dribble is essential. This requires a different kind of focusing skill.

In order to read the action when dribbling the court, your concentration must normally be wider; so when you square up to shoot, you must employ a more narrow or pinpoint type focus.

Start playing Personal Best off several dribbles, alternate two-dribble moves to the right and left. Keep a Personal Best score and keep calling the **Sight! Feel! Yes!** commands on each shot.

Vary your moves, direction and position on the floor, and extend the time limit of 10 minutes to as long as you want. Make it a rule to keep shooting until you beat your Personal Best.

At camp, it's not uncommon for motivated players to score over 100 consecutive baskets (the camp record is 265).

MODELING THE PRIME TIME PLAYER

Let's look into the mind and body of the money player and examine what's there. Imitation offers the quickest route for acquiring the shooter's groove.

What do you think would happen if you duplicated a star shooter's strategy, attitudes and physiology (body language)? Modeling the best with VAK is one of the fastest ways to improve your shooting proficiency. Think of it as a three act mirroring process.

Act One: You model the good shooter's body language before the shot is taken.
Act Two: You model the shooter's stroke.
Act Three: You model the shooter's reaction after the shot.

Okay, now let's model.

Stand on the three-point arc with a ball in your hands (which you will not use). Place yourself directly behind a good shooter about to play Personal Best. Observe the shooter confidently toss, turn and shoot jumpers (or dribble and shoot). As you watch, simultaneously recite the three command words (**Sight! Feel! Yes!**) with the star's shot. As you study the shooter, imagine what it would feel like if you were inside the shooter's body.

Act One: Note the shooter's unrushed, smooth shooting rhythm. Begin to capture the feeling of his confidence as he moves to shoot. Think of yourself inside the shooter's body. Imagine yourself moving with the same kind of self-trust and positive expectation.

Act Two: Begin to verbally coordinate the three shooting words with the model's shooting action. Feel that you are incapable of missing as you repeat "Sight! Feel! Yes!" with each of the winner's shots. In your mind **act as if** you are also the best! Become fully aware of the good shooter's perfectly relaxed stroke and fully extended follow through.

It's time to adopt the prime time shooter's code: **Never shoot a shot to make it—shoot it because it's there!** Although at first this attitude may sound stupid, the more you think about it, the more it makes sense. Can't you sense a shooting freedom in all good shooters? Without mastering your overconcern for making the shot, you'll never enjoy that freedom. "Never shoot a shot to make it," and "letting it happen" are the two best shooting suggestions I can offer you. Their design is to neutralize the overtrying effort of I've got to make this shot. When you try to "make it happen," the tendency is to shoot a flat and hard trajectory.

On the other hand, an attitude of "let it happen" or "never shoot a shot to make it, shoot it because it's there," sends your subconscious the same set of signals the good shooter's subconscious receives. Does this mean I want you to keep repeating these two shooting mantras day after day until your subconscious believes you? You bet I do! Since it's been listening to a "make it happen" shooting attitude all these years, your subconscious needs time to accept the new freedom you're giving it. Only then will you enjoy an incredible sense of poise, control and freedom. Plus a smooth, free stroke.

Act Three: After each shot, hit or miss, always respond with the same mindset. Never show frustration. Don't overreact on hits either. A happy **Yes!** or a cool **Clear!** is sufficient. A steady sense of composure sends your subconscious the right kind of feedback.

Modeling the best is a short cut method to success that can be achieved while watching television, sitting on the bench during a game, or in practice. Become a wise observer. Mentally study the best shooter you can find and coordinate the three powerful command words of **Sight! Feel! Yes!** with the star's stroke.

MENTAL PROGRAMMING FOR SHOOTING SUCCESS

What would be the effect if you just repeated **Sight! Feel! Yes!** to yourself 100 times a day? I mean no ball ... no basket ... no shot ... just a stack of 100 verbal suggestions pouring into your subconscious every day of the week!. Your user friendly subconscious would be receiving 100 successful shooting experiences! Thanks to the phenomenon of the cybernetic loop, when a word and an experience are associated and stored together, recall the word and you recall the experience. Check it out. Repeat the name of your favorite food 50 times and see if your mouth salivates.

Think of the daily verbal recital as 100 shooting successes being recorded by your mental computer. That adds up to 700 made shots a week . . . 3000 a month!

Do this for a week: Before falling asleep instead of counting sheep, count 100 **Sight! Feel! Yes!** commands. Add some visualization to the verbalization. Imagine that you're shooting all kinds of shots in a game. On each smooth shot recite **Sight! Feel! Yes!** nice and easy.

RECAPTURING THAT GOOD SHOOTING FEELING

Expect to be challenged by an occasional shooting dry spell. Should you hear yourself grumbling "This stuff doesn't work," or "It's not my night," insert a new floppy disk into your computer by repeating the word **Yes!** until you've regained that winning feeling. **Yes!** does not have to be spoken out loud. You can say it quietly (but sincerely) to yourself. I don't want you "institutionalized" before you become "lionized."

BANK SHOTS

You are going to have to learn to program two new high powered command words for developing your shot off the glass. The anchors **High! Soft!** will be substituted for **Sight! Feel!**

- **High!** replaces **Sight!** and is recited as you locate the spot on the backboard where you will bank the ball.
- **Soft!** is recited to provide you with the correct sense of **feel** as you shoot the bank shot.
- **Yes!** and **Clear!** are still the final anchor words, associated with the outcome.

A MINUTE OF BANK SHOTS

The evidence procedure for testing your shooting proficiency off the glass is different from Personal Best. Scoring is based on the total number of short bank shots you can make in one minute, not how many shots you can make in a row.

You'll learn the method by modeling a good shooter and linking **High! Soft! Yes!** to the shooter's focus, feel and finish. Then, you'll retest your bank shot, and compare the before and after scores.

- With a partner feeding you the ball, shoot short bank shots from three spots on the floor (left, center, right) … no more than two or three steps away from the basket.
- Change shooting positions after each shot.
- The feeder counts the shots made in one minute.
- **High! Soft! Yes!** command words **are not** employed.

THE MODELING EXPERIENCE

The best shooter in the gym becomes the model, shooting bank shots (with a feeder). Watch the shooter bank in one successful short jumper after another.
- Observe the high degree of completions.
- Feel the success. Mentally jump inside the body of the shooter and feel as if **you** are taking and making the shot.
- Start to recite the three words, **High! Soft! Yes!**, coordinating the command words along with the shooter. **High!** with sighting of the appropriate spot on the backboard, **Soft!** on the stroke, **Yes!** with the successful finish (**Clear!** on the miss).
- **High! Soft!** is spoken in a smooth, continuous delivery.
- Feel the confident release of the shot and its soft kiss off the glass.
- Make it a first person experience. You're inside the body of the shooter … taking the shot.
Before you retest your bank shot, verbally repeat the command words **High! Soft! Yes!** 50 times. Now with a feeder passing you the ball, go for a minute of bank shots. Score the results and compare it to the score of your first test.

You can also work on your bank shot without a feeder by playing Personal Best. Bank shots

THE POWER SERIES

Start at the baseline under the right side of the basket.

Dribble to the right elbow, directly in front of you, reverse-and drive to the basket (same side), stop and shoot a power layup (off both feet). If you miss, keep shooting until you make the shot.

Then, immediately grab the ball as it goes through the basket and dribble across the lane to the left elbow, reverse and drive back to that side of the basket, stop and shoot a power layup (off both feet).
Next two shots ... stop, pump and shoot. (Off both feet.)
Final two shots ... across the lane for reverse layups.

should be taken off the dribble and without a dribble. Mix it up. Enjoy your new found best friend … the backboard.

DEVELOPING THE POWER LAYUP

Not finishing off your drive opportunities? You don't have to experience the embarrassment of missing those inside shots anymore. Not with what you know about modeling. Here's what you can do:
- Model the forceful drives of successful others with the anchor words **Low and Hard!**
- Anchor their shot completions with **High! Soft! Yes!**
- On a stop and/or pump, anchor the action with the word **Stop!** It's important you learn how to successfully power-stop before you shoot a power layup.

The next time you watch a game, study the hard moves and strong finishes of the power players you see. With every hard drive you observe, anchor the player's drive with the words **Low and Hard!** (forcefully, to yourself). With every successful finish, link the command words **High! Soft! Yes!** (confidently, to yourself). Then, when you work on your moves in practice or mentally program these same moves at night, repeat the anchors … **Low and Hard! … Stop! … High! Soft! Yes!** with the appropriate action. (Add **Clear!** on missed layups.)

Coaches: (Try this at the beginning of the season.) On all layup drills, have your players recite out loud, the words **Low and Hard!** on their drives, **Stop!** on the two foot gather, and **High! Soft! Yes!** on their shots. They will be anchoring both their own drives and their teammates. As each player drives and shoots, the entire team shouts the anchor commands … **Low and Hard! Stop!** and **High! Soft! Yes!** This reinforces the anchors and keeps the players focused. Encourage those players who have trouble finishing their drives, to repeat **Low and Hard! … High! Soft! Yes!** 50 to 100 times a day. Instruct them to mentally program every other drive in slow motion. This will help them feel the successful finish.

THE POWER SERIES

You will shoot a series of six power layups. The object of this challenge is to complete all six shots in the fastest time possible. Have someone time you. With a basketball in your hands, start at the baseline under the right side of the basket. The timer shouts "Go!" and you:
- Dribble to the right elbow, directly in front of you, reverse direction using a drop-step, drive to the basket (same side), stop and shoot a power layup (off both feet). If you miss, keep shooting until you make the shot.
- Then, immediately grab the ball as it goes through the basket and dribble across the lane to the left elbow, reverse and drive back to that side of the basket, stop and shoot a power layup (off both feet).
- After you score, grab the ball and dribble across to the right elbow, reverse direction without a stop, and drive back to the basket and stop. But this time before you shoot, execute

a strong pump fake. Quickly secure the ball as it goes through the basket, and dribble hard to the opposite elbow and back to the basket on that side. Stop, pump and shoot until you make the shot. Now, for the last two shots, dribble the ball to the same elbow you just drove from on the left side, then drive diagonally across the lane for a reverse, left-handed layup on the right side. Then dribble to the right elbow and across the lane to the left side of the basket for a right-handed reverse layup (your sixth and last shot).

Let's review:
- First two shots ... stop and shoot. (Off both feet.)
- Next two shots ... stop, pump and shoot. (Off both feet.)
- Final two shots ... across the lane for reverse layups. (The last two shots are taken off one foot.)
- Shots that require a stop employ the anchor word **Stop!**.

How To Program More Power Into Your Power Series

Model the best! It's that easy. Observe the quickest player in the gym execute his or her Power Series. As the model drives, forcefully recite (out loud) **Low and Hard! Stop!** On each shot **High! Soft! Yes!**

Before you go for your Power Series again, recite 25 times: **Low and Hard! . . . Stop! . . . High! Soft! Yes!** Enjoy the results!

Now that you know all about the **Ultimate Shooting Method**, what are your plans? **The Method** will contribute to your dream of becoming a prime time shooter. Why am I so sure? Because it has for so many others who were willing to commit to it. Give it a three week test run, starting today.

GOOSENECK: THE PRIME TIME SHOOTER'S STROKE

Good shooting is both a mental and physical game. The **Ultimate Shooting Method** teaches the inner aspects, but flaws in shooting technique have to be corrected, too. Shooting consistency also depends on the correct principles of balance, hand and elbow position and follow through. Since athletes think in pictures not words, teaching in images quickens learning time. Here are a few shooting form image representations:

- For the correct placement of your shooting hand, the thumb and index finger of the shooting hand form a 'U' shape. This helps properly spread your fingers.
- The thumb and index finger of the support hand form a 'V'. This helps prevent the support hand (especially the thumb) from getting involved with shooting the ball.

- **Gooseneck** is a good word-picture for creating the proper arm follow through. Make your arm extension feel as if it's a graceful and beautiful **Gooseneck**.
- Always lift your shooting forearm straight up for several inches (like an elevator going up the shaft) then extend your **Gooseneck** up and out.

- On the follow through picture your shooting hand two feet directly above the rim. Suggest to yourself that all you have to do to make the shot is flex your wrist and let the ball drop straight down into the basket.

With the process of mirroring, good shooting form can be acquired quickly. All you have to do is physically model the specific body language of someone who has already mastered the physical principles of shooting. At camp the modeling procedure is called the **Gooseneck-Off**.

The Gooseneck-Off: By explicitly mirroring the physiology of someone who has already mastered the physical elements of shooting, you'll have a fast and sure method for developing your own stroke. Copy the physical stroke of a good shooter to the smallest detail.
- Pair off with a player (the model) who has the most picture perfect stroke on the team. Position yourselves a step away from each other.
- Neither you or your model are holding a basketball.
- Place your shooting arm twelve inches from the good shooter's arm. Both forearms should be straight up and down. Picture the forearm as a vertical #1 (straight up, perpendicular to the floor).

STEP 1

Act as if you have a basketball in your hands. Imagine that ball is resting on the pads of your fingers. Spread the fingers of the shooting hand comfortably with the thumb placed against the palm of your nonshooting hand. The fingers of the support hand are all facing upward as if they are about to shake the hand of God. The wrist and fingers of your support hand will not flex during the action of the shot. Remember, the position of your forearm is mirroring your model's straight forearm.

STEP 2

The model physically shoots several imaginary shots using only the upper part of his body (arms only, no legs). At the same time, physically mirror the model's perfect stroke. Be sure to duplicate the graceful motion of the full follow through and the relaxed action of the wrist. Relaxed wrist action is essential to achieve the shooter's touch.

STEP 3

Develop the correct position of your feet, by setting your left foot forward (assuming that you are righthanded), so that you're standing about a yard away from the model. Holding the imaginary ball over your shooting shoulder bring your back foot forward to shoot and say **Sight!** Then, as you elevate and follow through on the shot say **Feel!**. Physically shoot the imaginary ball and recite the commands together. Repeat the modeling exercise ten times.

Add **Yes!** after the follow through. On the **Sight!** word, pinpoint a spot upon which to focus. By centering on your partner's right eye as the visual target, you are sharpening your concentration skill.

STEP 4

Do the **Gooseneck-Offs** standing back to back with your partner several feet apart. Pretend to toss the imaginary ball away from your body. Physically jump out, and act as if you're catching the ball. With the imaginary ball over your shoulder, pivot and face your partner, shooting smoothly, without hesitation. Time it so that you both toss, pivot and shoot simultaneously. Copy the model's form and smooth rhythm exactly, even the confident facial expression. Detail everything down to the shooter's relaxed and smooth wrist action after the release of the imaginary shot. Be sure to recite the command words simultaneously with your model. Can you focus on the self-assured tone of the good shooter's voice? Repeat the action at least ten times until you feel that your stroke and the model's are identical and connected. You will be sending the same kind of signals that the good shooter sends (and receives) from his own subconscious.

Coaches: Use the **Gooseneck-Offs** before and after shooting drills. Make it a practice to match up good shooters with weak shooters and play follow the leader... gooseneck style!

A MAJOR SHOOTING TIP

A shot can be missed right, left, short or long. If your shot is moving right or left, try this:

- On your follow through, point the index finger (pointer finger) of your shooting hand directly at your visual target on the rim.
- Keep the finger pointed at the rim until the ball drops.
- Be aware that the last finger to touch the ball is the pointer finger of your shooting hand. Toss the ball over your head (at least a dozen times) and feel your pointer finger touch the ball last. Point that finger in the direction of your toss.
- If you're missing short or long, imagine your fully extended arm and hand two feet directly over the rim. All you have to do to score the basket is drop the ball down into the basket.

More On The Court Shooting Drills

Here are several shooting drills we use at camp incorporating the Method in a competitive situation. The key advantage of the drills is the shooter has the opportunity to make a lot of shots.

One Minute of Jump Shots
- Three players to a basket (one ball); a shooter, passer and programmer (observing).
- The shooter faces the basket and takes jump shots moving around (two to five steps away from the basket), always employing the shooting commands.
- The passer feeds the shooter and keeps score of the total hits in one minute.
- The programmer stands further away from the basket, holding a basketball and, observing the shooter while verbally linking the **Sight! Feel! Yes!** commands to the shooter's commands. The programmer never shoots the ball, only holds it.
- Rotate roles after one minute until every player gets to shoot. Record the results.

Second Minute
- All shots are taken off several dribbles.
- No bank shots.
- Employ the word commands and record the results.

Third Minute
- All shots are bank shots without a dribble. **(High! Soft! Yes!)**
- Record the results.

Fourth Minute
- Shots are a mixture of bank shots and straight in shots.
- All shots are taken off the dribble. Vary your moves.
- **High! Soft! Yes!** on bank shots ... **Sight! Feel! Yes!** on straight in shots.
- Record the results.

Say Clear! on all misses.

Beat The Pro

This is the players' favorite.
- The shooter plays 1 on 1 against an imaginary superstar who is on defense.
- The object of the game is for the shooter to convert ten shots, before five shots are missed. Each made basket is worth one point for the shooter.
- Two points are automatically awarded to the imaginary defensive pro, whenever the shooter misses a shot.
- Ten points wins.

- The shooter tosses the ball away from the basket (2 to 7 step range), pivots and either shoots or executes a decisive move and drives for a shot. All moves must be strong and game-like.
- Bank shots and straight in shots are varied with the appropriate command words recited.
- No layups.
- **Clear!** after misses.
- Before the game the shooter must identify the name of the imaginary Pro. The more famous, the better. Have fun beating the legend.

Coach: Recognize a player who **Beats the Pro** ten times or more in one practice.
- Chart each player's total number of **Beat the Pro**, **Personal Best** and **Minute Drill** scores daily. Reward athletes in some way when they improve their scores by 10 or more.
- From time to time, incorporate the modeling technique for all drills. Just add a player who is assigned to study the shooter and recite the appropriate anchor words with each shot.

Give **The Method** three weeks of your court time. You won't be disappointed with the results. As you read this, thousands of shooters have discovered the great shooter within them by employing **Sight! Feel! Yes!** Now, it's your turn.

A CONFIDENCE BUILDER: THE POWER FIVE

Your shooting success will be in exact proportion to the level of confidence you possess. The **Power Five,** unusual as it is, effectively builds and locks in confidence ... in seconds.

You may hesitate in using the Power Five technique or sharing it with others because it's too weird! But don't let that stop you. Think of it as an opportunity to have some fun! Three weeks of strange behavior is a small price to pay for a better shot.

Stand in front of a mirror (close the door behind you), make a fist with your right hand and place it against the glass. Sincerely look into the eyes of your reflection and say out loud: **"My shot is incredibly great and my talent is awesome!"** Get that silly grin off your face. You need sincerity. Say it again. Tell yourself with a confident and enthusiastic voice, **"My shot is incredibly great and my talent is awesome!"** Repeat the affirmation several times. Your subconscious does not have to immediately endorse the commendation, only hear it. Consider it planting season and you're sowing a positive seed. Trust the subconscious to cultivate the growth process. Without a strong belief in yourself nothing great will be accomplished. Nourish these positive seeds on an hourly basis! As absurd as it sounds, repeat the affirmation to yourself as often as possible every waking hour for 21 days.

Linking The Affirmation To Real Success. After a string of baskets, make it a habit to tell yourself, "My shot is incredibly great and my talent is awesome!" By associating the affirmation to real shooting success, you are reminding your ever-listening subconscious, "See, I told you I have a great shot!" For 21 days, I want you to bombard your subconscious with the verbal belief that your shot is incredibly great and your talent is awesome. Make sure your body language, facial expression, tone of voice and belief system are in harmony as you play this **act as if** game

Coach: Show some courage! Commit to using this affirmation as a part of your daily practices.

Pair off your athletes before and after shooting drills. Have them place their right fist against their partner's right fist as they take turns telling each other ... **"Your shot is incredibly great and your talent is awesome."** Before returning the favor, the recipient responds with an appreciative "Thank you." Coach, gather your troops in practice and from time to time ask them, **"How's your shot?"** Encourage them to answer in unison, **"My shot is incredibly great and my talent is awesome."** It's not nonsense. There may be scattered smiles or nervous laughter from some. Don't let the characters on your team discourage you. They're usually the players who need the encouragement most.

Have fun with the Power Five and remember always ...
"Your shot is incredibly great and your talent is awesome." It will be! Count on it.

An Affirmation For Shooting Detachment

Are you an emotional shooter who lives and dies on the outcome of each shot? Unless you learn how to become less attached to the outcome of your shot, you will never become a consistent shooter. Never, never, never!

Here's our cybernetic best for telling your subconscious to stay cool:

"I am a shooting machine."

This affirmation, spoken in the most machine-like monotone you can create, will teach detachment. Keep in mind that voice tone with a strong mechanical rhythm is the key. How you say anything (especially to an impressionable subconscious that is always listening) is just as important as what it is you are saying. Make it a habit of reciting this simple but profound affirmation before foul shots, after timeouts, after missed or made shots, and especially before you fall asleep at night. Then observe if your emotions and the finish of your shot aren't better controlled in battle. Start thinking and talking to yourself as if you are a shooting machine and it will be impossible for you to get emotionally tied to the shot. Are 100 affirmations a day too high a price tag for a more consistent shot?

FREE THROW SHOOTING SUCCESS

"When I go to the line I'm thinking 'all net.' When I don't think that, I'm likely to miss."
Larry Bird

If it's true you've been blessed with this terrific computerized inner success system between your ears, why is it your free throw shot has a personality all its own? Frankly, there is nothing wrong with your inner equipment that a little reprogramming can't fix. This is how you can dramatically improve your free throw shooting ... in a very short time.

- Employ a simple free throw verbal routine.
- Move your body, talk to yourself and believe you are the best free throw shooter in the world regardless of where your shot ends up. You will **act as if** until you find the shooting groove you've been looking for.

The verbal routine will:
1. Set up your subconscious for a successful response.
2. Eliminate unneccessary thinking while you're shooting.
3. Allow you to respond to a miss or hit with the same mindset and composure.

Let me ask you, is it your habit after setting an alarm clock for a wake-up call, to get up every two hours during the night to check if the alarm mechanism is operating? I think not. If you did you wouldn't get a good night's sleep. Since your subconscious and the alarm clock are cybernetically designed (and equally reliable), shooting free throws successfully should be no different from setting the alarm. You simply set it and forget it. Trust is a must. No thinking allowed. Thinking, as you already know, interferes with doing. The key to our free throw method is simple: **keep the judgemental left brain of yours busy so that it doesn't interfere with the trusting.**

THE CT FOUL SHOT VERBAL ROUTINE

Stand two steps directly in front of the basket (in line with the foul line) with a ball in your hands.

1. Focus at the basket and imagine a basketball cleanly dropping through the middle of the rim. Say **Yes!** as you mentally see the ball pass into the center of the basket. The tone of your voice must be full of confidence.

2. Now take your eyes off the rim and look directly at the ball as you bounce it (one, two or three times). Say the word **Bounce!** on each dribble. This keeps your conscious mind (and eyes) busy as you shoot. **If your shot is very erratic, make it a habit to use one Yes! and one Bounce!**

3. Pick up the ball after the last bounce, immediately focus at the rim and say "Sight!" … begin your stroke and say **Feel!** allowing the ball to follow any trajectory it wants. Don't force the shot. **Let it happen.** Keep the **Sight! Feel!** smooth and continuous.

4. On all successful finishes say **Yes!** (with the same tone you used at the start of the routine). Calmly say **Clear!** on misses.

Review … Say:
1. **Yes!** (on the imagined shot)
2. **Bounce!** (on each dribble)
3. **Sight!** (focus on the rim)
   Feel! (on the stroke)
   Yes! (on the successful finish) or **Clear!** (on the miss)

THE SHOOTING PROGRESSION

Using the verbal routine, convert two shots in a row from two steps in front of the rim. Then move two steps further back and shoot until you make two in a row from this spot. Now, move back to the foul line and keep shooting until you establish a shooting groove of 5 or more shots in a row.

Feel free to personalize the routine any way you feel comfortable including the number of preshot bounces or even incorporating different words. Think of yourself as an unemotional shooting machine. The shooting outcome is not important. What is vital is keeping your body language, facial expressions and tone of voice aligned and confident. You are in the process of programming a reliable and trustworthy cybernetic device. Your subconscious is a careful listener. Positive thinking doesn't work if body language and self talk aren't in step. Remember, your cybernetic system is a feedback device. As soon as you stack up enough baskets … it will produce the reliable shot you want.

SOME FREE THROW SHOOTING DRILLS

1. **Play Personal Best from the foul line.** See how many baskets you can make in a row. Establish a Personal Best score and beat it, daily.

2. **Model the good free throw shooter:** Three players to a ball. The shooter is two steps in front of the basket ready to shoot. A retriever (who feeds the ball back to the shooter) is under the basket. The programmer is standing two steps directly behind the shooter. The role of the programmer is to study the shooter and coordinate his own routine with that of the shooter using an imaginary ball. This provides the programmer with an opportunity to practice the follow through without the pressure of having to make the shot.

- After two shots are converted consecutively, the programmer becomes the shooter, the shooter in turn becomes the feeder, and the feeder becomes the programmer.
- The next set of shots are made two steps further back, closer to the foul line.
- When all three players convert two from this spot, they move to the foul line where they again take turns shooting.

SHOOTING TIPS

On each shot, the programmer (who is always standing behind the shooter) must physically and verbally mirror the action of the good shooter. The shooter uses a real ball, the programmer an imaginary ball in unison with the real shooter. Each employs his or her own personal routine.

Coach: Incorporate your favorite free throw shooting drills ... but always employ **The Method's** verbal routine.

PROGRAMMING OFF THE COURT

Recite the entire series of verbal commands twenty-five to fifty times each night before you go to sleep or when you awaken. Verbal programming can be accomplished any time or any place, but is most effective when you are totally relaxed.

Yes! ....Bounce! Bounce!...Sight!...Feel!...Yes!

Make certain you express the verbal commands with the same smooth rhythm and flow you use when shooting foul shots in actual competition. The more sense of confidence you link to the commands, the greater the benefits.

> Remember if your shot is very erratic, employ one **Yes!** and one **Bounce!**
> **Yes! ... Bounce! ... Sight! ... Feel! ... Yes!**

GOING TO THE MOVIES OF YOUR MIND

Apply the verbal programming to a mental movie.
- Close your eyes and imagine that you are shooting a crucial free throw in a big game. Feel the pressure of the moment. Your team is down one ... and you've got a crucial 1 and 1.
- Visualize your teammates and opponents lined up awaiting your first shot. Feel yourself

confidently standing at the line. Sense the texture of the ball in your hands. As you focus your eyes on the front of the rim, say **Yes!** and visualize the ball where you expect it to be ... already in the basket.

- Feel yourself bouncing the ball, saying **Bounce!** on each of your two deliberate bounces. Feel the quiet confidence as you bounce the ball.
- Pick up the ball and coordinate **Sight! Feel! Yes!** to your shooting action. Visualize the ball's straight trajectory and the final splash of the net as the shot drops. Congratulate yourself. Nice job under big time pressure. You're cool as ice.

Play this visualization game on the silver screen of your mind. Create all kinds of game situations from the foul line. Include a score, time factor, fatigue and especially the successful finish. Be sure to make the mental heroics a first person experience.

Before we move to the defensive end of the court, you must understand that your shot from the floor or the line will be "incredibly great" only when you successfully develop the feeling of certainty, confident body movement and cool inner dialogue of the great shooter. I must emphasize that shooting consistency results when you align all three. Two out of the three is not enough. The CT techniques you learned in this chapter will guide you each step of the way in the direction of all three. But until you get prime time results ... **act as if** you already have. Promise you will and you'll soon rejoice ... **"Yes, my shot is incredibly great!"**

DEFENSIVE SYNERGY:
THE WHOLE IS GREATER THAN THE SUM OF ITS PARTS

"Teamwork is the essence of life. It makes everything possible from moonshots to building cities to the renewal of life. And a good team multiplies the potential of everyone on it."

Pat Riley

Offense wins games! Players know that. Defense wins championships. Coaches know that. Regardless of your opinion... you can bet the ranch that ... **DEFENSE IS THE NAME OF THE GAME!**

Analyze any successful high school, college or professional program and you'll find a commitment to defense. In the 1992–93 season, St. John's, a young and inexperienced team picked to finish 9th in the Big East Conference, dedicated itself to playing a stingy team defense which led to an unexpectedly successful season. The University of Connecticut's Coach Jim Calhoun explained St. John's surprising success this way, "They're not the most talented team we've faced in the league, but they understand the concept of **We** comes before **I** and **Us** before **Me** better than any team we've faced."

After a slow start punctuated by an embarrassing loss to Indiana, St. John's turnaround began with a team meeting where the entire squad committed to going all out. No pacing, no alibis. Nothing held back. No matter what happened on the offensive end, they would all come to play on the defensive end of the court and pay any price to win. Each player agreed to commit his energies to team defense. Overnight, a team short on talent was playing on the same page. The **We** and **Us** replaced the **I** and **Me**. Defense became the name of the game for St. John's. Throughout their remarkable season they pressured the ball, closed the passing lanes, helped each other out, got their hands on the ball for countless deflections and steals, and rebounded with tenacity. Individually they lacked size, quickness and experience, but on defense, they performed aggressively and together. For St. John's, **The whole became greater than the sum of its parts.**

And that brings us to the doorstep of what this key chapter is all about... how to increase the defensive effectiveness of a team so the whole becomes greater than the sum of its parts. The process is called **Defensive Synergy.** Second to none, **Synergy** offers the most direct route to immediate **team success** than any other CT method in this book!

> The following information on **Defensive Synergy** is directed to the coach reading this book more than the athlete. Since it requires team participation and commitment, share **Synergy** with your coach and ask your coach to test its effectiveness in the gym during practice. I've seen what **Defensive Synergy** has done for my program and others. I know what **Synergy** has done to the intensity of our camp games as a result of the extraordinary motivational powers it generates.

Coach: How can **Synergy** help your team? It multiplies (not adds) the energy production of everyone on your team, producing a sustained sense of team purpose and unity—from the best player to the weakest link.

SYNERGY: THE TEAM PLAN

In those rare moments, when every player on a team is enthused, energized, focused and 100% committed to playing defense, the team is in a state of synergized power! **The definition of synergy is combining the energy of two or more people in a joint action.** When this occurs, a multiplying effect is produced. Synergy is the process of pooling together the abilities and strengths of five players for a common purpose–**to prevent the opposition from scoring an uncontested shot.**

When a team is defensively synergized, everybody is focused and energized! No "good look" or easy shot is allowed. The basket is protected from intruders! The opposition is forced to work exceptionally hard for shots, usually ending up with a forced shot or a basket that requires a number of difficult passes or a great deal of luck.

BUILDING DEFENSIVE SYNERGY

When five players form a team, they bring to the table five different levels of enthusiasm, energy, talent, and endurance. During the course of a game, these factors individually fluctuate depending on a large number of physical and emotional elements. Any distraction for a single player can become an irreparable crack in the team's defensive wall. Reasons for a diminished defensive effort can range from fatigue, to a bad night of shooting, to a bad call. A distraction can cause an otherwise hustling player to suddenly lose his or her commitment and energy to play defense. Interest is lost in pressuring the ball, denying the pass, or hedging.

But what about the tough teams that somehow manage to stay focused and energized regardless of adversity? What's their secret? The answer is discipline, top physical conditioning, and their desire based on a sustained sense of purpose.

If you're not a **get in your face** coach, the obvious question is, "How can the necessary discipline, conditioning and a sustained sense of purpose be achieved?" The answer is **Synergy**.

A Defensive Team Is As Strong As Its Weakest Performer

When four players are playing physically tough, hard defense, contesting every shot, pressuring every pass, banging the boards, and one player isn't (for whatever reason) the entire team loses its defensive efficiency not by one-fifth, but by 100%. The ball invariably finds its way to the uninspired defensive player's man.

If you believe a team is as strong as its weakest player (as I do), then it's time to motivate the unmotivated, commit the uncommitted, and energize the unenergized.

The First Step: Establish A Set Of Defensive Rules

Before you can incorporate Synergy into your practice and get its bonding benefits, you need to clearly establish your team's defensive rules. Let me tell you mine:

> 1. Pressure the ball.
> 2. Support the ball.
> 3. Box out.

Three simple basic defensive rules.
- Good defense begins with applying tough pressure on the ball by challenging each shot and pass.
- Good defense requires teammates helping each other out. Players more than one pass away from the ball, should be aggressively stepping (hedging a step or more to the ball) to prevent all driving and passing lanes.
- Last but not least, good defense is predicated on not allowing your opponent to get to the offensive boards for a second or third shot.

Soon after **Defensive Synergy** became an integral part of our daily practices, I noticed an increase in the intensity and effectiveness of our team's defense in scrimmages and games. All players appeared to be giving it their best on every play. The strong were stronger and so were the weak. And we were winning more games!

THE SILVER BULLET

Turning the me-too into we-too is achieved by drawing on the entire team's energy force. You'll expend less energy while your players do all the work ... and they'll have fun while they're working.

The advantage of **Synergy** is you won't have to introduce a single new defensive drill. Everything stays the same ... except the results will be better.

This is what we do at camp to introduce **Synergy**. We divide the athletes into teams of four. Each team of four forms a separate circle, joining hands. Taking a strong, wide defensive stance, they shout in unison the first camp rule of defense ... **"Pressure the Ball! Pressure the Ball! Pressure the Ball!"** Nothing is held back. At the top of their lungs they scream their commitment to pressure the ball (three times). The cumulative effect is their body language, facial expressions and tone of voice generate an incredible **power state of mind** for every player.

In concert, the players loudly chant the second rule of defense (three times) ... **"Jump to the ball! Jump to the ball! Jump to the ball!."** And then, the final rule ... **"Box out! Box out! Box out!"**

The act of joining hands allows each player to feel the conspiring intensity of the group. Try the same aggressive chanting without the hands joined and the players immediately feel the difference.

The screaming of the rules becomes even more fun as the four player teams compete against each other to see which group is the loudest and craziest. The unaggressive and uncommitted are quickly exposed. But after we acknowledge and reward the teams that show the most enthusiasm, the meek and shy soon get plugged in. The camp games are never the same after synergy is introduced.

For some of the more macho players who would rather not hold hands, just remind them that those mammoth NFL athletes they see on televison each Sunday have no trouble joining hands in their defensive huddles. Certainly, your players can join hands in the privacy of their own gym. Any embarrassment they may momentarily feel by joining hands will be a distant second compared to the embarrassment of being a part of an uninspired and losing defense!

SYNERGIZE YOUR DRILLS

Coach: You can reinforce all defensive skills and attitudes by forming **Synergy Circles** before and after every defensive drill. For example, on rebounding drills, the players join hands and shout, "Box-out! Box-out! Box-out!" Circles can be in groups of of 4,5,6 or include the entire team.

Teams can synergize before the game or at halftime in the locker room. Everybody joins hands (including coaches and managers) in one big cooperative circle and chants some point you want them to emphasize

Synergy Circles can be subtle. After a timeout, I've seen five players join hands and quietly remind themselves of a defensive rule or point of emphasis, like **"Get back on 'D'!"** or **"Stop #24!"**

THE GAME OF WAR

War is our special half-court game that uses synergy as its base of operation. It not only teaches the rules of defense, it's as fun to play as it is exciting to watch. Here's how it's played:

- War is a 4 on 4 half-court game.
- There is a third team under the basket (out of bounds) waiting to get into the game.
- Action is continuous. As soon as a team scores a basket, they remain on offense. The defensive team which gave up the score is replaced by the team waiting off the court.
- If the defensive team secures the rebound, intercepts a pass, forces a turnover or deflects the ball out of bounds, they become the offensive team. The original offensive team is knocked out, changing positions with the team off the court.
- The team entering the game always plays defense first.
- The only way to play offense is to play successful defense.
- Each basket is worth one point. No free throws are shot, but a defensive foul knocks out that defensive team.
- After a score, the offensive team does not have to wait for the new defensive team to set up.
- In order to reset their offense, all a team needs to do is dribble or pass the ball beyond the foul line, yell **"Set up!"** and attack (or shoot).
- The first team that scores 7 points wins the game.

THE SYNERGY RULES OF WAR

No team can come on the court unless they first synergize a defensive rule (usually the one they last violated or a specific rule the coach wants emphasized). They circle-up off the court (behind the basket), join hands and emphatically shout a defensive rule three times. The circle opens up into a straight line of four players with their hands still joined (except for the outside hands of the end players). The line is facing the court ready to enter the game ... as soon as a team is knocked out..

Rule: Since the offense does not have to wait for the defense to come in, incoming and outgoing teams are forced to hustle into the game to pick up their assignments or off the court to synergize without delay. War can get chaotic as teams run on and off the court.

Rule: Emphasize that the team being bumped off, must quickly sprint off the court (this simulates a defensive fast break), join hands, synergize, open their circle forming a straight line with their hands still joined, and wait for an opportunity to reenter.

Coach: Commit to synergizing and playing **War** every day in practice. I know of no better way to increase your team's hustle, endurance, sense of purpose and the skills and attitudes of winning defense.

Can you hear the cry of your fans behind your bench encouraging your team with a call of ... **DEFENSE! DEFENSE! DEFENSE!** Can you see your team challenging the opposition's every shot, denying every pass, smothering every drive, battling for every rebound, diving for every loose ball, and taking one fearless charge after another? I can! **Use Synergy and I promise .... so will you!**

SYNERGY: THE WRITTEN PLAN

The use of goal cards is a technique that further crystalizes a team's excitement for playing defense.

Coach: A few days before a game, in front of the team on a chalkboard, write the word **Synergy** under which you boldly write the number **48**. This number represents the amount of points you feel you must hold the opponents under in order to win. **Note:** Whatever score you choose, it must be one that is realistic while still challenging your team's defensive juices.

Divide the score by four and write the number 12 (four times) on the board, further defining your team's defensive goal by quarters. The objective is not to allow more than 12 points per quarter. Consider it a shutout quarter if your team limits the opposition to single digits. Now develop a synergy plan with your team.

1. **Establish a clear cut set of team goals.** Discuss what your team must do to attain the defensive score of 48. Discuss your opponent's offensive tendencies. Assign defensive matchups. Identify primary offensive threats. Determine with the team which defensive rules must be emphasized and which opponents should draw the most attention. Defensive roles and individual expectations are clearly defined. Under the number 48 on the board, list 3 to 5 defensive strategies that must be realized to achieve a defensive score of 48.

For example:
   1. Contain the guards.
   2. Deny #21 inside.
   3. Get back on "D".
   4. Pressure all perimeter shots.
   5. No second shots (especially #12).

Make sure that you keep everything on the board in view of the players before the game, at halftime and after the game as a reminder of your team's commitment to defense. Use the halftime break to evaluate the list of requirements and your first half success. Involve the players in the evaluation by asking for a show of hands whether each strategy was attained.

2. **Make a contract.** A few days before the game, players write the number 48 using a black magic marker on a 3 by 5 goal card imprinted on the back with the 3 basic rules of defense. Then, they list the same specific goals listed on the chalkboard.

3. **Mentally program it.** Ask your players to find time at home to mentally visualize the final score of a "48" lighting up on the opponent's side of the scoreboard. They should program by quarter ... **12, 24, 36 and then, 48** ... on their mental screen and envision what they have to do on the court to achieve these scores. They should feel themselves pressuring the ball, stopping the dribbler, preventing baseline penetration, boxing out, creating steals and deflections.

The first time I used this technique with my own high school team, we held the opposition under 45 points for five consecutive games. One team only scored 39 points. The string was finally broken in a game where the opposition scored a basket at the buzzer. After the game, I asked the player who allowed the baseline drive that resulted in the final basket if he had programmed the 45 score? He admitted he hadn't! (A coincidence?)

Be fair to your own expectations and your players. Set a realistic attainable defensive goal (perhaps a score of 55 or 60). If the team falls short of attaining a team objective, don't give up on the goal card technique. Evaluate the game video (or defensive charts). Then, encourage those players who did not execute well to double their mental programming activities for those defensive skills they performed below par.

There's an additional benefit of the use of goal cards. Even if your team loses, setting specific strategy objectives allows players to achieve partial victories. After a loss, it's important to focus on what they did right, not what they did wrong. With enough small victories, in time they'll earn the big ones.

ANOTHER USE OF GOAL CARDS

The goal card (see page 33) is an excellent tool for defensive skill development. It allows you to center your focus on a specific deficiency. For instance, write on a goal card the word or words that represent a single defensive skill or rule that needs developing. Perhaps you're not stopping the opponent's point guard from penetrating the paint. Now write the cure on a goal card ... **stop penetration** or **quick feet.** The prescription must be positive and short (2 to 4 words). Words like **don't** or **avoid** are not to be used.

Use your goal card as a constant reminder for mentally rehearsing a skill or attitude. You should sign the card and date it. Signing the goal card does not guarantee commitment ... but it's a good beginning.

GRABBING THE DEFENSIVE REBOUND

Do you have trouble holding on to a rebound? Does the ball mysteriously squirt loose? Is it poor hands, lack of concentration, confidence, strength, aggressiveness, or maybe heredity? Stop analyzing and start programming a better set of hands. A pair of hands that hold on to a rebound!

VAK with **Velcro!**
1. Start by presenting your subconscious with clear cut instructions. Write on a goal card the command ... **"Velcro the rebound!"** You'd like the ball to stick to your hands on all rebounds like two pieces of velcro that instantly bond. Give your subconscious two weeks to come up with a better set of hands.
2. Imagining your eyes as a video camera, mentally video tape the best set of soft hands you can find in the gym. Study those sure hands as they rebound and catch. On each rebound and reception you see, say to yourself ... **"Velcro!"**
3. Once you've anchored **"Velcro!"** to the action. Start tossing a ball over your head and on each catch, say **"Velcro!"** out loud. Toss the ball off the backboard, grab the rebound and shout **"Velcro!"** (at least 12 times). Imagine the ball sticking to your hands like you are wearing a pair of velcro gloves.
4. Every night before you go to sleep say **"Velcro!"** at least 50 times. As you do, imagine a ball coming off the boards and sticking to your hands.

No, you won't have to shout **"Velcro!"** in games ... but your subconscious will remind your hands ... **"Velcro!"**

TAKE THE CHARGE!

"Take the charge!" How many times have you heard a coach yell out these instructions? It's easy for the coach from the safety of the bench to advise you to sacrifice your body for the good of the team.

Let's be frank. Do you really want to take the charge? Don't you need a good reason? Remember, reasons come before results. Here's a list of possible whys.

- Earn more playing time.
- Turn a game around.
- Demoralize the opposition.
- Be a hero.
- Make a contribution.
- Teammates, coach and significant others will approve.
- Earn a scholarship.
- Love the challenge.
- You just want to!

The reason you haven't been taking the charge is that taking the charge is outside your comfort zone. That's good news. Now you have another reason to take the charge. It will expand your comfort zone.

If you're serious about wanting to take the charge, CT can help. Let's VAK it!

V: Observe someone taking the charge and memorize the action. Make it a mental movie you can watch at night. Add the sight of fans on their feet shouting the defensive hero's name. See the coach's and teammates' elation. Sense their gratitude for the courageous act.

A: Anchor the charge with the word **"Great!"** Each time you see a heroic athlete take a charge say to yourself, **"Great!"**

K: Before you fall asleep at night, visualize the star taking the charge. Then jump into the mental video and make the experience first hand and slow motion. Feel yourself taking it squarely on your uniform numbers. Feel yourself decisively stepping into the path of a hard driving offensive player. Wham! Feel the contact of the collision. No sweat at all and no pain! You're feeling Great! **You are incredibly great! Hear the fans ... they're shouting your name!**

Repeat the programming for several days and you'll know ... **What lies in front of you and what lies behind you are small matters, compared to what lies within you!**

THINK DEFENSE

Listen to coaches argue about their defensive strategies and you come away with the belief that there is more than one way to get it done. One coach in particular has a very unique approach to teaching one of his key defensive rules.

When I was writing my first book back in 1978, I had an unforgettable opportunity to observe one of the finest college coaches work his team in practice, Pete Carril of Princeton. Year after year, Princeton's team defense was one of the stingiest. After practice, we talked defense. I asked Coach Carril if he forced the opponent's offense to the middle or the sideline. He responded, "Middle". I asked him which foot he taught his players to lead with?

Coach Carril's answer startled me. "I don't care about foot position. I want our players to think the ball into the middle. I don't want them worrying about what their body is doing. Think him where you want him to go. That's all the instruction the body needs."

Simple enough instructions for the subconscious to comprehend ... with or without a Princeton degree. From that day on, my defensive coaching was never the same.

Think the ball off the baseline!
Think the dribbler to stop!
Think rebound!
Think steal!
Think charge!

If you want to live your basketball dream ... THINK DEFENSE!

THE FROG THAT BECAME A PRINCE

If you think you've got the slowest feet in the world, guess again. They belonged to a high school player I coached by the name of Derrick Roland. His major inability? Staying between his man and the basket. Watching Derrick play defense was as much fun as watching paint dry. Regardless of how much time we drilled quickness and slide technique, Derrick had trouble containing the dribbler or beating the offensive man on the cut. That is until one day in practice when I was forced into creating our first modeling technique. This is what happened:

While drilling one-on-one full court, Derrick was playing his typical matador defense. Suddenly, I had a cybernetic brainstorm. I had just begun to experiment with cybernetics in practice. Stopping the drill, I asked everybody to watch the quickest feet in the gym play 1 on 1 defense. They were Jose's feet. I instructed the players to focus their attention on Jose's agile feet as he smothered the creative moves of one of our best offensive players. I told the players not to analyze Jose's defense, just to observe the lightning quickness of his feet.

This is what I said to my team: "Think of your eyes as a video camera, filming his feet. Mentally jump inside Jose's basketball shoes and feel what it would be like if you had his quick feet." As they watched Jose's incredible foot speed, I told the players to verbally connect the words **"Quick! Quick! Quick!"** with each defensive slide they saw.

The key was that first step. I wanted Derrick to visually memorize what he had to do on the first recovery step–cutting off the driver–and then program that response into his mental computer via the modeling procedure.

Then, I asked the players to close their eyes and imagine themselves as Jose playing with his same containment ability. "Repeat **Quick! Quick! Quick!** to yourself as you imagine yourself successfully containing the dribbler," I instructed.

Anxious to evaluate the results, I had the players continue competing full court 1 on 1. It was like magic. Derrick was sticking to his man with a tenacious effort I had never before witnessed. His first step was awesome. The defensive tempo of the drill had picked up for everyone. It was a dramatic step foward for both Derrick and our program.

By the way, if you're interested in what happened to Derrick Roland, he went on to play at a Division III School, Potsdam State in upper New York. There he became a small college All-American leading his team to two national titles. Derrick's success didn't stop there. He became an all star in the Continental Basketball Association. A brief tenure in the NBA was cut short by a knee injury. Not a bad basketball journey for an athlete with slow feet!

What happened to Jose? After graduation his family moved off Long Island and I lost touch with him. Wherever you are Jose … I'm still grateful for those quick feet of yours. Without them, I'm not sure if **our frog would have ever turned into a prince.**

Say … what are you waiting for? Stop complaining about your slow feet. Start looking around for a pair of quick defensive feet you can model.

Part Four

*"The young boy looked directly above to the stars that lit up
the clear autumn night and wondered out loud,
what is beyond that. . . and beyond that. . . and beyond that?"*
Mordecai Shapiro

151

BECOMING A CLUTCH PERFORMER

"Even when I went to the playground, I never picked the best players. I picked guys with less talent, but who were willing to work hard and had the desire to be great."
Earvin Magic Johnson

Each competitive situation offers a creative opportunity for success. The so-called money player in sports is the athlete who is at his or her best under the stimulus of a challenge. John F. Kennedy once said, "There are no great men or women, only great opportunities."

Do you want to be a prime time money player? There is a price to pay and a progression to learn.

1. First, learn skills under conditions where you will not be over-motivated. Over-motivation leads to overtrying which leads to incomplete plays. At the beginning, skills are best learned under conditions where there is little pressure. The more completions during the learning process, the better. For example, when developing passing, catching and shooting fast break skills, run the court at three-quarter or 7 speed until there is a consistency of completions. Avoid overtrying at any cost. Act cool and stay cool. An overtrying effort interferes with thinking and doing. Your automatic success mechanism becomes jammed by too much effort (notice the flat trajectory of your shot). Control your effort speed and completions will become the name of your game.

2. The effort speeds apply to mental practice, as well. At the start the imagery should include no competitive or emotional details. Make your mental movies purely instructional. You are watching the action and not participating in the action.

3. Now, run the action of your movies at a slow motion speed. Half speed is perfect. Enter the action. Let it become a first person, inside-out action movie. Feel yourself finishing off the play exactly as planned.

4. In the final phase, quicken the action and make your mental exercise an **everything on the**

line game experience. Your mental practice must be as game-like and combative as you can make it. The opposition is aggressive … your team is down a point … time is running out! Unless your mental movie approximates the excitement and uncertainty of an actual game, prime time programming will be ineffective. Did you hear the roar of the friendly crowd at the end of your impressive performance or the displeasure of the opponent's home crowd?

5. Learn to react to a crucial game situation with an aggressive rather than a defensive attitude. You must want to respond to a challenge, not hide from it. Keep your purpose in mind. Life is short … your playing career is even shorter. The fear of making a mistake shouldn't bother you if you realize that the worst outcome is not the mistake itself, but the loss of an irretrievable opportunity by failing to seize the moment.

The secret of the clutch performer lies in the attitude of aggressively accepting every crisis as a creative opportunity. The worst thing you can do is hope you won't screw it up. What you're doing is adopting the same evasive attitudes by which underachievers live their lives. Be fearless. Accept the challenge of the moment for what it is … a fleeting opportunity.

6. Learn to evaluate so-called life and death situations in true perspective. Before it's too late, you must understand what you do on the court today is only tomorrow's trivia; an event that no one remembers or really cares about (except you). No game is composed of life and death situations … just many small challenges. If you fail at one … learn from it and get ready for the next one. Prime time players do not live in the past or the future … only the present. Be a **here and now** person! The philosophy that everything depends on one single play is pure nonsense! There are hundreds of plays in a game.   What's the difference if you miss a jumper in the first period or the closing moments of a game?

Everything to gain and nothing to lose is a great attitude to live by. If you think about it, how can you lose something you never had? That's not negative thinking. It's a great strategy for reducing anxiety and increasing your risk taking ability.

7. Reframe that feeling in your gut (before and during a game) as excitement … not fear or anxiety. Excitement is an empowering emotion that supports peak performance. All successful athletes experience excitement in competition. When directed toward a positive goal picture, excitement generates additional strength, speed and courage…the fight part of the fight or flight syndrome. A negative goal picture is nature's way of equipping you for escape and a losing effort.

8. Still tentative in prime time? Ask yourself this question: "What's the worst thing that can happen to me if I fail?" Imagine looking into your crystal ball. You are in the future, a short time after the end of the current season. Now look back to the past season. Because you played it safe and never took chances, can you see the pile of lost opportunities you left behind? Since you didn't play aggressively and fearlessly when the game was on the line, what do you think your teammates and your coach are saying about you now? What do you think about yourself? Not a pleasant picture is it?

Now try this one on for size. You just completed a season in which you stepped up in the clutch to take that last shot or make that last big defensive play that turned the game around.

More than several times you succeeded. I want you to look in the crystal ball and tell me about the image of yourself looking back at you. Do you see an inner strength, a vitality, a look of determination and courage in your facial expression? What do you think your friends, teammates, coach and parents are saying about you now that you've played so courageously and decisively? Not a bad feeling...is it? So which image in the crystal ball do you prefer to see after the season? The choice is yours.

You might want to note what Charles Barkley said about hosting *Saturday Night Live:* "Anyone who gets up here and tells you they're not nervous is lying. But don't expect success until you're not afraid of screwing up." Sounds like pretty good advice for the court, too.

You've Got To Love It

"When love and skill work together, expect a masterpiece."
John Ruskin

Loving The Basketball And Rim

There are three essential ingredients necessary for a successful basketball journey. They are the three basics ... the ball, the rim and your dream. You need all three every day of your basketball life if you seriously expect the best from yourself. The dream, without daily exposure to the ball and the rim, never transcends beyond the pleasurable, fanciful daydream stage. The ball and rim, without exposure to your dream, remain nothing more than fun objects to play with. Combine all three and a life of exploration, adventure, and growth awaits you.

Now love all three unconditionally and chances are, self-fulfillment also awaits. The sooner you build a feeling of love, sacrifice, and commitment with the ball and rim... the sooner you will enjoy the benefits of the relationship.

Obviously you love your dream or else you wouldn't have progressed this far into this book, but do you love, sincerely love, your ball and rim with the same passion? Love is an absolute must.

My favorite definition of love is looking for good. Do you see only the best qualities in your basketball and the rim, or do you see frustration, anger, disappointment and betrayal every time you pick up a ball and stare at a rim? **"Love,"** Eric Seigal wrote in his book *Love Story*, **"means never having to say you're sorry."** Do you enjoy a forgiving relationship with your ball and rim? You ought to, because the great shooters do.

Observe the way the great shooters hold, bounce, shoot and pass their basketball and you will see a magical rapport that goes beyond respect. Look carefully and you'll find a sense of oneness and bonding between the great players, their ball and the rim.

With the good shooter, the relationship is less intense. At times, there is a feeling of closeness similar to the love that exists within all great shooters and their ball, but, on this less consistent level of performance, the relationship is more fickle. Should the ball act deviously for just a moment, the relationship quickly cools. There are good days and bad. Maybe it's because the good shooter's love is too conditional and based on immediate gratification.

For poor shooters, the ball-rim relationship is tenuous at best. Unfortunately, their association has been built on the negative feelings of disdain, distrust, disrespect and aversion. Their relationship is so painful, you don't even want to be on the same team with them. In fact, their relationship generates so much tension, it affects the relationship between you and your ball.

Fixing the blame is not the issue. Fixing the relationship is. May I offer you some ball-you-rim counseling advice? You will have to be the strong one and change. Don't expect the ball and rim to meet you halfway. Hopefully, you'll listen to my advice with an open heart and head. The relationship surely is worth saving. I suggest that you first learn how to love the ball. There ... I've said it and I'm not ashamed.

LOVING THE BALL

1. Spend quality and quantity time, alone, with your ball. You cannot talk love ... you have to live it. When you are not shooting or dribbling it, keep it close at hand. Put it on your lap while your watching TV. Put it in your bed at night and sleep with it. Enjoy its company. Notice when you awake in the morning that it's there, within reach. Before you pick it up, stare at it. Isn't it a magnificent, perfect and beautiful companion? Now pick it up in your hands and feel its smooth, grainy, expensive leather coat. Perfectly designed!

2. Your ball loves to be bounced, especially by your caring hands. Because of its resiliency, it won't damage easily, but remember it enjoys the soft, quick, low bounce the best. So bounce it often ... with either hand. Do tricks with it. It loves creativity. Once it understands what you expect from it, notice how consistently it obeys your commands. Imagine that there is a string attached from the ball to your dribbling hand and no matter how quick or hard it bounces off the floor, it dutifully returns to your hand. You know why? Because it wants to. You are its master and friend. With time and experience, it will realize who is boss. Keep bouncing it, thousands of times, until it fully understands how important it is to you ... as you are to it. It won't go anywhere without you. And without it, neither will you.

3. To increase your sensitivity with your ball, close your eyes when dribbling. If the ball occasionally eludes you, don't show anger or disappointment. The ball is your companion and should occasionally be allowed to express its own personality. Its shape is perfect ... its personality isn't. Is yours?

   After an occasional erratic response, communicate with your ball by softly and quietly bouncing it, alternating hands, until you and your ball are one. This will take time ... be patient. The relationship can only endure if you and your ball trust one another.

4. The ball loves travel by air. Reward its trustworthiness with countless flights. Start each day with casual tosses over your head while lying in bed, sitting in a chair or standing. On each

Did you know that two balls can fit
through the rim at the same time?

soft toss, allow the ball gracefully to leave your shooting hand touching your pointer finger last. The familiarity and trust you develop with these tosses will pay remarkable dividends when you get to the court.

Find a basket and begin shooting all inside shots (2 to 3 steps away). Shoot hundreds of them from all angles (straight in, off the board, off the dribble). Since the ball treasures finishes over misses, those inside shots are priceless.

Do not show any boredom while shooting. The ball will mirror your apathy and fall short of its target. Have faith it will travel in a straight and sure trajectory. If it wanders off from time to time . . . let it. Your relationship is being tested. Only when you keep the faith, will the bonding process continue.

By the way, the ball does not like a jerky stroke or a short-arm follow through. So keep your stroke confident, smooth and fully extended.

LOVING THE RIM

5. It's essential you love and appreciate the rim with equal fervor. Spend some quality time, alone, with the rim each day. Ball in hand, move around the orange steel rim and study its shape, color and details. Toss the ball over the front of the rim and step under it. Observe how small the ball appears as it drops into the basket. This will help you appreciate the full width of the rim. The fact is the rim is exactly twice the size of the ball! Two balls can actually pass through the rim at the same time! Now, stand several steps away from the rim and focus on the steel loops (underneath the rim) that hold the white nylon net. Accept the rim for what it is . . . a perfectly designed implement for success . . . your success.

    Become one with the rim. You can, if you ask yourself the question, "What would it be like if I were a steel rim?" Stare at the rim until you feel the transformation. Now that you're a rim . . . sense the quality of strength, sturdiness and reliability that lies within you.

6. You are now one with your ball and the rim. The three of you are bonded into a single entity. Start to shoot, but don't make a conscious effort to score. Let the ball take any arc it wants. Allow the shooting action to happen . . . don't make it happen. Easy does it. No unnecessary rushing. You're not shooting the shot to make it. You're shooting the shot because it's there. Nothing more than an opportunity. Whether the ball drops or not is okay with you. You are still one with the ball and the rim regardless of what happens. Just keep your eyes softly focused on the rim and consider each shot as an opportunity to become more intimate with your two friends. Lasting relationships are never based on good times alone, but rather on how well the bad times are handled. Misses are wonderful opportunities to show the ball and the rim you still love them. Soon, you'll notice fewer and fewer shots are off target.

    Find a rim that is unattached without a net and step through it. Feel how wide and accommodating it is. Squeeze two basketballs, side by side, through the rim.

    Now that you know all these things, are you willing to bring a feeling of true kinship involving the ball, rim and yourself into one loving family? Stephen Covey writes a simple mission statement for the family.

"To love each other...
To help each other...
To believe in each other...
To wisely use our time,
talents and resources...together."

So what are you waiting for? Have a family meeting ... right now! Start communicating your love to your basketball and the rim. It could be the beginning of a beautiful relationship.

Am I being silly or serious ... you decide!

MORE INNER GAME STUFF

"Things won are done. Joy's soul lies in the doing."
Shakespeare

YOUR BLUE RIBBON PANEL OF TOP COACHES

Whether you are an athlete or a coach, how would you like to be able to consult with Dean Smith, Mike Krzyzewski, Bobby Knight, Nolan Richardson, Pat Riley, Roy Williams, Rick Pittino or any other top coach before each game, or better yet, employ their professional advice while devising a game strategy or solving a problem? You can!

Within your mind, there is an infinite storehouse of ideas, know-how and power. Ralph Waldo Emerson said, "There is one mind common to all individuals." He was talking about the ocean of the universal mind whose inlets reach out to the minds of all people. Many great inventors, writers, composers and philosophers believe their creations came from a source outside themselves.

All of us have access to this universal mind, as we have access to the endless amount of information, facts and ideas that we've stored in our memory. All kinds of data accumulated from attending camps, reading books and magazine articles and sharing ideas with fellow athletes and coaches have been indelibly recorded in your brain for future use. We also have a capacity for acquiring knowledge that transcends the sensory experience ... an extrasensory capacity, a creative capacity to remember a thought that we never knew before.

Have you ever had a creative idea, an inspiration, a sudden revelation or intuition that solved a problem for you? Sure you have. This book is proof that I have tapped a greater power. I often wonder how I accessed these thoughts. It truly is beyond me! This same creative process is available to all of us, all the time. We only have to learn how to tap the creative process of our subconscious to get answers to life's problems and challenges.

What does this magical process entail? Nothing more than clearly identifying the problem, presenting it to your subconscious mind before falling asleep and being smart enough in the morning to trust the hunch your subconscious produced for you while you slept.

Your subconscious mind is a priceless resource whose powers you must learn how to uncover. Working twenty-four hours a day, every day, it can do its best work while you sleep. Operating below the conscious level, the subconscious enjoys a freedom to operate. During sleep, there is no conscious thinking to jam this impeccably creative device.

THE SLEEP ON IT TECHNIQUE

Coach, let's say you want to develop a game plan for your big rival. You're worried because you're uncertain how to defend their inside offense. Should you zone them and pack it in tight, or cover their guards with a pressure full court man defense. You're unsure about a couple of other things. Especially bothering you are your match-ups and who will be your fifth starter...a problem you've been struggling with all season. Every five minutes you change your mind. Fearful you'll make the wrong decision, you rethink it again. Your overconcern is making it more difficult to come up with a game plan you have confidence in.

Try this sleep on it technique. Before going to sleep, silently present the problem to your mighty subconscious. While relaxed and lying in bed, ask it to solve the specific problem you're having. Relaxation is essential. It opens a direct avenue to your subconscious. Use the same breathing technique you used in the visualization procedure that helped you get into the Alpha State.

With your eyes closed, visualize yourself sitting at a large conference table. Sitting at your side, are nationally known coaches (all of whom you hold in high regard). They are there for only one purpose ... to determine the best game plan for Friday's important game. Present them with all the facts and figures about your opponent's tendencies. Include the strengths and weaknesses of your own team, too. The more complete your scouting report is, the better. Now present the various options you have. Expect no immediate answers ... you'll have the right one in the morning.

During sleep, your subconscious mind will take over and determine the best strategy for you to take. The creative power of your success mechanism will scan the mentally stored facts which you provided, select the pertinent data, tie it all together (perhaps even filling in some vacant spots by tapping a few ideas from the Board), and reliably serve you the answer in the form of a hunch the next morning.

I've used this method almost every night while writing this book. At the beginning, nothing I wrote was really on target. I knew I had a lot to say, but the words and thoughts were not flowing. One night I created a board of successful writers (authors whose books I admired), and asked them to help me. The next morning, I couldn't believe the incredible state of concentration and creativity I was experiencing as I wrote.

Let me give you an on-the-court experience that was solved by my coaching board. I was struggling with a problem the night before an important Christmas Holiday Tournament game. We had won the first game and were now in the finals. I wasn't sure who to start. Joe or Felton. Neither one was impressive in the first game, although Felton had a decided edge because of his size and quickness. Joe wasn't as athletic and just wasn't playing well. I submitted the problem to my blue ribbon panel before falling asleep. I detailed the advantages and disadvantages of both. In the morning, the answer my success mechanism surprisingly produced was Joe. I couldn't believe it. Felton was my strong conscious selection. Before the game, my assistant coach, disappointed with my decision (as I was!), tried to talk me out of starting Joe. When the game ended, Joe was not only our high scorer, he was the game's hero. With the score tied and time running out, he stole a pass and scored on a breakaway to win the game. Joe scored 19 points! His previous best was 11 points.

Call it luck or coincidence, explain it any way you want. There have been too many sleep on it success stories for me not to believe in its merits. Judge for yourself. Give it a try and become a believer in the power … that lies beyond.

POST GAME ANALYSIS: REFRAME AND LET GO!

After a game never dwell on mistakes too long. Make it a habit to briefly evaluate what went wrong and before you consciously dismiss the emotional debris of the mistakes from your mind, reframe the mistakes into valuable learning experiences. Remember the three step reframing method:

1. See a star successfully finish the same action you didn't (a baseline drive, missed jumper, fumbled pass, whatever).
2. Jump inside the winner and feel yourself redo the action in slow motion speed.
3. Abandon the star. Now it's you again with an identical opportunity, but this time feel yourself complete the action.

After a game — when emotions are still high — never place judgements on yourself or your teammates. You don't want to entertain any detailed analysis or self-recrimination after a loss. Stop punishing yourself. If you're a coach, don't make it a habit to right the wrongs immediately after a game. I suggest words like… "Forget it!", "Clear!", or the great last line from the novel, *Gone With The Wind*… "Tomorrow's another day."

I've heard coaches critique a game to death in the locker room after a loss. If you're a coach who lists game objectives on a chalkboard before a game, I see no problem having your team, with a show of hands, vote on whether these objectives were achieved, but go no further. Remember, coach. … "tomorrow is another day." Analysis rhymes with paralysis. Overthinking rhymes with overstinking.

Incidentally, make certain that the first practice after a tough loss isn't a workout of drudgery and punishment. Make it as much fun as you can. Have players switch positions or perhaps have the last two players on the bench choose (and captain) teams for drill competition and scrimmages.

YOUR OPPONENTS HAVE SUCCESS MECHANISMS, TOO

One year, the only loss our high school team experienced was at the hands of a team we defeated by 40 points earlier that season. Our invincible team lost by 20 embarrassing points to a team whose center was out with an injury! Overconfidence … maybe. A mistake? No way! Our opponents systematically destroyed us in every phase of the game. With a greater sense of purpose than we had, they simply set and employed their success mechanism to its maximum capacity.

We were ready to be beaten. Prior to the game, I recall our players setting their success mechanism for a poor performance level. Their body language, facial expressions and the way they talked in the locker room before the game all contributed to a partially plugged-in success mechanisms. I reminded them to no avail, that our opponents also had success mechanisms.

Determined not to relive their embarrassment, our proud opponents had set their subconscious for the game of their lives. When I went over to congratulate them, I remember experiencing the same goose bumps I usually had after one of our big wins. I had the greatest respect for what they accomplished. Although, I was at the wrong end of the miracle, I felt thrilled to be a part of their great event.

Did the best team win? That's irrelevant. What is valid is a team with less talent beat a team with more talent because they communicated a stronger, more powerful reason to their subconscious.

What's the lesson? **You're not the only one with a success mechanism!** Respect your opponent.

WINNERS NEVER STOP SETTING GOALS

For the senior who has played his last game, there is a natural let down. Reaching the end of the season for a graduating athlete means the end of his high school career. When I coached, the end of a season was also a heavy time for me.

When both player and coach get involved in setting new goals, there is a feeling of rediscovery. New goals bring with it a renewed sense of energy. Real and lasting happiness comes from the work in striving toward goals. Never stop setting goals … no matter what.

A CYBERNETIC THEORY ABOUT OFFICIALS

Have you wondered why close calls by an official too often seem to favor the better team. Are officials dishonest, or are they out of position when they make a bad call? You may think I'm crazy, but I have seen so many calls that should have gone to our opponents go our way just because we were the favorites.

There's a cybernetic explanation for this phenomenon. Before the game starts, the official knows which is the better team. He carries into the game an image of the winner in his mental computer. It's there … exerting a strong effect on his subconscious. His habit maker responds as expected. A conditioned response is produced during a close call. The official blows his whistle favoring the better team.

There are times when the poorer team appears to be receiving beneficial treatment from the referee. My cybernetic explanation still holds water. The official may be overcompensating for his pre-game decision as to which is the better team. His reaction is to respond in the opposite way, spontaneously opposing his pre-game notion and giving the benefit to the underdog.

I'm also a great believer in the pain and pleasure principle regarding the decisions of an official that favors the home team. Homers are nothing more than the natural reaction of an official aware of the emotional reward of a crowd pleasing call versus the pain of a call going against the home team. Officials are not dishonest. They are human.

Do not overanalyze officials. There are bad calls on and off the court. Learn to live with them. Be respectful and trusting. You've heard this before … life is a self-fulfilling prophecy. You get what you expect. No matter what happens, expect the best call from the men and women in striped shirts, and most of the time you'll get their best. Check it out.

THE SHOE SQUEAK THAT WON A CHAMPIONSHIP

Would you believe a referee's shoe squeak contributed to the outcome of a high school championship game? I was there and this is exactly how it happened. A player, driving towards the basket, looked as if he was fouled. Play stopped because the referee on the baseline appeared to have blown his whistle. Except it wasn't a whistle. It was the loud squeaking noise of the official's shoes on the floor. There was no call. The offensive team just stood around as an alert defensive player picked up the ball, dribbled the length of the court and scored. The game eventually ended with the team that scored the opportunistic bucket winning 77 to 75. That earlier squeak turned out to be the difference!

There is a point here. Whether coaching or playing, never allow a sound or negative thought distract you from the task at hand. It wasn't the referee's fault or the sound of his noisy shoes. It was the players' responses to the sound that made the difference. The winning team wasn't distracted, the losers were. It was noted psychiatrist and Holocaust survivor, Viktor Frankl, who said, "Our greatest power is the freedom to choose our response."

As a player, what value do you link to the sound of your coach's whistle in practice, or to your coach's excessive instructions during timeouts? It'll be your response, not the sound of a whistle or the coach's words, that freezes you or allows you to play at your best.

Most coaches coach the way they've been coached. If there was a whistle blower in their lives, chances are they will be whistle blowers, too. It doesn't make them right or wrong, good or bad. Coaches who like to overcorrect mistakes mean well. That's probably the way they've been taught. They're only guilty of being themselves.

Stop overanalyzing the strategies and actions of others. You're no victim unless you choose to be one. Learn what you can from what significant others say and do. But in the end, if you don't get to live your dream, I don't want to hear that you blamed your coach, the referee, the home court, heredity, your parents or the bad breaks of life. Accept full responsibility for your actions and reactions. That way, the only one in charge of your destiny … is you.

SUCCESS STORIES:
ACHIEVERS, CONTRIBUTORS AND HEROES

"That's why we call them heroes. The best thing they ever do, is point to the best in us all and say, 'If I can . . . you can, too!"
Billy Dean, from his song "Once In A While"

ACHIEVERS

Since the **Yes, I Can!** basketball camps and clinics have been in existence, thousands of athletes have achieved a higher level of performance as a result of CT. Over the years, there have been some exceptional stories of achievement. I remember presenting a shooting clinic in Denmark in front of several hundred skeptical athletes and their coaches. The demonstrator, who missed all ten of his freethrows before learning our preshot routine, suddenly converted twenty-four consecutive foul shots employing our verbal method. There was the camper who increased her personal best to 265 consecutive jumpers, and a girl who increased her vertical jump a full six inches, touching the rim for the first time in her life.

They were all outstanding achievers, yet I would be the eternal optimist to think that every **Yes, I Can!** camper could experience such dramatic basketball breakthroughs. Still, I can say this with confidence: the vast majority of athletes who attend our camps, noticeably improve their skills as a direct result of our program.

Although I receive a large number of letters and phone calls from athletes and coaches confirming success as a result of employing CT, one could say that it's all subjective proof. What is undeniable testimony are the scores on the campers' achievement cards on the last day of camp. Compare them to the scores of the first day and you have validated proof of the dramatic effect of Cybernetics Training on basketball achievement.

CONTRIBUTORS

Is improving your consecutive best, or being able to jump higher your main purpose for reading this book? Beyond skill improvement, what else is there? For some of you, it could be increasing your contribution to the team by learning how to aggressively step up when the game is on the line. However, the campers I am most proud of are not the ones that have gone on to the NBA or become college stars (although I've enjoyed their talent and commitment). The athletes I respect most are the ones who come to camp as the proverbial role players and decide to shed their play-it-safe security blanket, redefine themselves and reach for the unreachable. Because they exceed everybody's expectation, they become living role models, proof positive anyone can live the impossible dream. Far above the rest, they have become my greatest reward because they are telling others, "If I can, so can you.".

HEROES

From time to time, there have been campers who have taken extraordinary action under the most challenging of circumstances and, in the process, become heroes. In a real sense, they permanently influence the lives of others.

Allow me to share with you several memorable success stories. You be the judge . Were they achievers, contributors or heroes?

Keith was a one-armed camper who refused to accept his disadvantage as a reason not to play hard or drive both ways to the basket. When I asked for a volunteer to demonstrate our shooting method, he was the only one willing to step in front of 250 campers without a trace of self-consciousness. He proceeded to stroke a half a dozen hits in a row. Think of this courageous athlete with one arm the next time you have an opportunity to step up. I can tell you this: there were an inordinate amount of players taking the charge, diving for loose balls and playing with reckless abandon during that week of camp. Even the coaches were taking the charge and diving on the floor during the coaches' games.

Ed was another disadvantaged athlete, though you'd never know it by the way he played. He had lost a leg in a farming accident when he was eight years old and decided having one leg wouldn't prevent him from playing his favorite sport. He was going to be the best one-legged basketball player in the state of Ohio. And he was! Forced to compete with an unwieldy prosthesis, he made the junior varsity as a sophomore, getting about twenty minutes a game. At camp he achieved one of the top scores in the side-step quickness test and earned the right to be the demonstrator for others to mirror. The mixture of intensity, pain, determination, and joy on his face inspired everyone to extend themselves beyond their capabilities. Interestingly, no one complained of blisters, body aches and long hours at that camp session. For the entire week the air was filled with positives and optimism. Everywhere you looked, campers were encouraging one another. It was a special week I'll long remember.

One of the most inspirational campers I have had the privilege of knowing has to be Joyce Hovest. At the time of her first camp, she was 14 years old. With a heart full of unmatched courage and inner strength, Joyce was able to battle her leukemia into total remission. I will never forget watching her at camp, in an unbearably hot and humid gym, refusing to take a break during the rigors of the one minute skill challenges. Players and coaches watched in awe.

Her mother told me when Joyce contracted the dreaded disease in the fall after her first camp, she promised herself, the doctors, friends, parents and anyone who would listen, she would be in attendance at the **Yes, I Can!** Camp that next summer. The doctors and nurses were skeptical, but they had no idea how deep Joyce's inner strength was. Wearing her **Yes, I Can!** shooter's cap and T-shirts, and placing the same positive slogans we used at camp on the walls of the hospital room, Joyce was constantly reminding herself: **"If I believe it … I can achieve it."**

She was committed to full recovery. She would accept no restrictions or limitations. Not only did Joyce attend camp the next two summers, she competed in two sports at school. After graduating from high school and college with impeccable academic honors, Joyce created a scholarship fund for others inflicted with leukemia so they might complete their dream as she lives hers. In my mind, Joyce will always be one of life's illustrious warriors whose spirit is cut like a precious gem … designed to last forever.

My list of exceptional success stories wouldn't be complete without Peter Quinn. While hustling home after a soccer practice, Peter decided to take a short cut. As he hurdled a four foot snow fence, his foot became stuck on the top of the fence and he landed poorly. The anterior, medial and lateral ligaments of Peter's right leg were all severed, and to make matters worse, the peroneal nerve which is responsible for lifting his foot was damaged beyond repair. Regardless of his commitment to rehabilitation, Peter would have to live the rest of his life with a permanent dropped foot … forced to drag his right foot even when walking.

The first time I met Peter was at camp two summers before the accident. Enthusiastic and trusting, he was like a human sponge absorbing everything he was exposed to at camp. His skills and physical attributes were good. His resolution was excellent. In the drills and games, Peter's tenacity and determination had no boundaries.

When I first heard about his accident, I called him at the hospital. Before I could get in a comforting word, it was Peter assuring me he would be playing basketball and soccer again. "Count on it coach," he said. "No drop-foot is going to stop me." I remember sending him Robert Schuller's inspiring book, *Tough Times Never Last, But Tough People Do*. I know that he read the book several times. If Dr. Schuller knew Peter's story, he would share my pride.

You may be interested in knowing what happened to Peter and his drop-foot. Here's a partial list of his athletic achievements:
- High School All-County and All-League in soccer as a goalie.
- 10 consecutive shutouts.
- All-League in basketball (in a very competitive conference).
- 13 points and 9 rebounds a game as a six foot senior.
- A full soccer scholarship to college.
- Led his college team to the National Final Four Championship.
- 18 shutouts (16 consecutive) in his freshman year.
- All New England Conference goalie.

Incredible, considering that all of these achievements were accomplished basically on one working leg! Peter came back to camp first as a camper and then, as a coach. During the closing ceremonies at the New York camp it became a tradition for Peter to tell his story of overcoming adversity with the power of belief. There are few dry eyes in the gym when he talks.

Peter is now coaching freshman basketball at a high school on Long Island. You can bet he's coaching **yes, you can** basketball. Recently he said, "The best thing that ever happened to me was the accident. It taught me well how to help others faced with tough situations."

Would you like to know the strangest story of them all? The girl with the nine month headache! What you are about to read is absolutely true, written by the girl, Jennifer, in her own words. A few weeks after Jennifer experienced our camp, she attended a retreat camp in Colorado where she wrote this story. Another camper, the niece of Dr. Ron Slaymaker, director of the Kansas **Yes, I Can!** camps, received a copy of the story and sent it to her uncle, who sent it to me. These are her own words.

No More Headaches

"You're ... gonna ... take ... four?" the school nurse drawled out slowly just as I had heard her do so many times before.

"Yes," I replied dully, taking the aspirin out of the bottle. "I can take that many for migraine headaches." I showed her the prescription on the side of the bottle. She shook her head as I swallowed the pills and walked out of the room.

"How long is it going to take her to figure that out?" I thought, angry at the stupidity of the nurse.

I clenched my teeth, trying to deal with the pain of the headache. It was as if my head were a rubber band, stretched to the limit, and about to break. I kept waiting for the pain to go away. I don't know why; it never had before.

"Jennifer Kimball," said the nurse as I got up from my waiting room chair to go and see the doctor.

"We got back the results from your CAT scan," the doctor said. "There is nothing wrong with you, physically. You're just putting too much pressure on yourself." I was getting tired of hearing those words. I had heard them from my parents, my teachers, even my friends.

It was so frustrating! Didn't they understand that I knew what was wrong with me? What's wrong with wanting to be the best? What's so terrible about giving 100% to everything you do? How can I learn from my mistakes if I don't remind myself of them?

If I had stopped pushing myself to do the best I could, my grades would have gone down, I wouldn't have made "A" team in basketball, and I wouldn't have had first chair in band. Besides, you can't just snap your fingers and change your life!

For nine months straight, I had a headache. I woke up with it in the morning and went to bed with it at night. The headache was a definite damper on my abilities. It's hard to compose a song when you're not sure if your head is still attached to your body.

My headache wasn't the only thing that showed the stress I was under. I was hurting emotionally, too. The warm feeling I had always had before was gone. It had been replaced by a cold emptiness. It was like I had a huge gap in my middle. Something was gone. It left me with little energy; it stole my smile. I was left with no soul. Just an empty body. I knew something had to change.

School was finally out, and it was time for my full summer to begin. First on the list: basketball camp.

"I frowned at the man standing in front of the classroom which was jam-packed with basketball campers. "Rules," I thought. "Yuck!"

He stood calmly, waiting for everyone to be seated. "Sit back in your chair, feet flat on the floor, hands on your lap, palms up."

Everyone did as he said, most of us having no idea why.

He took us through a "progressive relaxation and imagery workout."

"Geez," I thought. "This was supposed to be a basketball camp."

"I am going to improve your game by changing the way you think," the man said, whom I now knew as Stan Kellner. I turned to my friend and gave her a "what now?" look. She shrugged her shoulders, indicating that she knew no more about what was going on than I did.

Three or four times a day we went to these mind improving sessions. I thought they were stupid and a waste of time, but I had to admit, I always left with more energy than I came in with. Through all of this I still had my headache, though at times not as bad.

My camp coach, noticing my lack of self-confidence was always reinforcing my good points and rarely brought up any mistakes I had made while playing.

I walked off the court after one game, silently cursing myself for missing two of four important free throws. "Way to play, Jennifer." I spun around to see my coach smiling, knowing I didn't agree with his statement. "What do you mean?" I asked, half mad. "I missed two of my free throws."

"But," coach said calmly, "I put you on their best shooter and you held her to zero points." I thought about this for several seconds, finally accepting that I had done something right. I'd done a good job! Maybe I wasn't so bad?

"Thanks," I said to the coach. Smiling, I noticed the cold emptiness inside of me disappear. I'd barely sat down when I noticed something was different. All of a sudden I realized what it was. My headache was gone!

I had never felt so happy or relieved in all my life. It must have been quite a sight to my friends to see me crying and smiling and laughing all at the same time. With tears still streaming down my face, I went to thank my coach. I told him that my headache was all gone and that it was all because of him. He hugged me and told me that I was the one who had made it go away and that I could get rid of them forever if I would just have confidence and believe in myself.

To this day, I have had no more headaches. The cold, empty feeling inside of me has been replaced by a warm, happy, contented feeling. I am eternally grateful to a basketball camp and a very special coach.

What cured Jennifer's headache? Certainly her coach's positive outlook and encouragement helped. Also, Jennifer didn't realize she was putting herself into a pressure cooker each time she aimed at perfection. By being her own worst critic, she was her own worst enemy. Her habit of overlooking what she did right and remembering only what she did wrong, didn't help her.

But, everything at camp was so positive, she was forced to focus on what was right, rather than what was wrong. She started to feel good about herself. She never did experience a severe or lasting headache again. I know, because she came back to camp that next summer … bright-eyed, smiling and headache free.

This last story involves the saving of two lives, and may be the most remarkable of them all. In 1988, I arrived home after completing a summer of camps. One of the first letters I opened was from a camper by the name of Kim. She wrote about how much fun she had at camp, complimented the staff, and said she couldn't wait to come back next summer. It wasn't until page three that I discovered how much of an impact camp had been in her life. This is what she wrote:

"After camp, my girl friend and I went on a canoeing trip down the Illinois River in Missouri. It was cool until we hit the rapids. That's when we lost control of our canoe, and as it overturned, we both were tossed into the water. How stupid can you be? We had forgotten to put on our life jackets. They were tied to the canoe! I tried to swim to the canoe that became wedged between two rocks, but I couldn't make any headway against the strong current. Then, the worst thing happened. My girl friend in a panic grabbed me from behind and started to pull me under. I swallowed a lot of water. No way was I going to make it to the canoe. Then clear as a bell I remembered what you told us at camp about fear. You said it was False Evidence Appearing Real. Guess what? I suddenly became calm and somehow fought my way through the rapids to the canoe with my girlfriend hanging on to my ankle. We untied the life jackets from the back of the canoe and put them on. Holding each other's hands, we floated down the Illinois River until we got to a turn in the river called Eagles Bluff. Exhausted, we crawled on to the shore. Soon a park ranger found us and told us how lucky we were to be alive. He said two 15-year-old girls had died in a similar canoeing accident two weeks earlier!"

One last salute, if I may? I would like to acknowlege all the many achievers, contributors and heroes—athletes and coaches alike—whose lives have touched mine. By wanting more for themselves, they made it possible for me to develop this program and write this book. To the athlete or coach who is reading this book, may I also take the liberty to congratulate you in advance of your triumphs?

There are no words more appropriate to express my sentiments than the lyrics of the song *Here's To The Winners*.

"**Here's to the winners … lift up your glasses.**
Here's to the glory … still to be.
Here's to the battles … whatever they're for,
That ask the best of us and then we give much more.
Here's to the heroes … those who move mountains.
And here's to the miracles … they make us see.
Here's to all brothers … and here's to all sisters,
But especially, here's to the winners … that all of us can be!"

BEYOND THE ABSOLUTE LIMIT

"Attitude determines altitude."
Unknown

Congratulations, you made it this far! Have you gotten the results you wanted? Without outcome, it's tough to stay with any training program, especially one like CT that works inside-out.

Have the **Ultimate Shooting Method** and the daily **Personal Best** shooting games grooved your shot? What about your freethrow ... power moves? Are your hands softer, feet quicker, and your baseline game more aggressive? Be honest, are you handling frustration better and finishing more plays?

Even with a starting effort of 100%, unless there is a return for your efforts, no one expects you to stay with the methods of CT for long. There is no dream-breaker more devastating than the condition of no results!

If you haven't achieved the level of skills and the attitudes you wanted, it will come down to this: how strong is your dream? Without a big enough reason to pursue your basketball dream, your inner journey will be as unrewarding as it is short. Regardless of the degree of results you are getting, the bottom line remains ... nothing succeeds like success, unless it's persistence. Staying power is the common denominator in any success formula. Face it! You will not always get what you want or when you want it ... only when you earn it.

So, how about those of you still not getting the degree of outcome you want? Review the **FAST Formula for Success.** Remember the letter **F** represents **finding a compelling reason** to keep you headed in a forward direction. Whether it's the thrill of the challenge, self-discovery, personal pride or the love of the game, **you must understand why you want what you want**. There is a big difference between like, want and need. Like-to won't get lasting results. Want-to may. A need that grows out of desperation provides you with the best chance to fulfill your dream. Not attaining what you want immediately tests your resiliency, but also inspires a need factor winners seem to have.

When tough times challenge you, stop thinking short range and start thinking long term. Look into your crystal ball and imagine the benefits of the inevitable success that awaits you, not the temporary frustration of the struggle. Empower yourself by asking, **"What will I gain in the long run if I hang tough,"** or better yet, **"what will I lose if I don't stay with it?"**

Be your own success coach. Tell yourself that you don't need immediate dividends to continue. The hunt for self-discovery and change is difficult, but it is worth it. Someone once said, "It's not what you get in the end that's important, it's what you become in the process." These new habits of thinking and doing that you are developing along the way will last your lifetime. So, just keep reminding yourself, **"One step short of success is failure,"** and keep going.

F, finding a powerful why provides you with the energy to apply yourself to the rest of the **FAST Formula of Success.** Continue to **A, act as if**, **S, see what you want**, and **T, take action** ... until you get the best outcome of all—**freedom.** Listen to this verse written by Dennis Waitley:

> **"Mirror, mirror on the wall**
> **help me hear my inner call.**
> **All I ever want to be ... is free**
> **to be that person ... me."**

Free from what? Try the ultimate freedom:
Free from the fear of making a mistake or missing a shot...
Free from overconcern and overtrying...
Free of frustration, anger and disappointment...
And free to be yourself.

How do I know all of this will happen? That's easy. Have you forgotten? You have a reliable success mechanism ready and willing to support the hunt for your dream.

It was only after a coach asked me a very probing question that I realized exactly what the centerpiece of the Cybernetics Training Program was.

A COACH ASKS A GOOD QUESTION

On the final day of a Kansas camp, a high school coach challenged me with an interesting question. He asked me if he could bring back just one cybernetic technique to his own program which one should it be?"

I understood the coach's real concern. Too much inner game stuff could complicate life in his gym. I knew he observed the positive results at camp. But what if there were no immediate results for his team or worse yet his players rejected his inner game efforts?

I wondered, if there was a yellow brick road I could offer this coach ... a single method, technique or drill more valuable or effective than the others? Was there that one incredible drill that would lead his team to the pot of gold? Asking me to place a value judgement on the various techniques of CT was like asking a mother which child is her favorite. I had no preference. From the

Ultimate Shooting Method to **Defensive Synergy**, depending on the commitment invested, all produced outcome. My easy answer… "It would depend on your program's need."

But before I responded, my mind suddenly shifted gears and the obvious occurred to me. Yes, there was a single **cybernetic strategy** that would irreversibly improve the quality of his players' performance. But it wasn't a method or drill. **It was a simple truth;** the most meaningful CT enlightenment of all:

"Each athlete is equipped with a powerful internal success mechanism."

I told the coach, "If your objective is to bring back just one cybernetic lesson, let it be this. Tell your players to **trust** in the existence of an inner device for success. All else you learned is secondary without this **trust.** Explain that the final **T** of the **FAST** formula also represents trust. If they'll trust, in advance, that this mechanism exists, they'll be more trustworthy on the court."

Of course, I told the coach he could play it safe and not say anything at all about their inborn gift. "Do the next best thing," I said. "Just coach **as if** every player on your team has the inner equipment to succeed. From your star to the last man on the bench, believe, feel and coach as if every one of your athletes has this reliable success support system working for them. Before long, they'll be mirroring your faith and playing with an extraordinarily higher level of confidence and freedom. Then, after you observe their improved play, you'll find yourself wanting to employ more of what you learned at camp. There'll be no CT restrictions. Because you've activated your own success mechanism, don't be shocked to find yourself coaching with more determination, patience, trust and effectiveness."

Whether you are reading this book as a player or coach, my advice to you is the same. There's no more empowering belief for creating a better life than constantly reminding yourself of the power of your fantastic internal success equipment. Think of it! It's right there within you as you read this book: shoot your jumper, snag a rebound, power to the basket, and prepare to live your dream. Give your subconscious positive goals and feedback, and it will work its magic, producing the skills and attitudes you'll need to fulfill your destiny.

Want additional proof? Go no further than the existence of this book. Do you think that I could have written a book of this magnitude without an uncompromising trust in my own internal success system? I'm the same fellow who had trouble graduating from high school, getting into college and winning games. Once I started to trust in the power of my internal gift, I was able to discover my own true worth. The **Yes, I Can!** program and this book are direct results of this trust. Isn't it time for you to let go of skepticism and believe in the presence of your own success system, too?

There is a story told in the mountain country of the great Northwest of a skier faced with the worst of all mishaps. While skiing down the side of a mountain, the skier, unable to negotiate a sharp turn, suddenly found himself soaring off a cliff. Hurtling off into space and headed towards the rocks below and a certain death, the skier, halfway down, managed to grab hold of a branch of a tree growing out of the side of the mountain. Realizing his life was only momentarily saved, he screamed, "Help me! Help me! Is there anybody up there that can help me?"

Suddenly a powerful voice from the sky responded, "I can."

The skier cried, "Who are you?"

The voice answered, "You know who I am."

Desperately the skier pleaded, "Whoever you are, please help me ... now, before it's too late!"

"I will," the voice from above explained! "But if you believe ... really believe, I want you to let go!"

The skier, quickly considering his options, shouted back, "Is there anybody else up there that can help me?"

Now it's your turn to answer the question. "Do you believe ... really believe you have been gifted with a powerful inner success mechanism?" If you can learn to trust it...the power will come. You'll be able to let go of the fear, frustration, overtrying, overconcern, self-doubt, and oppression of the past. They've been holding you back long enough. Let go, now! Start trusting and become the player and person you are meant to be.

How To Take It Beyond The Absolute Limit

From the start of this book, you and I have focused on achieving your basketball dream. Once you've attained this dream, what then? Another dream perhaps? With the awareness of your inner success system and the CT know-how for shifting these resources into high gear, any dream is possible if you are willing to pay the price.

Are you ready to turn the corner and see what else awaits you? Are you willing to commit to an even more glorious dream? To go for the big one, taking yourself **beyond the absolute limit** of what you think you are capable of becoming? I'm talking about a dream few people have and a place few people go ... the highest level of attainment, where fulfillment is the ultimate reward. Curiously, reaching this level requires a performance and effort we are all capable of producing.

Before I tell you about this lofty place, just for a moment do this: imagine that your basketball destiny is a building—a four story structure. While we're into metaphors, I want you to picture your subconscious as the elevator and your belief system as the operator capable of pushing the floor button of your choice.

Let's take a look at your choices. On the first floor, you'll find those athletes who play basketball for the fun of it. Nothing wrong with the athletes on this floor except they rarely pick up a ball or pay the price between basketball seasons. Since the game isn't that important to them, you won't find them working diligently on their playing weaknesses or shot. They value entertainment over hard work. They are easy to spot. See their pained body language and bored facial expressions during drills. They would rather play than prepare. "When are we going to scrimmage, coach?" is their favorite line. I warn you, if you decide to get off on the first floor ... it's crowded.

The second floor is for players looking for the winning edge. They practice and play hard, but their game, unfortunately, is saddled with one glaring deficiency ... they're afraid to screw it up! They tie their shoelaces just like any big play performer. But when their team needs a huge effort, they play as if their laces are tied together. Afraid to make a mistake, their play is tentative and predictable. Risk taking is not a part of their game-plan, neither is mastery. No matter how hard they try, they end up becoming the proverbial role player.

The third floor is for prime time athletes who strive to be the best they can. They thrive on competition and never worry about taking chances. When the game is on the line, you'll find the ball in their hands. Their major quality is not talent alone, but their fearlessness. They are not afraid to fail, make a mistake or miss a shot. Trusting themselves and taking action with the game on the line is second nature. They are the winners who become champions, receive trophies and earn scholarships.

For years, I thought this was the highest level an athlete could strive for or arrive at. I was wrong. There is a floor above, a fourth floor for those willing to take it **beyond the absolute limit** and enjoy an even greater reward. Interestingly, athletes who make it to this upper level may not be the most talented or even garner the most playing time. But don't make the mistake of not carefully studying them. They are excellent role models quietly leading by example. If you are looking for the highest level of return, pay close attention to the athletes who reside on the fourth floor. They can teach you so much more about life fulfillment than any of the highly glorified and publicized winners on the third floor.

- These are the athletes who are value-driven by an inspiring inner strength of character.
- The key to the decisions they make both on and off the court are guided by such values as hard work, determination, discipline, compassion, optimism, loyalty, unselfishness, caring, courage, trust and respect.
- Although they may not be the best athletes on the team, you won't find any better role models to emulate.
- Because they do and say the right thing at the right time, their greatest quality is they make you feel very good about yourself when you are with them.
- Incidentally, those who make it to the 4th floor never set out to lead the field or become the standard bearer of high principles for others to follow. They never consciously seek the spotlight as a leader or a hero.
- Heroism isn't the name of their game, but integrity and team contribution is.
- They are the kind of athletes not interested in how many shots they get during a game, but if their shots are good ones. A bad shot to them means a teammate didn't get a chance to shoot a better one.
- Regardless of the playing time they receive, you won't hear them complain.
- Their habit is to come to each practice ready to work.
- They never learned how to point a finger of blame. When things go wrong you'll never find them fixing the blame, only fixing the problem.
- They may not always agree with their coach's strategy, but no one will ever know it. Loyalty is important.
- Another quality is their habit of never talking about others behind their back.
- However, they are not shy in telling teammates who habitually break training rules or are performing selfishly to straighten out.
- When teammates commit playing mistakes or miss shots, they are the first to encourage them to hang tough.
- Those who qualify for the 4th floor love the thrill of the challenge. The tougher the practice, the better.
- Watch them do their wind sprints and you'll be inspired.
- In games you'll always find them hustling at both ends of the court no matter what the score.
- Optimism is their middle name. They see the glass half full, recognizing what went right

176

in practice or a game.

- For them, setbacks are temporary and offer good opportunities for lesson learning.
- They never take criticism personally, or sulk or indulge in self-pity parties after a loss or a game in which they didn't play much.
- Since they stay in great shape, they never seem to get sick or miss a practice or game.
- When they are injured, they miraculously recover.
- Responsibility is their middle name. Coaches trust them implicitly.
  So do their teammates.
- It goes without saying . . . they are the first to arrive at practice and the last to leave.
- Whenever the coach talks, their eyes are always glued on the coach.
- They are exceptional listeners and learners. They observe, study, and remember.
  We're not talking I.Q., but sincerity of purpose and focus.
- They have an inner eye to see the big picture . . . not what is, but what will be.
- They need no external motivation from their coach or well meaning parents telling them what to do. They are self-assigners.
- Since they know what they want, they have no trouble challenging themselves in practice and between seasons.
- In spite of the fact that they are not the biggest, quickest or best, they are without a doubt the most determined and resilient.
- They never discovered the secret of quitting.

Have you heard enough? Do you understand who I'm describing? It's the person you can be! What's stopping you from going for the **Big One** and exhibiting these same extraordinary inner virtues as you pursue your own dream. Think for a moment about all the pleasure you'd give and have if you lived each day of your life with these same inner strengths of character. Don't you dare tell me you can't take it beyond the absolute limit. Think for a moment about those people who have helped you become who you are. What were their inner qualities you admired most? Well, decide right now to model their qualities of thinking and doing.

Why not set a goal to create a life demonstrating your best inner qualities? Start by establishing a shopping list of empowering values that you are willing to live by each day of your life. Prioritize your own values by putting a number next to each one. Put a 1 next to the most important, 2 next to the second most important, right on down to the least important. Here is a partial list of values that have helped guide the decisions I've made on my own life's journey. What are yours?

Faith	Family	Contribution	Optimism
Integrity	Success	Work Ethic	Dedication
Know-how	Preparation	Persistence	Risk Taking
Courage	Caring	Freedom	Adventure
Happiness	Discipline	Self-motivation	Friendship
Passion	Team Work	Fun	Trust

You may have noticed neither comfort or security is on my value chart. They only interfere with the hunt for success. However, work ethic, dedication, know-how, preparation, persistence and risk taking rate high on my value list.

Can you see how the power of your values acts like a compass, guiding the decisions you make each day? When your values are inconsistent with your primary goals, the results will be conflict and self-sabotage. On my own team I have observed talented but self-serving athletes travel life's journey with a faulty value compass. Since they weren't clear on what was truly important, they often made decisions which in the long run led them away from their full potential and lasting happiness.

I have seen athletes have their lives ruined by the use of drugs and alcohol because they valued immediate gratification over self-discipline. I have observed athletes redefine their sense of integrity placing a higher value on self-interest than team contribution.

One such case was the bizarre incident that occurred at a Long Island high school, coincidentally as I was writing this final chapter. The event clearly illustrated the power of wrong values leading a team astray. The destiny of a boys' basketball team and their coach were sadly altered when the team guided by the wrong principles quit on their coach! The team just walked off the court and forfeited the game. It seemed the players were upset at their coach for shouting at the star player about the careless way he was warming up before the start of the game. The coach challenged the star to either get his head into the game or hand in his uniform. The player decided to turn in his uniform. The team conferred at midcourt and decided to follow their star into the locker room. They forfeited the game and the next one as well, refusing to play unless the star player was reinstated. The coach rejected the team's ultimatum and rather than waste the rest of a season (that had started out so hopefully), the coach resigned. Ironically it would have been his last season. He had planned to retire no matter how the season finished. After 27 seasons , 375 wins, 13 Coach of the Year honors and an equal number of championships, he concluded he had enough.

The players' main complaint was that the coach was unreasonable and spoke to them harshly. I know this coach as a colorful but caring man who had his own unique way of motivating his players. More than a few times he took money out of his own pocket to send a player to summer camp. In fact, he had loaned $1000 to the father of the player who walked off the court. Figure that one out.

The coach's real problem, as I saw it, was that he demanded more from his players than they were prepared to give back. The star's real problem was being misguided by a self-serving principle of false pride. The team's real problem, aside from playing a sorrowful game called **follow the follower**, was that not one player had the courage and integrity to do what was right and support the coach.

I recommend that you clarify your basic values before it's too late. There is nothing more fundamental to the core of every decision you make, nothing more essential to the dream you strive for, and nothing more important to your joy of living ... than your value system.

So this is my challenge to you ... to go for the **Big One** and take it **beyond the absolute limit**. Why not live a life demonstrating your most worthy inner qualities of character. Not for yourself, but for all the others watching. You see, whenever you do the right thing by following your highest values, you are providing a visible path of possibility for others to follow.

You may be thinking you're too ordinary or too set in your ways to deserve that 4th floor. Take the time to compose your own list of ordinary people with an extraordinary dream who found the power to accomplish the **Big One**. Let me start you off ... Mother Theresa, Martin Luther King, Albert Schwietzer, Mahatma Gandi, Helen Keller. Add the names of people you personally know who've improved your life, including your mother and father. Their formula was simple enough: a core of caring values and a desire to contribute.

With courage, commitment, passion, integrity, and caring don't be surprised as you look back to find others following your lead ... step for step.

This is the Big One! The 4th floor! The highest place you can ascend to ... beyond the absolute limit! It's there for the taking. Or should I say for the giving. Go for it and enjoy the processional effect it produces.

THE POWER OF THE PROCESSIONAL EFFECT

"By living our dream, we contribute not only to ourselves, but to everything around us."
John-Rogers

When you do a good deed for someone, who in turn does a good deed for someone else, who in turn helps another, it is called the **processional effect**. Unselfish service is contagious and has a habit of multiplying. By doing the right thing, who can predict how many others your selfless actions will touch down the line. Like the bee that flies from flower to flower gathering the fine dusty bloom of the pollen for its own purpose of making honey ... little does it realize it's also pollinating the flower.

Do you remember the movie *It's a Wonderful Life?* I'm sure you've seen this classic Christmas movie weave its magic on television. The story line revolves around the life of George Bailey (played by Jimmy Stewart), a loving family man who has dedicated his life to the service of others. But on this one Christmas Eve he has fallen on hard times. Thinking he has been abandoned by his family and friends, George stands alone on a bridge wishing he had never been born. About to jump into the black waters of the river below and end his life for the insurance money his death would provide his family, a guardian angel suddenly appears to save him. The angel, whose name is Clarence, will earn his first class angel wings provided he can keep George from killing himself. As a ploy, Clarence jumps into the river first and has to be rescued by George. Then, to prove to George that his life has value, Clarence grants George his wish of never being born. He accompanies George back in time to show him the impact of his nonexistence.

In visual flashbacks, he witnesses the drowning of his younger brother, who George would have saved had he been alive. This brother, had he not drowned, would have become a war hero, saving the lives of hundreds of fellow soldiers. Since George wasn't around to save him, he wasn't there to save the lives of the soldiers.

George learns that there were many others, whose lives were tragically altered because he was not there to help them. Clarence tells George, "Strange, isn't it? Each man's life touches so many other lives, and when he isn't around, he leaves an awful hole, doesn't he?"

George Bailey painfully realizes that his wish was foolish and asks his guardian angel for a second chance to live. In the emotional closing scene, having discovered he has had a wonderful life, George is back home, joyously surrounded by his family and friends, all there to help him. Clarence, of course, has earned his angel wings.

THE PROCESSIONAL EFFECT OF MY FIRST TEAM

After enjoying a run of championship seasons, you wouldn't think it was my first varsity team, winners of only seven games, that would be considered my most satisfying team. But no team had a greater **processional effect** on my life than my '66–67 team. Absolutely none!

Back in 1966, I coached varsity basketball for the first time. The team I inherited had won only one game the previous year and wasn't expected to do much better under my command. When I arrived, I promised the team if they did what I said and worked hard they would win. Unfortunately on the way to winning, a funny thing was happening. We were losing games!

We lost the first two games by double figures. The third game proved more than interesting. In a real sense, it would literally impact the rest of my life. Ahead by 15 points at one time, we went into the locker room at halftime with our proverbial tails between our legs. We had squandered the big lead and the score was tied. The momentum was in the other locker room.

As I started my halftime talk, I noticed my entire team was facing away from me. I was talking to their backs. Evidently, they must have had enough of me. Instinctively I said, **"You guys don't need a coach, you need a psychiatrist!"** And with that I stormed out of the locker room. The second half was about to begin with my team nowhere in sight. Were they still in the locker room? I remember asking my assistant coach if he thought they had gone home. Just then they bolted out of the locker room in a single file following their captain. With fire in his eyes, he said to me, "We're ready to kick butt, coach!" That's exactly what they did. They performed with such a remarkable sense of purpose we won going away by twenty points for their first win (and mine, too).

Although we never won a championship during the tenure of this team, it was their commitment to play tough and hard that set the standard of excellence that would follow, year after year. I've enjoyed a wonderful and rewarding life because of basketball. Perhaps I've helped some people get what they want, and I've never lost count of those that have helped me. But, frankly, no team has contributed more to my basketball destiny than the 1966–67 team. I'll always remember them as **the team that never quit**.

What do you think would have happened to my career if that team had decided to turn in their uniforms as the high school team did that quit on their coach? For one, I don't think I would have had the opportunity to write this book. You know something . . . I owe a lot to that Long Island high school team, and especially to the tough decision twelve young men made in the locker room back in November, 1966. A lot more than they'll ever know. I guess it's also a wonderful life when you're surrounded by people whose basic values are aligned with yours.

The next time you're faced with the choice between a tough decision or an easy one, think of the dichotomy of two high school teams ... one that supported its coach and the other that quit on him. If you still have trouble doing the right thing ... think of the processional effect of your decision.

THE PROCESSIONAL EFFECT OF AN ATHLETE'S DECISION

You can never tell when a difficult choice you make will affect the lives of others. The next time you're pondering a tough should I or shouldn't I decision, think of this story.

I received a phone call from Mitch Kupchak who, at the time, was playing power forward for the Los Angeles Lakers. My former player wasn't having such a wonderful life. What should have been the height of his NBA career had become a nightmare.

Prompted by a career threatening injury, Mitch was considering retirement. While driving to the basket in a game, he had blown out his knee. The medical prognosis was not encouraging. Even with a total commitment to rehabilitation, the doctors estimated the best he could hope for was 80 percent range of motion from his damaged knee. He understood he would never be the player he once was.

With hard work Mitch had accomplished much in his illustrious athletic life. He had been a high school All-American and an Atlantic Coast Conference Player of the Year from the University of North Carolina. Mitch also earned an Olympic Gold Medal and an NBA Championship Ring along the way.

To continue to compete professionally he would have to pay an enormous price of time and pain that the rigorous rehabilitation demanded. With a signed long term contract guaranteeing his financial stability, retirement seemed a viable consideration.

As we spoke on the phone, I sensed Mitch's indecision. Should he or shouldn't he retire? I warned him if he took the easy road and retired, in ten years he might look back to regret the decision. I explained, "The choices you have both involve pain. One the pain of regret, the other the pain of rehab? Which one will hurt more?"

Mitch realized that life doesn't go into rewind. Once he decided to quit, that would be it. So, Mitch decided to commit to the challenging road of rehab. The road back was expectedly slow. In the 1984–85 season, after a full year of rehabilitation, he became the ninth player on Pat Riley's eight man rotation. Getting little key playing time as Kareem Abdul Jabbar's backup, when on the court, Mitch still gave 100 percent of what he had.

The Lakers easily finessed their way past all Western opponents into the NBA finals against the rugged Boston Celtics. The first game went to the Celtics 148–114, in a game called by the Los Angeles newspapers the "Memorial Day Massacre." Boston with a much stronger and bigger line-up was able to unmercifully beat up on the Lakers on both ends of the court.

The talk in the L.A. papers was that the Lakers needed the physical play of the 6 foot-10 inch, 240-pound Mitch Kupchak. Although he couldn't run as he once did, the hope was that perhaps he could neutralize the Celtics' inside power game. With the Lakers 15 points behind in the second game of the series, a desperate Pat Riley inserted Mitch into the lineup. Mitch went right to work. Playing with reckless abandon, he dominated the boards, took a charge, converted several putbacks. His play seemed to be the tonic the Lakers needed. It was an inspired Lakers team that went on to win that game and three of the next four to clinch the championship.

I was there at the Boston Garden for the final game. Afterwards, I attended the championship post game party and watched the Lakers and their families rejoice in victory. There was Magic, Kareem, Riley, the Kupchak family, and of course the Lakers' number one fan, movie star Jack Nicholson.

I couldn't help wondering if there would have been a Lakers' celebration had Mitch chosen the easier path and retired two years earlier. Finding the courage to strive for his own impossible dream, he was presented with an opportunity to contribute to the lives of others. I remember looking around during the party on that warm Sunday evening in the spring of '84. ... I couldn't help thinking about the processional effect of one man's commitment to make a difference. "It's a wonderful life," I thought, "especially when living your own dream helps others live theirs."

Now you have another reason for living your dream. You can never tell whose dream you'll be helping.

THE REAL VALUE OF
YOUR BASKETBALL JOURNEY

"Give and it shall be given to you."
Luke 6:38

The joy of success is not the winning of a championship or even a game. The sense of victory can be compared to a rare flower that has blossomed on the top of a mountain. After struggling up the mountain path to find the flower, to have it within arm's reach... you realize that happiness lies more in finding the flower than in picking it.

The end of a game as the end of a season comes too quickly for us all. The real fruit of victory is not at game's end or at the conclusion of the season. It's rooted in the daily work and struggle in the practices and during the games. It is the feeling of satisfaction from overcoming obstacles and hardships, developing weaknesses into strengths, solving problems and attaining objectives. It is the process of becoming more than you were before. Arriving at the final destination is important, but the journey in between yields the greatest reward.

This point is made clear in an old Zen story about the pilgrim who mounted his horse to cross formidable mountains and swift rivers in search of a famous wise man. The pilgrim sought universal truth and wisdom that could bring him everlasting joy, happiness and self-fulfillment. After months of searching, the pilgrim located the wise man living in a cave. The wise man listened to the pilgrim's question and said nothing. The pilgrim waited. Finally, after hours of silence, the wise man looked at the horse on which the pilgrim had arrived and said, "Learn the lesson of the horse." The wise man smiled and retreated to his cave.

How do you interpret the wise man's answer and thus, the story's riddle? What truth could be learned from the "lesson of the horse?" Could it come from the horse's faithful service to the pilgrim carrying him dutifully over the treacherous encounters of the road, and bringing his master to his final destination? Is it the joy of serving and helping others over the road of life? When I think of the events of my own life that have brought me the greatest reward and satisfaction, I don't think of trophies or plaques. I think about the people I've been associated with and how they've helped me, and hopefully, how I've helped them even in some small way. Coaches ask me what keeps me energized all summer long traveling from one camp to another, staying in the gym from seven in the morning to eleven at night. The answer is the opportunity to help young people who want more ... get more. The inner reward for me is limitless.

I do not consider myself an achiever of enlightenment or even an extraordinary coach. I believe I'm an enthusiastic messenger. The knowledge in this book has come from others with far more intelligence and insight than I could ever possess, but I know this ... some of the teams I have had the privilege of coaching have won championships, other teams have not faired as well ... but it was an equal privilege coaching all of these young men. I have coached two players who have played in the National Basketball Association and have seen an equal number institutionalized for drug abuse.

I can remember being in Montreal in 1976 to root for a former player of mine, Mitch Kupchak, who was the starting center on the USA Olympic team. The thrill of seeing him receive the gold medal is still with me. As he leaned over to accept the Gold Medal, I could feel the weight of it around my neck. I can also remember returning home from that great event to find a basketball left at the front door of my home. Another former player, Raymond, had left it there for me. It was the ball he had used to score his 1000th career point. I later found out that Raymond had escaped from Pilgrim State Hospital, a drug abuse mental health center. He had gone home to get the ball and had walked the fifteen miles to my home seeking help.

The tragedy lies in the decision gap between these two ballplayers. Both Mitch and Raymond utilized their greatest God given power ... the power to choose. Mitch used it positively. Raymond chose the devastation of drugs. Both were capable of great achievement.

THE REAL VALUE OF COACHING

I can recall the elation of coaching a team that went undefeated, and just as clearly remember the trauma and disbelief that befell us hours after winning the championship game. Frank Mackwich, our assistant coach, had died suddenly of a cerebral stroke. He was 34 years old, a father of three girls and a dedicated husband and a teacher who was never short of time for helping others.

With similar anguish, I remember being at the hospital bedside of my friend Cliff Lennon. Cliff, a teacher and coach, was dying of cancer. He was in great pain as he dozed in and out of a morphine induced unconsciousness. Trying my best to comfort him, I recalled his coaching achievements and all the athletes he had helped. He looked at me as tears filled his eyes and said, "You got that one wrong. They were the ones who gave to me." In his dying moments, Cliff was never more right.

At Cliff Lennon's funeral over a thousand people, many of them his students, crowded into the small church to honor his memory. Father John Gilmartin eulogized him perfectly. "There are three kinds of people in this world. Those who believe in Santa Claus. Those who don't. And those who are Santa Claus! That was Cliff, all right ... he was the personification of Santa Claus."

Like Frank Mackwich, he had done so much for so many people, including me. Over the years, Cliff had been instrumental in the success of the **Yes, I Can!** camps. He had driven Long Island athletes hundreds of miles in his crowded van to attend camps in Ohio and Maryland. His coaching and leadership at camp were inspiring .

The hurt of losing both Cliff and Frank is still with me. It is hard for me to comprehend the meaning of these tragic events, of why bad things happen to good people. ... irretrievably lost were the lives of these two exceptional men. How strange it seems. They came, served and left ... ending all too soon their purpose in life ... to help others.

With the healing of time, I realized how fortunate I have been to have known them both. Two lives that were so inexplicably short in quantity but rich in quality. Father Gilmartin said, **"To live in the hearts left behind is not to die."** If this is true, they will both live on forever and ever.

Now do you understand the lesson of the horse? If you do ... your life will be as full of ever-lasting joy as it was for my two friends.

Are winning games and championships only illusions? Is helping others reach their destination what you should strive for? It's your call.

I can tell you this ... for every coach, each new season represents the ultimate opportunity to help improve the lives of players restricted by their poor self image, unaware of their natural instinct to succeed, and never knowing a sense of freedom and self-fulfillment ... unless you, their coach, show them the way.

You can begin by asking your players to determine specific performance goals for themselves and their team. Challenge them to find a strong reason why they are willing to commit to working toward their goals. Tell them what you know about their inner resources. Teach them the power of visualization, positive self talk, and acting as if. Show them how by living the **FAST** success formula yourself.

If you decide to employ CT, be faithful to its techniques. Remember, there has to be a sincere application if you want serious results. You may select certain parts of the program at first. This is understandable. Walk before you run ... but run you will, because awaiting you will be results as astonishing as they are rewarding.

With a little imagination, you will be free to seek out opportunities in other endeavors that interest you. The results will be equally satisfying ... perhaps even more so.

TIME TO START BELIEVING IN MIRACLES

There have been times when I have heard the desperate voice of an athlete or coach say, "It didn't work," assuring me they followed my Ultimate Success Formula. What went wrong? Where was the power of their success mechanism when they needed it? Listen to this story and judge for yourself.

Years ago when I was a high school coach, I had an enlightening conversation with a fellow teacher. His name was Richard, a very pious man. While I'm not in the habit of talking religion or politics, I surprised myself by asking him why he was so devout. "Was there a specific event that inspired your strong religious feelings?" I asked.

Richard said nothing for awhile. I could sense he was struggling internally about whether to respond. Evidently, his thoughts were quite personal. "Do you really want to know?" he finally asked. I assured him I did, and this is the story he shared.

"I was courting my wife, Barbara," he began. "It was just before we were to be married that she became very ill. There was some kind of obstruction in her digestive tract requiring surgery. After the operation, her condition worsened. Soon, she lapsed into a coma. She remained in a coma for weeks as her weight fell below 90 pounds. The doctors warned me to expect the worst.

From the start, I never stopped praying to God for her recovery. The harder I seemed to pray, the worse she got. Then one night, I stopped my pleading and said to Him, "Do what is best. I trust and believe in your power and wisdom. Take her if this is Your plan. Whatever You do I will understand and accept." I had not given up. I wanted to reaffirm my faith and trust in God.

The next morning, I visited the hospital early. The nurse greeted me with the incredible news that Barbara had miraculously come out of her coma during the night. As I entered her room, she was sitting up having breakfast."

Was it coincidence or Richard's reaffirmed trust in God? You decide. I do know this: **without uncompromising faith, no miracle can ever occur.**

On another note, a coach called me recently to tell me he had introduced the CT free throw routine to one of his players who was struggling at the foul line. The player proceeded to make 10 straight in practice. The very next night, the same player was fouled while shooting a three. With the game on the line, he missed all three foul shots. What went wrong? Was it his body language, self talk or belief system misdirecting his shots? Something was amiss. And something will remain so unless he develops a sincere trust in his ability to deliver in the clutch.

I'm not trying to give CT an escape clause, but without believing in your potential and your inner resources, your success will be sporadic. Think of it this way ... it's that feeling of self trust that eliminates the need to overtry and discover the best you have. Isn't faith the common ingredient in all religions as it is for all progress, human advancement ... and the final destination of your free throw?

No matter what happens, start believing in yourself ... in advance of the outcome and in spite of it.

For those of you who still can't accept the cybernetic definition of your success mechanism (the subconscious), let me introduce you to its other names:

The Unconscious

Free Will

The Spiritual Force

Call it what you want, unless you believe in its existence and trust its force, you will never be able to enjoy its benefits.

THE EAGLE THAT THOUGHT IT WAS A CHICKEN

The **Yes, I Can!** camp program isn't complete without the telling of the inspiring tale of *The Eagle That Thought It Was A Chicken*. What makes this story so wonderful is how it features the key elements of the **Yes, I Can!** program such as potential, the comfort zone, modeling, power talk, visualization, risk taking and persistence. The story also illustrates the responsibility we all have to use our inborn gifts to fulfill our true destiny. I hope it inspires you as it inspires me each time I tell it.

Once upon a time there was a chicken farm located at the foot of one of the great Rocky Mountains. It was one of the finest farms in the entire Great Northwest. Much of the credit for the success of the chicken farm was due to the dedication of the farmer who cared for the chickens.

Each evening after dinner, it was the farmer's custom to climb the foothills of the mountain that overlooked his farm. As the sun was setting behind him, he would marvel at the beauty of his farm, below. One evening standing on a bluff, he heard the hungry cry of a small bird behind him. The farmer turned to find a baby eagle alone in the nest, apparently abandoned and left to die. From the look of the eagle's emaciated body, it had a severely damaged wing and was close to death.

The farmer had a vision. He would nurse the eagle back to health at the farm and then, return it to the sky where it belonged. The farmer placed the eagle into one of the open pens with the chickens and began feeding it with an eyedropper. Soon the eagle accepted the same food as the chickens ate. With each passing day, the eagle grew bigger and stronger, but never once did it try to fly out of the pen. The farmer noticed the wild creature truly enjoyed being with the domesticated chickens. Eating, playing and sleeping with the chickens provided the eagle with everything it wanted. For the eagle, life appeared full.

Weeks passed into months as the eagle grew to full size. Remembering his promise, the farmer decided it was time to return the wild creature to the sky where it belonged. He was confident that a little jump start was all the eagle needed to fly.

Picking up the eagle, the farmer threw the bird high over his head. The eagle instinctively spread its wings and was about to fly, when it made the mistake of looking down towards the chickens with whom it had spent such a delightful time. Suddenly, the eagle lost altitude, spiraled down towards the chicken pen, and landed with an awkward thud.

The farmer was amused, but determined. Again, picking up the eagle, he climbed a nearby ladder, and threw the eagle up as high as he could. The eagle made the same mistake, and once again, landed with an embarrassing thud in the dust of the chicken pen.

"This bird thinks it's a chicken," the farmer mused. This time picking up the eagle by the neck (the farmer's frustration beginning to show), he walked over to the ranch house, climbed onto the roof, and proceeded to toss the eagle as high as he could into the air.

From the sheer force of the throw, feathers flew out of the eagle's body. Furiously the eagle flapped its wings and was about to become airborne, when it committed the same mistake of looking down towards the chicken pen. Once again, the eagle belly-flopped into the dust of the chicken pen.

"I give up," the farmer exclaimed, "This stupid eagle thinks it is a chicken." And so he did give up trying to get the eagle to fly.

This would have been the end of the story had it not been for a passing stranger. Walking by the chicken farm, he came upon the pen in which the eagle lived. Amazed by the sight of this magnificent wild bird living with the chickens, the stranger went to the farmhouse to inquire. The farmer explained the entire course of events: finding the abandoned eagle, nursing it back to health, and not being able to get the eagle to fly. The stranger listened to the story and then said bluntly, "I know I can get that eagle to fly. Please let me try."

There was a sense of confidence in the stranger's voice that impressed the farmer. "Be my guest, but I must warn you, that eagle absolutely thinks it is a chicken."

The stranger walked over to the chicken pen in which the eagle was sleeping and with the greatest of care picked up the eagle. Carrying the bird tucked under his arm, they headed toward the mountain and began the perilous journey to its top.

As you can imagine, climbing a mountain is no easy task, especially carrying a full size eagle. Ascending a mountain is akin to the journey of life (or even the journey of a long basketball season). Along the way, all journeys present challenges. This particular mountain was no exception. There were dangerously narrow paths, rugged rocks, fallen trees, deep rivers, even threatening cliffs. It took the stranger, eagle in hand, all day and all night to struggle up the mountain. At dawn with the sun rising in the east, they finally reached the very top of the montain.

What a strange sight it was. Silhouetted against the bright orange light of the morning sky stood the stranger holding the eagle in his hands. Staring straight into the confused eyes of the eagle, the stranger commanded in a confident voice, **"Thou art an eagle, spread thy wings and fly. You belong to the heavens!"** Instantly the stranger threw the eagle high over his head, again shouting... **"Thou art an eagle, spread thy wings and fly. You belong to the heavens."** As the eagle began to rise into the sky, it repeated the mistake of looking down. But this time the eagle was too high up to see the chickens, the chicken pen, or even the farm.

Then a wonderful thing happened to the eagle. Rising upward, it felt the force of the wind beneath its wings and the rush of the cold mountain air against its face. The eagle began to inspect the magnificent panoramic scene of the cloudless sky and the endless horizon with the rugged beauty of the mountains below. The eagle seemed to suddenly realize the infinite opportunities that free flight offered. An incredible feeling of excitement, power and freedom flowed through its body. It was unlike any other feeling the eagle had experienced living in the chicken pen.

Then the eagle heard the voice of the stranger crying out one final time, **"Thou art an eagle, spread thy wings and fly. You belong to the heavens."** And for the first time, it understood what the stranger was saying. The eagle finally realized that its destiny was in the sky and it began to fly effortlessly higher and higher. As it was about to disappear into the early morning sky, it dove toward the stranger, dipping its wings as if to say "thank you!" Before the stranger realized it, the eagle was gone.

The eagle never returned to the farm, nor did the stranger. There are evenings when the farmer, standing on the bluff and with the wind blowing just right, thinks he hears the joyous cry of a free flying eagle coming from the sky above the mountain.

So ends my favorite story of *The Eagle That Thought It Was A Chicken*. But the end of this story is really the beginning for all of us. Are you ready for the infinite opportunities of flight awaiting you on your basketball journey? I hope you are. Before getting airborne yourself, you'll have to hurdle the fence of your comfort zone and that means **paying the price** of some discomfort.

Trust your Cybernetic flight plan. Before you can fly, you have to firm up the reason you want to soar. Without a compelling reason, you'll find yourself spiraling downward into the dust of your own comfort zone at the first sign of trouble. Just remember what this book teaches. Any time you meet a challenge on your flight, simply act as if you can do whatever has to be done. Think, feel, talk to yourself and fly as if you are an eagle. After all ... you are one!

By the way, you can expect to see a lot more chickens than eagles on your personal journey through life. Just remember these two key rules for high flying and you'll be all right:

Rule #1 ... Ignore the chickens.
Rule #2. ... Pay close attention to the eagles.

Make it your habit to model the strategies of eagles, only. Hopefully your journey will be smooth and safe. But don't count on it! Especially in high flying, I don't have to warn you about the unpredictable crosswinds of life. They're there to test your resolve and make you stronger. When hardships happen remind yourself, **"Thou art an eagle ... spread thy wings and fly ... you belong to the heavens!"**

THE FINAL CHOICE IS YOURS

It is clearly up to you to select your basketball dream and the path you intend to take to achieve it. Whether you take the inner path of Cybernetics Training or not, make sure it's your dream you are reaching for and not someone else's.

The next step is to decide, specifically, what will bring you the most happiness and go to work to make it (and let it) happen. If you want a more accurate jump shot, additional aggressiveness on defense, or the ability to see the court better, the results will be in exact proportion to the time and effort you invest in the **FAST Formula for Success** or any other training program you decide to follow. Cybernetics Training has never been a get rich quick plan. Getting what you want requires focus, commitment and persistence.

After you've made your choices and lived your basketball dream ... what then? There is a road full of twists and turns that will constantly provide you with opportunities for growth and change, if you'll only keep your eyes open for these golden moments. Often the opportunities take the shape of problems, so don't be deceived.

And remember to live these three qualities of the overachiever every day of your life:
1. Pay close attention to the winners around you and model what you see, hear and feel.
2. Assign yourself ... don't wait to be told this is what you must do to improve. Motivate yourself by finding a reason why you must immediately take action. Then, take it!
3. Develop that feeling of success by using the power of visualization to see what you want ... never what you want to avoid.

Simple enough! Pay attention, assign yourself and visualize.
Got it? Good! Now, **live it!**

A Final Prayer

I leave you with a simple prayer that I learned from a 16 year-old camper in Ohio. Her parents taught it to her to keep her strong and on track during life's tests.

"By your own soul, learn to live.
If others thwart you, take no heed.
If others hate you, have no care;
Sing your song, dream your dream,
Hope your hope and pray your prayer."

I pray, hope and dream you find the courage, commitment and faith to sing your own song. Do you know its lyrics and tune? Just listen closely to your heart, and you will hear the melody. Let the unlimited power of your inner resources be the strong voice you'll need. Please trust the inner game plan detailed in this book. It will help you fulfill your greatest responsibility ... to become everything you are meant to be.

Before another moment passes, promise me ... you'll live an extraordinary life.
Why? Because there is no better way to enjoy your journey.

THE BUTTON MARKED SURPRISE!

Have you ever wondered what life in the gym would be like if you played perfectly...play after play, game after game, season after season? What if the CT process worked with such incredible perfection that every time you practiced or competed on the court, you never made a mistake or missed a shot. Wouldn't you feel sensational? Every play you were involved in, every shot you took, always ended in a completion! As long as you played basketball, there would be only one flawless play after another. Your game would be pure.

But, what if after a period of time thoroughly enjoying your mistake free performance, you noticed your perfect play was producing a strange feeling within you ... of all things ... boredom! Life on the basketball court was too predictable. Since there were no risks involved in competition — playing basketball seemed to lose its quality of adventure and excitement. Everything was the same! No misses! No mistakes!

Of course, frustration, disappointment and fear were gone, but that sensational up feeling was gone, too. You know what I am talking about. That fantastic feeling of stepping up in the clutch and doing something spontaneously great; or accomplishing something someone said you were incapable of doing; or rediscovering your touch and nailing those two foul shots to win a game; or working extra hard and long to improve a skill and then executing that skill in competition.

Because of your perfection, playing wasn't as much fun as it had been. The game had lost its attraction. Everything was so darn perfect.

Then, what if you walked into the gym, one day, to shoot around as you usually did — making one shot after another and you suddenly turned around to find at midcourt, a big red button resting on the floor. Walking over to get a closer look, you notice the word **"Surprise"** printed on its top.

Now, here is the decision that you must ponder: should you push this red button to experi-

193

ence the surprise it offers or walk away and keep things precisely the way they are . . . living in the monotonous rut of perfection?

After considering all of the possibilities, wouldn't you push the **"Surprise"** button to see what life's greater challenge has in store for you? If the answer is yes . . . which I'm sure it is . . . do you know where you would find yourself? **Exactly where you are right now . . . reading the last page of this book . . . hopeful of the prospects of a journey whose ending is as uncertain as it is challenging . . . feeling the imperfection but also feeling excited about the opportunity the imperfection provides!**

The next time you step on the basketball floor to live your dream, promise me you'll enjoy each basket, each miss, each success and yes, each learning experience, too!

GLOSSARY OF TERMS

The following words are your key Cybernetic stepping stones toward living your dream. Think of them as the means of communicating with your inner success system. By fully understanding their meaning, you will be able to stay firmly on course in the direction of your true destiny.

Act As If Method: The art of thinking, self-talking and moving as if you already are what you want to be.

Affirmation: A positive comment repeated over and over again until your subconscious accepts the suggestion as a belief.

Anchoring: The act of linking (and recording) a unique, sound, motion and feeling to a certain state of mind in order to access that state when needed.

Belief: A powerful thought that produces a feeling of certainty.

Brain (Split Brain): Communication between the two halves of the brain.

 Right Brain is the side that controls your visual and playing ability.

 Left Brain is the side that controls your verbal ability including all self-talk.

Brain Waves (Alpha, Beta)

 Alpha Rhythm: A relaxed and effortless state of rest when brain waves slow down to 7-14 cycles per second (such as in sleep or meditation). Excellent state of mind for mental programming.

 Beta Rhythm: A faster cycle of 14 cycles and up (a normal wakeful state). Excellent state for Power Talk and Anchoring.

Clear: The technique of programming an immediate response of composure after a missed shot or playing mistake. By reciting the anchor word "Clear!" the athlete is able to completely eliminate any emotional sense of failure or frustration from his mental screen and is able to play clear headed.

Coach: A lifetime learner who is committed to helping athletes become the best they can.

Comfort Zone: All the skill and attitude habits that you have done so many times they become easy to do again.

Comfort Zone Junkie: An athlete that allows a feeling of fear or unworthiness to discourage him/her from living his/her basketball dream.

Concentration: (Also called **Focus**) The ability to center your mental energies on a single object or action (pinpoint vision), and/or a large area (peripheral vision).

Confidence: A sense of unstoppable expectation.

Composure: (Also called **Poise**) An aggressively controlled state of mind.

Crystal Ball Method: The process of projecting yourself into the future to experience the pain of not committing to change and the pleasure that awaits you if you do.

Cybernetics: The science of communication that explains the similarities between the central nervous system and automatic controlled machines (such as the electronic computer).

Cybernetic Loop: The mental recording of an experience along with the associated sight, sound and feel of the action.

Erasure Technique: The amusing process of running a mental movie of a skill or attitude weakness forward and backwards so rapidly that you erase the negative anchor of frustration and fear that you have associated to it.

Feedback: Instructions (usually in the form of mental images) sent to the subconscious for processing. These input signals originate from your beliefs, self-talk and body language.

Flow: (Also called **The Zone** or the **Power State**) The effortless, wordless state of mind that produces peak performance.

Freedom: A total liberation from fear, overconcern, overtrying and negative thinking.

Goal: The first step of activating your inner success system with a specific challenge to improve a skill, attitude or activity.

Gooseneck: The full and relaxed extension and follow through of the shooting arm and hand.

Imaging: (Also called **Creative Imagination** or **Mental Visualization**). The repetitive act of creating imagined pictures or movies and wrapping them with emotion and feel.

Integrity: An honest and sincere state of mind.

Intensity: The state of mind that allows you to play with more energy and passion.

Luck: That moment in time when preparation and opportunity meet.

Modeling with VAK: Eliciting the winner's beliefs, self talk and body language into your own mental computer by mirroring what you see, hear and feel.

Negative Thinking: Anticipating what you want to avoid.

Opportunity: Inherent in all problems.

Optimism: A way of looking at life. Where all problems are not considered permanent, nor taken personally, nor allowed to affect other areas of one's life.

Pain And Pleasure Principle: The twin forces that shape your life. Everything you do is out of your need to avoid pain or your desire to gain pleasure.

Perfection: An illusionary state of mind that destroys dreams.

Positive Thinking: The act of looking for good.

Power Questions: Asking smart questions that empower you, such as "What's good about this?"

Power State: The ultimate state of mind that supports peak performance. The combination of the three inner essential states of confidence, concentration and composure.

Power Talk: Inner conversations or key words that empower you.

Power Thoughts: Thinking in positive, end-result images.

Pressure: The life and death situation that is rarely life and death! The inside-out force that you exert on yourself making the situation more important than it really is.

Prime Time Player: (Also called the **Money Player**). A clutch performer who is unafraid to fail. Any athlete who is willing to step up when the game is on the line regardless of his/her level of talent.

Psycho-Cybernetics: The science that considers the mind and nervous system as a wonderful automatic success system that can be programmed.

Purpose: Adding a powerful reason to a goal.

Reframing: The process of learning from an experience. Changing states by finding a positive outcome in an unfavorable event.

RAS or Reticular Activating System: The internal focusing device that permits you to screen what is important and what isn't.

Self-Confidence: The unstoppable feeling of self-trust.

Self-Esteem: A degree of self-worth produced by your self image.

Self Image: How you envision (imagine) yourself performing.

Serendipitous Events: (Also called **Sychronicity**). Unexplained happy coincidences based on a powerful need or desire.

Success: The process of striving for a goal.

Subconscious: Your automatic and powerful habit maker that controls all performance and behavior.

Synergy: The whole is greater than the sum of its parts theory. The multiplying of individual energies in a united effort to create a more powerful force. Turning the I and Me into the We and Us for a stronger effort.

Ultimate Shooting Method: (Sight!Feel!Yes!) Combining three key words to the shooting process in order to lock into a successful focus, feel and finish of your shot.

Whoosh Method: A state changing technique that allows you to regain a high level of confidence, concentration or composure after a run of bad breaks.

Value: A belief that is most important to you. More powerful than talent and luck, your value system determines the direction and speed of your basketball journey.

THE KEY OPERATING PRINCIPLES OF THE SUBCONSCIOUS

There are rules for operating the subconscious as a success mechanism. They hold the key to the best season you've ever had ... so get to know them.

1. Activating the powers of your success mechanism begins with the setting of a specific goal. Understand that you are always setting goals and not all of them are positive. Any time you use fear, guilt, anger or unworthiness as your counselor, you're setting negative or low expectation goals. If you are afraid to make a mistake ... you've set a goal for mediocrity.

   The goal should be in a form of a clear-cut basketball skill or attitude you want to master. Clear-cut means just that. If you want to improve your shooting for example, you must define the shooting skill you want in specific terms. For example...off the dribble, no dribble, straight on, bank shot, power layup or three. Never be fuzzy with your subconscious unless you want fuzzy responses. Ask and you shall receive ... that is if you ask in specific language.

2. The goal alone won't empower your subconscious. **Purpose will!** Combine a goal with a serious reason why you want to achieve the goal and you have an energy state of mind called purpose. The more important the why. ... the better the chances are you'll achieve the results you desire. Only with a compelling reason will you find the necessary energy for total commitment to the daily mental programming methods of CT.

   There is unlimited energy whenever goals are linked with reasons. The success equation works this way:

   > **Goal + Why = Purpose**
   > **Purpose = Energy**
   > **Energy = Success**

   Goals are chosen ... purpose is discovered. Find your purpose and your life will always have a forward direction.

3. Make a written success contract with your subconscious. By writing a two or three word statement on a goal card describing a word picture of the final result you want, you are informing your subconscious that you are not pleased with the status quo of the way things are going for you on the court. **You want change! Now!** The written contract becomes a constant reminder that will help you turn the "invisible into the visible."

   Keep your focus on the goal by duplicating the goal card and placing it on the mirror in your room or on the inside door of your school locker or inside cover of a book you normally carry around.

4. If a picture is worth a thousand words, then visualization is worth a thousand efforts. You think in terms of pictures because your subconscious works best from pictures. So always visualize the goal as an accomplished fact in a big, vividly bright moving picture. Make it a habit to think in terms of the end result images and your goal-striving subconscious becomes the ultimate dream fulfillment mechanism.

5. You gravitate in the direction of your dominant thoughts. One of the most important operating laws of your subconscious is that your dominant thoughts are processed first. Think "mistake" and you move towards it. Even if you think about something you don't want to happen, the chances are it will, because your mind moves towards your thoughts not away from them. Words like "don't" or "never," are processed. Forget them. Promise yourself "I'll never miss an easy lay-up again!" and you just guaranteed a missed chippy on your next try.

6. Your subconscious will appreciate it if you make the imaging procedure vivid, clear and big. See it, feel it and do it as often as you can is the rule.

7. **Repetition is the mother of skill** applies to visualization. The more often you repeat the visualization process the better the impact on your subconscious.

8. Avoid the fear of making a mistake. The fear of making a mistake is far worse than the mistake itself. In fact, start considering mistakes as valuable **learning experiences.** Rename mistakes as the chief suppliers of all essential software instructions for your subconscious. As long as you keep your goal firmly in mind, your subconscious is equipped to make the necessary adjustments. Learn this formula:

> **Success comes from good judgement;**
> **good judgement comes from experience;**
> **experience comes from bad judgement.**

Now, go out and make some mistakes! It's the only way to succeed.

9. Trust comes before **trustworthiness.** Trust your subconscious to be trustworthy and it will. Learning to **let it happen** on your shot is a true sign you are trusting your subconscious. Simple rule: Winners **let** . . . losers **try.**

10. Always keep your conscious mind busy with expectations of success. The best way to eliminate negative thoughts is by focusing your thinking and self talk on a positive expectation. Haven't you usually gotten what you expected?

11. Never use the words, **"I can't do this."** (**"I can't"** really means **"I won't."**) Your subconscious takes you at your word. Overcome this tendency by thinking the three magical words of **"Yes, I Can!"**

12. Your subconscious will accept any thought it believes to be true. This law of belief is the law of your success mechanism. Start to believe in what is best for you, not what is easiest

to achieve. Whatever your conscious mind assumes to be true, your subconscious will bring to pass. Maybe not always with the speed you want. Delays are not denials.

13. Your subconscious does not know the difference between a real experience and a vividly imagined one. Learn the power of visual lies!

14. Although your mechanism works best in pictures, words when linked to pictures, also become a powerful programming tool. Whenever you talk (even idle talk), your subconscious is paying careful attention!

15. Your beliefs, self talk and body language provide the three most powerful sources of feedback for your mental computer. If you don't like the way you're playing, change the way you think, talk and move.

16. Your success mechanism works below the conscious level. When your mind and body are relaxed and you are in a sleepy state (alpha level), your dreams and goals are dealing directly with the subconscious. When accessing the alpha level, you're eliminating any negative interference that might originate from the conscious mind. Take advantage of the fact that your subconscious mind accepts positive visualization more willingly on this level.

17. Your subconscious works 24 hours a day, 365 days a year. Right before sleep it's especially susceptible to suggestion. Awaiting sleep, present your success mechanism with a problem to solve or a skill that you want improved. Start the mental wheels moving before you go to sleep, and in the morning you'll have a solution or a better skill.

18. Never become overly concerned about the outcome of your performance. Overtrying strains your mechanism.

Let me leave you with three words regarding successful operation of your subconscious ...EMPLOY AND ENJOY!

POWER QUOTES

"What would you attempt to do if you couldn't fail?"
Robert Schuller

"The play is the thing!"
Shakespeare

"Imagination rules the world."
Disraeli

"There is no road to happiness. Happiness is the road."
Wayne Dyer

"Live with passion!"
Anthony Robbins

"You've got to have a dream if you want to make a dream come true."
Rodgers & Hammerstein

"Genius is ninety-nine percent perspiration and one percent inspiration!"
Thomas Edison

"Life is a banquet... and most of us are starving to death."
Auntie Mame

"Love is something you do."
Stephen Covey

"We are what we repeatedly do."
Aristotle

"Man is what he believes."
Chekhov

"Nothing happens unless first a dream."
Carl Sandburg

"Never, never, never quit."
Winston Churchill

*"The greatest thing in this world is not so much where we are,
but in what direction we are moving."*
Oliver Wendell Holmes

"I see no virtue where I smell no sweat."
Francis Quarles

"Boldness has genius, power and magic in it."
Goethe

"Feedback is the breakfast of champions."
Anthony Robbins

"Some people are so busy cutting wood, they have no time to sharpen the ax."
Stephen Covey

"The more you do, the more you discover you can do, and the more you want to do."
Julie Ridge, Long Distance Swimmer

204

"The ancestor to every action is thought."
Ralph Waldo Emerson

"Life is either a daring adventure or nothing."
Helen Keller

"To conquer fear is the beginning of wisdom."
Bertrand Russell

*"My first dose of athletic confidence came to me when I was eighteen years old.
Something happened that opened my eyes and chilled my spine.
On this particular night, I was sitting on the bench watching
McKelvey (star of the team) take an offensive rebound and move quickly to the hoop.
It was a move I couldn't execute. Since I had an accurate vision of his technique
in my head, I started playing with the image right there on the bench, running back
the picture several times and each time inserting a part of me for McKelvey.
Finally, I saw myself making the whole move, and I ran this over and over.
When I went into the game, I grabbed an offensive rebound and put it in
just the way McKelvey did. When the imitation worked,
I was so elated I couldn't contain myself."*
Bill Russell, NBA Great

*"Each time I visualized where I wanted to be, what kind of player I wanted to become, I
guess I approached it with the end in mind. That way I knew exactly where I wanted to go."*
Michael Jordan, NBA Great

"Just being good at something changed my entire self image."
Larry Bird, NBA Great

"You are here to enrich the world. You impoverish yourself if you forget the errand."
Woodrow Wilson

"Winning starts at the beginning... set a goal."
Stan Kellner

"A mind stretched to a new idea never returns to its original dimension."
Oliver Wendell Holmes

"They can because they think they can."
Virgil

"Accept the challenge so that you may feel the exhilaration of victory."
George S. Patton

*"Don't be afraid to take a big step if one is indicated.
You can't cross a chasm in two small jumps."*
David Lloyd George

"By perserverance the snail reached the ark."
Charles Spurgeon

*"Your failure mechanism is your natural tendency to follow the path of least resistance.
Your impulse is towards immediate gratification with little or no concern for the long-term
consequences of your actions."*
Brian Tracy

"Whether you think you can or you can't, either way you're right."
Anonymous

"The greatest pleasure in life is doing what people say you cannot do."
Walter Bagehot

*"If one advances confidently in the direction of his own dreams, and endeavors to live
the life which he has imagined, he will meet with success unexpected in common hours."*
Henry David Thoreau

"Success is simply a matter of luck. Ask any failure!"
Earl Wilson

"The last of the human freedoms—to choose one's attitude in any given set of circumstances, to choose one's own way."
Viktor Frankl

"You'll see it when you believe it."
Wayne Dyer

"If you always live with those who are lame, you will yourself learn to limp."
Latin Proverb

"All can hear, but only the sensitive can understand."
Kahlil Gibran

"There is a little robot that goes around with me,
I tell it what I'm thinking, I tell it what I see.
I tell my little robot all my hopes and fears,
It listens and remembers all my joys and tears.
At first my little robot followed my command,
But after years of training it's gotten out of hand.
It doesn't know what's right or wrong,
Nor what's false or true.
No matter what I tell it now...it tells me what to do."
Denis Whaitley